How I Got
Published

Famous Authors Tell You
in Their Own Words

Edited by Ray White
& Duane Lindsay

WRITER'S DIGEST BOOKS

www.writersdigest.com
Cincinnati, Ohio

Visit our Web sites at www.writersdigest.com and www.wdeditors.com for information on more resources for writers. To receive a free weekly e-mail newsletter delivering tips and updates about writing and about Writer's Digest products, register directly at our Web site at http://newsletters.fwpublications.com.

11   10   09   08   5 4 3 2

Distributed in Canada by Fraser Direct, 100 Armstrong Avenue, Georgetown, ON, Canada L7G 5S4. Distributed in the UK and Europe by David & Charles, Brunel House, Newton Abbot, Devon, TQ12 4PU, England. Distributed in Australia by Capricorn Link, P.O. Box 704, Windsor, NSW 2756 Australia.

Library of Congress Cataloging-in-Publication Data

How I got published : famous authors tell you in their own words / edited by Ray White and Duane Lindsay. -- 1st ed.

p. cm.

ISBN 978-1-58297-510-8 (pbk. : alk. paper)

1. Authorship--Marketing. I. White, Ray, 1950- II. Lindsay, Duane, 1951-

PN161.H65 2007

070.5'2--dc22

2007025310

Edited by Jane Friedman
Designed by Claudean Wheeler
Cover photograph by Nick Schlax/iStockphoto.com
Production coordinated by Mark Griffin

Table of Contents

Why You Should Buy
This Book (Everybody Loves
a Good Story)

This is a book about success. Ours ... theirs ... maybe yours.

It's about how to get published. Got a book or a short story? Got a dream you want to make real? You'll find out how to make it happen right here.

In these pages you'll meet a lot of the authors you love to read. You'll meet them when they were you: struggling, unsure, not yet famous.

You'll meet them when they went to writers conferences, manuscript in hand, hope in heart; when they had a box full of rejection letters; when they were broke and the choice was food or fixing the car to get to work. You'll see hope and determination and, in every case, success.

Every one of these authors got published.

So can you.

This book covers that huge place where people are poised to jump before they discover if they can fly—the days when the writer had nothing but a manuscript or an idea or a story and a desire to get published.

How did they do it? We're not telling the story of what happened later: the book deals, the second novel, the grind of publicity tours. We're going to tell you how they went from unknown hopefuls to "Oh, my God; someone is interested." We'll cover what made the phone ring or the computer voice say, "You've got mail!"

You'll meet Clive Cussler, J.A. Jance, Dave Barry, John Lescroart, David Morrell, Stephen White, Greg Bear, Gayle Lynds, Stephen Coonts, Christopher Moore, David Brin, and many more. You'll read the stories they sometimes tell at seminars or to friends. You'll read their answers to the question, "How did you do it? How did you get started?"

And of course, you'll get a lot of tips—from us and from them—about how the industry works and how to find your own way in.

You can't help but come away feeling energized and upbeat.

Another part of the book is specific advice on learning how to write. Not generic "how-to," but definitive tips. (Set a goal, make a calendar and stick to it, offer yourself a fine mix of self-congratulations and serious butt-kicking.)

You'll learn to write by writing as a business with specific rules and goals. And you'll learn to heed the advice of the bus driver who was asked how to get to Carnegie Hall: "Practice, practice, practice."

There's nothing arcane or mysterious about it. You learn by doing, by paying attention and always—*always*—being persistent. There's no luck involved. The definition of luck is, "The place where persistence meets preparation." We'll show you how to prepare. The authors will inspire you to keep going—to be persistent.

You'll learn how to see yourself as accomplishing something rather than failing at it, how to court criticism for its value. As author David Brin said, "Criticism is the only antidote for error."

Your success will come when your preparation meets persistence. This book will provide a heady dose of both with practical rules and inspirational real events.

Everybody loves a success story. This is ours … and theirs.

What's yours?

The Three J's:
Judo, Jazz, and Japan

BARRY EISLER

Enter the intriguing and dangerous world of John Rain—half-Japanese, half-American assassin—at your own risk. His is a world made authentic by Barry Eisler's experiences and training in the martial arts and his employment in the CIA's directorate of operations. Eisler is the award-winning author of *Rain Fall, Hard Rain, Rain Storm, Killing Rain* and, most recently, *The Last Assassin.* Visit his site at www.barryeisler.com for more about his books, as well as his highly informative For Writers section.

If you're writing fiction, you almost always need to have a completed manuscript to find an agent. And you need an agent to find a publisher. I had received about fifty rejections after sending the manuscript for my first book, *Rain Fall*, to as many agents, but some of them offered good suggestions, so I kept on revising.

Eventually, a friend of a friend who worked at a publishing house suggested I send the manuscript to a few agents with whom she worked, one of whom was Nat Sobel, the gentleman who represents me now. Nat saw promise in the early manuscript but knew it wasn't ready for prime time; he offered suggestions for improvement that were as extensive as they were excellent, and, about two years later, he judged the manuscript ready to go. I'm glad to say that his judgment was spot-on.

Then Nat had a great idea: he set up a series of meetings with Japanese publishers through his Tokyo-based associated agent, Ken Mori of Tuttle Mori, and we auctioned the rights in Japan before offering them anywhere else. Because *Rain Fall* is set in Tokyo, because the protagonist, John Rain, is half Japanese, and because I speak Japanese, we got a lot of interest and a big two-book deal from Japan. *Publishers Weekly* picked up the story in the States, and two months later Nat sent the manuscript around to about twenty U.S. publishing houses. Putnam liked the book so much that they pre-empted the auction and bought *Rain Fall* as well as its sequel, *Hard Rain* (which wasn't even written yet).

Strangely enough, I didn't start the series as a series — I started it as a standalone. But Putnam and all the other publishers who bought the rights to the manuscript insisted on a sequel, and one thing led to another. Looking back, I'm almost chagrined that I didn't spot the series potential. John Rain is such a fascinating and three-dimensional character that one book wouldn't have been nearly enough to explore his world.

I think that, in life, there are things you can control and things you can't (or, to think of the whole thing as a continuum, there are things relatively amenable to your influence and things relatively unamenable). The things you're responsible for, and therefore the things that can be the source of legitimate pride or shame, are those you can control.

If you want to be a writer, the thing you can almost totally control is finishing the book. Finding an agent, getting published … that all takes a certain amount of luck and timing (although of course your hard work on what you can control will affect these less controllable factors, too). So my attitude was this: I wanted to be published, but if it didn't happen, I didn't want it to be my fault. I wanted to be able to look in the mirror and say, "Okay, you didn't manage to get published, but you did everything you could to make it happen, and you finished the book, so you've got nothing to be ashamed of." That attitude — in a sense that fear of one day feeling that if I didn't make it I might think it was my fault — is what kept me going for many years with no external signs of success.

As for promotion, you have to approach your most accessible markets first. Of course you want your books sold by the millions at Wal-

Mart, airport kiosks, and supermarkets, but how do you get there? Start by attacking your niche markets. If you write mysteries or thrillers (or crime, or suspense—let's just call it mystery for short), this means doing signings at the independent mystery booksellers, attending mystery fiction conventions, and otherwise building relationships in the community. The mystery market is a ready-made demographic eager to hear about your book.

Part of this for me was identifying the "hooks" in my story: that is, the aspects that would appeal to identifiable submarkets. In *Rain Fall*, the hooks were what I came to think of as the Three Js: judo, jazz, and Japan. Or, more broadly, martial arts, jazz, and Asia. I contacted various media outlets in these areas and got interviews and other coverage.

How can you identify your own submarkets? Go to a magazine store and see if there's anything in your book that's covered in a monthly magazine. If so, there's a submarket you can approach. Just as you have to build to a bookstore mass-market presence, you also have to build a media presence. Yes, it would be nice to be featured on the cover of *Time* magazine, but to get that far you'll have to pave the way, and niche media will be your stepping stones.

I also toured for the first book—only five cities, but I made sure my publisher knew that the results were good, and since then, the tours have gotten progressively bigger and more effective: ten cities for *Hard Rain*; twenty for *Rain Storm*; thirty for *Killing Rain*; and I can't even count how many places I've visited on the current two-month, coast-to-coast-and-back-again extravaganza for *The Last Assassin*.

Remember, booksellers are your sales force, and you want to build good relationships with them. Most of all, I recognized early on that I had to impress my publisher, Putnam, with my efforts and my successes to persuade them to keep coming back to me. There's a tremendous amount your publisher can do for you if they think your books will provide a good return on their investment. Your job is to make them understand that it's in their interest to invest more.

"Did You Know Your Agent Died?"

C.J. BOX

C.J. Box is the best-selling author of eight novels, including the mystery series featuring Wyoming game warden Joe Pickett. So far, C.J.'s books have won the Anthony Award, La Prix Calibre 38, the Macavity Award, the Gumshoe Award, the Barry Award, and an Edgar Award—placing him in pretty select company. A Wyoming native, C.J. has worked as a ranch hand, fishing guide, small-town reporter, and editor, a background that lends authenticity to his work. His Web site is www.cjbox.net.

O*pen Season*, then titled *Joe Pickett* after my game warden protagonist, was completed in manuscript form four years before it was acquired by Putnam. In the four years between completion and sale, an agent was supposedly showing it around, but I never really confirmed that. For an entire year I heard nothing, and for good reason: he had died. No one told me. My editor overheard a (living) agent talking about *Open Season* in a bar during a writer's conference. She asked the agent for a look at the manuscript. Before leaving the publishing industry for good to seek honest employment, the agent passed along the inquiry to me.

Of course, previous to this, I had written three full unpublished novels and an unfilmed screenplay. My children did not know I wrote because I didn't want them to think of their dad as a failed novelist. They didn't know I wrote fiction until I had a book contract.

Just your typical twenty-year, overnight success story.

Say No to Nothing — The Right Attitude

DONALD BAIN

Nearly every agent and editor knows the work of Donald Bain. He is the author or ghostwriter of more than ninety books, many of them best-sellers, including *Coffee, Tea, or Me?* and thirty Murder She Wrote stories. His 2006 autobiography, *Murder He Wrote: A Successful Writer's Life*, published by Purdue University Press, is widely available. His Web site is www.donaldbain.com.

B ack in the early sixties, I was a writer-without-portfolio. I hadn't written a thing aside from countless news releases as part of the PR jobs I'd held. But that didn't deter a New York lawyer, Dan O'Shea, from signing me up as his first client in a one-man literary agency he'd launched. I had plenty of ideas for books and movies, but that's as far as they went—ideas, which are a dime a dozen.

Naturally, Dan had an obligation to find me work, and he decided I should join a stable of writers churning out articles for a group of magazines published by a company called Magazine Management. The magazines were referred to as "men's adventure magazines" and carried such titles as *Male, Stag, For Men Only, Man's World, Action for Men,* and *True Action.* I was familiar with some of them because my cousin, Jack Pearl, a prolific writer who had written the original biography of General Patton and become well-to-do by writing historical romance novels under the name Stephanie Blake, had done some pieces for them. It seemed that every writer in New York wanted to write for these publications, and I soon learned why. The money was good and the writing was easy.

Dan waltzed me up to Magazine Management's offices and introduced me to Hans Ashbourne, an editor who oversaw a number of the titles being published. Hans was a delightful guy, intelligent, witty, and always impeccably dressed. He claimed to be descended from European royalty and preferred to be referred to as Count Ashbourne. That was fine with me. I would have been happy to call him King if it meant getting assignments.

The three of us had a long, happy lunch that day. When it was over, The Count invited me to submit article ideas to him directly, which Dan later explained didn't always happen. I was in. I'd been accepted into the stable at Magazine Management, and what a stable it was — Mario Puzo, Mickey Spillane, Bruce J. Friedman, and dozens of other good writers, many of whom would go on to considerable fame. Puzo, of course, wrote *The Godfather.* I remember sitting in the waiting room and listening to him explain how he was analyzing the structure of bestselling novels, which he would use when he got around to writing an epic novel of his own that he'd been contemplating for years, about organized crime. Spillane, a delightful guy, would go on to define the hardboiled novel. And Friedman, who put in a stint as an editor at Magazine Management, achieved literary fame with such novels as *Stern* and *A Mother's Kisses.* No matter where anyone from the Magazine Management roster of regular writers ended up, we all had one thing in common: assignments to write for these strange magazines paid a lot of rent and put plenty of food on our tables.

One day each week, the writers gathered in a waiting room for their fifteen minutes with Ashbourne, to pitch him new ideas. You summed up each proposal in a single paragraph and used your time with him to verbally embellish your latest inspirations. While all articles were to be "nonfiction," most of them were made up by the writers, flights of fancy with bogus facts to back them up. Some of my pieces demanded quotes from psychologists and psychiatrists, but who had the time to seek out and interview real ones? I created a fictional shrink whom I quoted liberally in myriad articles. I wrote under many pseudonyms — Christopher Blaine, Stanley Jacob, Hugh Lambert, Cornelius Dailey, and John Southwick — and had pieces in Magazine Management's magazines every month for more than a year.

I really scored one day, however, when instead of fifteen minutes with Hans in his office, he took me to lunch, over which he described "an exciting new project." He was going to start running excerpts from soon-to-be published bestselling novels, with banners across the covers heralding it. I assumed, of course, that Magazine Management would buy the rights to such novels. I was wrong. The Count explained that he wanted me to write exciting stories that *could* have come from novels. They were to be twice as long as the usual pieces and I would be paid double. I agreed and went on to write four of them, beginning with an except from "the soon-to-be-published" novel *Flight From Erotica*. The "excerpt" was "I Fly the Charter Passion Route."

Like most writers toiling for Magazine Management in those days, I went on to bigger and better things, beginning with *Coffee, Tea, or Me?* which sold, along with its sequels, more than five million copies worldwide and was made into a TV motion picture. There have been more than ninety other books since then, including thirty in the *Murder, She Wrote* series of murder mysteries based upon the popular TV show, more than twenty bestselling novels ghosted for a well-known person, westerns, comedies, investigative journalism, and romance novels. But I look back on those days writing for The Count and his outlandish magazines as precious days. No matter what the project, you learn from every piece of writing you do — or at least you'd better. As my wife, also a writer, says, "You have to exercise writing muscles."

I learned a lot from grinding out those pieces, and to this day find writing to be a continuous learning experience. I also developed a philosophy back then that has held me in good stead throughout my writing career: "Whatever I'm writing at the moment is the most important thing I'll ever write, and maybe the last."

I can picture many young writers turning up their noses at writing for a publisher like Magazine Management, considering it beneath their literary talents and aspirations. Over the course of my career, I've had suggested to me hundreds of projects: some worthwhile, many silly or outright stupid. But I've never summarily dismissed any of them. I've always been willing to at least hear what they're about before deciding against becoming involved. I believe that, along with mastering the craft of writing and learning to channel creativity into a workable structure, attitude plays an equally important role.

Publishing is a business, and aspiring writers who take the time and expend the effort to learn about that business and what it demands give themselves a leg up on success.

Publishing is a business, and aspiring writers who take the time and expend the effort to learn about that business and what it demands give themselves a leg up on success. Many books ago, I found it financially necessary to take on a few writing projects that I would otherwise have turned down. While they don't rank among my most treasured memories, nor do I point to them with pride, I'm glad I did them. I learned from those writing experiences. They helped sharpen my writer's tools and made me a better craftsman, like a carpenter who becomes increasingly familiar with his tools and as a result can go on to more creative carpentry. In other words, while I was writing those books, they were the most important things I'd ever written, maybe the last.

Practical Demonkeeping

CHRISTOPHER MOORE

Anyone who enjoys sidesplitting laughter, devilish twists, and sheer, unadulterated fun will be unable to resist Christopher Moore. He also comes up with some of the greatest titles and subtitles around: *The Lust Lizard of Melancholy Cove*; *Practical Demonkeeping*; *Lamb: The Gospel According to Biff, Christ's Childhood Pal*; *Island of the Sequined Love Nun*; and *You Suck: A Love Story*, the sequel to *Bloodsucking Fiends: A Love Story*. Visit his site at www.christophermoore.com.

I was in my early thirties before I sold my first book. Until then, I'd sold exactly one short story, to a black men's magazine, and I've yet to this day ever to see a copy of the magazine.

My novel *Practical Demonkeeping* was out to market for eleven months before it sold. At the time, I was working as a waiter in an Italian restaurant and as a part-time DJ, as well as doing paste-up for a newspaper. I'd given my book to a friend, who worked in Hollywood, and she'd given it to an agent, who agreed to represent the book in Hollywood. I'd also managed to get an agent in New York through the same connection, but there were no bites on the book.

One night, the week before Thanksgiving, my Hollywood agent called me at work, which he had never done. He said that Disney wanted to buy the rights to my book outright for $300,000, but they had to have an answer by 8:00 P.M. or the offer was withdrawn. (I guess there were four other studios preparing offers as well.)

I stumbled away from the phone, into the restaurant bar, where the regular drunks started giving me financial advice. "Buy real estate." "You need to get into stocks." "Get yourself a tax lawyer." Stuff like that. The phone rang again, and it was for me.

"I can't talk now, I have to get garlic bread to Table Five. Tell them you couldn't get hold of me, but you're authorized to close at $400,000."

My agent said that they were up to $350,000, but they still had to know by eight o'clock. (I think it was about six o'clock at the time.) The restaurant was getting busy and I had a full section. I go, "I can't talk now, I have to get garlic bread to Table Five. Tell them you couldn't get hold of me, but you're authorized to close at $400,000." (At the time I was sweating losing my six-dollar tip on Table Five, so I wasn't really used to talking about numbers like that.)

He said, "They'll never believe that."

I said, "I gotta go. My garlic bread is burning." And I hung up and grabbed my garlic bread from under the broiler.

By this time I was completely spun out. I took my apron off, put it on my bus person, told her, "It's your section now — congratulations, you're a waiter," and bussed for her.

My agent called an hour later. He said, "We closed at $400,000."

I said, "What did you *say*?"

"I told them that I couldn't get hold of you but I was authorized to close for $400,000."

I said, "What am I paying you for?"

Anyway, I gave my shifts at the restaurant to people who needed them, but it was almost eight months before the deal closed. In the meantime, I lived off of kiting credit cards — advancing one to pay rent, then getting a new one and advancing that one to pay the other one. I had about thirty grand in credit card debt by the time I got paid.

Mainly I ate at a friend's diner, who gave me grilled ham-and-cheese sandwiches on credit until I got paid. (He'd also given me, on credit, the computer I used to transcribe the book—saying I could pay him if I ever got the money. What a guy!)

From there, *Practical Demonkeeping* sold in sixteen countries and has been re-released in the U.S. at least eight times. I've been making my living as a writer for the last fifteen years now. And although Disney spent millions to hire screenwriters, the movie of *Practical Demonkeeping* has never been made.

I Decided to Take a More Devious Approach

CLIVE CUSSLER

Clive Cussler practically invented modern action-adventure writing. His highly entertaining tales span both history and the globe, and the scope of his plots is truly amazing. He is the author of *Raise the Titanic, Sahara, Inca Gold, Flood Tide,* and numerous other Dirk Pitt adventures and nonfiction works—far too many to list here. He is truly the master of his field, and no serious reader of adventures should fail to devour all of his books, including *The Sea Hunters* and *Sea Hunters II,* two nonfiction novels that detail his true life adventures. Clive received the Lowell Thomas Award, bestowed for outstanding exploration, and is a fellow of the Royal Geographic Society in London and the Explorers Club of New York. Find out more about Clive at www.numa.net.

A fter I'd finished my first two manuscripts, I decided I needed a literary agent. I was working at the time in Los Angeles as creative director for a large advertising agency so I had often used talent agencies to shoot TV commercials, but I did not know any literary agents. Calling on the casting agencies for information, I assembled a list of about twenty agents in New York.

Rather than go through the rigamarole of letters of query, synopsis, etc., I decided to take another, more devious approach. I had the art director of the agency create a letterhead for the Charles Winthrop Agency. (I thought Winthrop was a classy name. Besides, I lived on Winthrop Drive when I was a kid.) Anyway, the art director came up with this very artistic letterhead. I did not insert a phone number and used the address of my father, which was in a better neighborhood than mine.

I then wrote a letter to the first name on the list, Peter Lampack of the William Morris Agency. It read,

> Dear Peter,
>
> As you know I primarily handle television screenplays, however, I've run across a pair of book length manuscripts which I believe have a great deal of potential. I would like to pursue them, but as we discussed, I'm retiring. Would you like to take a look at them?
>
> (Signed) Charlie Winthrop

I mailed off the letter and ten days later my father said I had a letter from New York:

> Dear Charlie,
>
> Sure, on your say so, I'll take a look at the manuscripts.
>
> Peter Lampack

I mailed off the manuscripts with no great expectation and buried myself in producing TV commercials for Budweiser beer. About three weeks later, my father calls and says there's another letter from New York. I opened it and was amazed to read,

> Dear Charlie,
>
> The first manuscript is not bad, but the second one is quite good. Where can I find Clive Cussler and sign him to a contract?
>
> Peter Lampack

Stunned that it had been so easy, "Charlie Winthrop" fired off a letter giving Lampack Cussler's address. The contracts came; I signed them and started another book. It took three years before Peter finally got me published. The bosses at William Morris told him to dump Cussler; he wasn't going anywhere. But bless his heart, Peter hung in.

The first book came out as a paperback that did marginally well. The second was a hardcover with a printing of 5,000 copies, and it sold 3,200. The third book, *Raise the Titanic*, was the breakthrough book: it reached number two on the *Times* list (but had a perfectly awful movie made on it).

I went to New York. Peter and his wife, Dianne, and my wife, Barbara, and I went out to dinner to celebrate the movie deal. I believe the restaurant was the Sign of the Dove. Waiting for dessert, I turned to my wife and said, "I think the time has come."

I had been with Peter for six years and never told him the story, for fear he would throw me out the door, but now I was his biggest client and could run the risk. So I laid bare Charlie Winthrop with great trepidation. When I finished, Peter looked totally blank. Then he laughed himself under the table. When he recovered he said, "Oh my God, I always thought Charlie Winthrop was some guy I met when I was drunk at a cocktail party." Peter took it in good humor, and we've been together for thirty-seven years with no contract, simply a handshake.

The final shot. I was left with 998 envelopes and letterheads with Charlie Winthrop's name on them. Being a cheap screw, I wrote my next book on the back of Charlie's stationery.

Interview With Dave Barry

Dave Barry is a Pulitzer Prize–winning humor columnist and the author of many hilarious books. Among his fiction works are *Big Trouble* (made into a movie starring Tim Allen) and *Tricky Business*, as well as *Peter and the Starcatchers* and *Peter and the Shadow Thieves*, which he coauthored with Ridley Pearson (appealing to all ages, though allegedly children's books). His nonfiction works are numerous and side-splitting—*Dave Barry Hits Below the Beltway (A Vicious and Unprovoked Attack on Our Most Cherished Political Institutions)*, *Boogers Are My Beat*, *Dave Barry's Complete Guide to Guys*, and *Dave Barry's Money Secrets*, to name a few. For deliberately provoked laughter visit his Web site at www.davebarry.com.

When and why did you decide to become a journalist?

I always liked to write, and when I was a college graduate with a bachelor's degree in English, journalism seemed like the only career that involved a) writing and b) getting paid.

Did your occupation influence what you write about?

In a way. Since I was writing serious news stories, when I turned to humor columns, I often wrote about things in the news. Of course I also made a lot of stuff up.

What steps did you take to get your first agent?

My first agent, Al Hart—who is still my agent, twenty-five years later—approached me. He saw some columns that I'd written and wrote me a letter asking if I'd thought about writing a book. As it happened, right around the same time a book publisher approached me about publishing a collection of columns, so I needed an agent.

How did you decide which agent or publisher to sign with, if more than one were interested?

It was just Al. We met for drinks and hit it off right away. So we shook hands, and that was that.

Are you still with him?

Yup.

How did you or your publisher promote sales of your first book so it sold well enough for you to get a contract for your next one?

My first book, a collection of columns called *Bad Habits*, didn't sell many copies. But shortly after it appeared, a different publisher, Rodale Press, asked me to write a humorous do-it-yourself book for homeowners. I got a huge break when that one came out. Somehow, I got booked on the *Tonight Show*. Johnny Carson gave me a wonderful interview, and the book sold well enough that I ended up doing four more for Rodale.

What advice can you offer to beginning writers about getting an agent and getting published?

You have to be patient, and you have to be realistic. It's very difficult to get published and damn near impossible to have a book that sells well enough to make you real money. That doesn't mean it doesn't happen, or won't happen to you; it just means that you have to accept that the odds are against it. If you go into the book world with the attitude that you deserve great success, you will probably wind up making yourself and those around you miserable. If you like to write, that's wonderful. Let the writing itself be the source of your happiness. If you view it only as a means to fame and fortune, you will not be happy.

My Life in Writing

J.A. JANCE

J.A. Jance is the *New York Times* best-selling author of the J.P. Beaumont series, the Joanna Brady series, three international thrillers featuring the Walker family, and *Edge of Evil*. The following biography is taken with permission from her Web site at www.jajance.com.

As a second-grader in Mrs. Spangler's Greenway School class, I was introduced to Frank Baum's Wizard of Oz series. I read the first one and was hooked and knew, from that moment on, that I wanted to be a writer.

The third child in a large family, I was four years younger than my next older sister and four years older then the next younger sibling. Being both too young and too old left me alone in a crowd and helped turn me into an introspective reader and a top student. When I graduated from Bisbee High School in 1962, I received an academic scholarship that made me the first person in my family to attend a four-year college. I graduated in 1966 with a degree in English and Secondary Education. In 1970 I received my M. Ed. in Library Science. I taught high school English at Tucson's Pueblo High School for two years and was a K–12 librarian at Indian Oasis School District in Sells, Arizona for five years.

My ambitions to become a writer were frustrated in college and later, first because the professor who taught creative writing at the University of Arizona in those days thought girls "ought to be teachers or nurses" rather than writers. After he refused me admission to the program, I did the next best thing: I married a man who was allowed in the program that was closed to me. My first husband imitated Faulkner and Hemingway, primarily by drinking too much and writing too little. Despite the fact that he was allowed in the creative writing program, he never had anything published, either prior to or after his death from chronic alcoholism at age forty-two. That didn't keep him from telling me, however, that there would be only one writer in our family, and he was it.

He made that statement in 1968 after I had received a favorable letter from an editor in New York who was interested in publishing a children's story I had written. Because I was a newly wed wife who was interested in staying married, I put my writing ambitions on hold. Other than writing poetry in the dark of night when my husband was asleep (see *After the Fire*), I did nothing more about writing fiction until eleven years later when I was a single, divorced mother with two children, no child support, and a full-time job selling life insurance. My first three books were written between four and seven in the morning. At seven, I would wake my children and send them off to school. After that, I would get myself ready to go sell life insurance.

I started writing in the middle of March 1982. The first book I wrote—a slightly fictionalized version of a series of murders that happened in Tucson in 1970—was never published by anyone. For one thing, it was twelve hundred pages long. Since I was never allowed in the creative writing classes, no one had ever told me there were some things I needed to leave out. For another, the editors who turned it down said that the parts that were real were totally unbelievable, and the parts that were fiction were fine. My agent finally sat me down and told me that she thought I was a better writer of fiction than I was of nonfiction. Why, she suggested, didn't I try my hand at a novel?

The result of that conversation was the first Detective Beaumont book, *Until Proven Guilty*. Since 1985 when that was published, there have been fourteen more Beau books. My work also includes eight

Joanna Brady books, set in southeastern Arizona where I grew up. In addition there are two thrillers, *Hour of the Hunter* and *Kiss of the Bees*, that reflect what I learned during the years when I was teaching on the Tohono O'odham reservation west of Tucson, Arizona.

One of the wonderful things about being a writer is that everything — even the bad stuff — is usable.

The week before *Until Proven Guilty* was published, I did a poetry reading of *After the Fire* at a widowed retreat sponsored by a group called WICS (Widowed Information Consultation Services) of King County. It was June 1985, five years after my divorce in 1980 and two years after my former husband's death. I went to the retreat feeling as though I hadn't quite had my ticket punched and didn't deserve to be there. After all, the other people there were all still married when their spouses died. I was divorced. At the retreat I met a man whose wife had died of breast cancer two years to the day and within a matter of minutes of the time my husband died. We struck up a conversation based on that coincidence. Six months later, to the dismay of our five children, we told the kids they weren't the Brady Bunch, but they'd do, and we got married. We now have four new in-laws as well as three grandchildren.

When my second husband and I first married, he supported all of us — the two of us, his kids, and mine. It was a long time before my income from writing was anything more than fun money — the *Improbable Cause* trip to Walt Disney World; the *Minor in Possession* memorial powder room; the *Payment in Kind* memorial hot tub. Seven years ago, however, the worm turned. My husband was able to retire at age fifty-four and take up golf and oil painting.

One of the wonderful things about being a writer is that everything — even the bad stuff — is usable. The eighteen years I spent married to an alcoholic have helped shape the experience and character of Detective J.P. Beaumont. My experiences as a single parent have gone into the background for Joanna Brady — including her first tentative steps toward a new life after the devastation of losing her husband in *Desert Heat*. And then there's the evil creative writing professor in *Hour of the Hunter* and *Kiss of the Bees*, but that's another story.

Another wonderful part of being a writer is hearing from fans. I learned on the reservation that the ancient, sacred charge of the storyteller is to beguile the time. I'm thrilled when I hear that someone has used my books to get through some particularly difficult illness, either as a patient or as they sit on the sidelines while someone they love is terribly ill. It gratifies me to know that by immersing themselves in my stories, people are able to set their own lives aside and live and walk in someone else's shoes. It tells me I'm doing a good job at the best job in the world.

How I Got Started and How I Keep Going

F. PAUL WILSON

F. Paul Wilson has authored more than thirty books, including *The Tomb*, *The Keep*, and several other Repairman Jack adventures, in genres ranging from science fiction to horror to thriller. In addition to appearing on *The New York Times* best-seller list, his novels have won the Prometheus Award, the Porgie Award, and the Bram Stoker Award. His character Repairman Jack is one of the most intriguing characters in all of fiction. For a complete booklist and to keep abreast of Paul's work, visit his Web site at www.repairmanjack.com.

I sold my first novel thirty years ago. Half my lifetime ago. It may not seem like yesterday, but it doesn't seem *that* long.

First novels are unpredictable.

For one author it's the best thing he will do in his career, something into which he empties so much of his heart and talent and experience that he's left with too little fuel to light much of a fire under future work.

For another it sets the course for an entire career: He's found the key in which his voice is most comfortable and he sticks to it.

For some writers that first novel gives no hint as to what is to come, the restless been-there/done-that school where every new work is a departure from the last.

And then there's that first novel, not terribly uncommon in the science fiction field during the seventies, in which the writer is learning his craft in public.

My first novel, *Healer*, was one of those.

When I started writing—seriously writing for publication (I'd been writing stories since second grade)—I was twenty years old and a junior at Georgetown. That would be 1967. I made my first magazine sale in 1970 as a medical student. Others followed. Years later I decided to expand one of those magazine stories into a novel.

In 1972, during medical school, one of my sales to John W. Campbell for *Analog* was a novelette titled *Pard*. At a nickel a word it paid a fair number of bills. I intended to continue the story of Steven Dalt, a man who shares his brain with an alien; that alien, Pard, was conscious down to the cellular level, making Dalt potentially immortal. However, I had no room in my life for writing during my fourth year of med school and my rotating internship the following year. But after joining a family practice group in 1974 I found I again had time to scratch the writing itch.

Starting with *Pard* as a springboard, I picked up Dalt's story a few decades after the end of the novelette and tracked him (in outline) on a peripatetic course through the centuries as he becomes a mythical figure known as The Healer.

But I needed a publisher. Naïve as can be, I decided to start at the top and work my way down.

(Now, you've got to understand that writing was something I wanted to do, *had* to do, but had never thought of as a career because I never dreamed I could make a living at it. So, I simply wrote stories and sent them out. I figured I'd do the same with my novel.)

In regard to the realities of the publishing world, the word "naïve" doesn't quite capture my state at the time. We need a new term to properly gauge my level of naiveté.

Doubleday seemed like a good choice—after all, they published Isaac Asimov, so I guessed they could publish me. Agentless, I sent off the novelette plus the outline of the rest of the book (a not uncommon practice in 1974). A couple months later I heard back from Sharon Jarvis, Doubleday's SF editor at the time, offering a whopping two-thousand-dollar contract for world rights.

Wow. My first book proposal had been accepted by the first publisher I'd sent it to.

As the saying goes: How long has this been going on and why didn't anybody tell me about it?

Looking back later I realized that *Healer* had a significant advantage in that its anchoring novelette originally had been purchased and published by John W. Campbell Jr., the Zeus of modern science fiction. That pedigree gave it a definite leg up on the average, over-the-transom proposal in Sharon's office.

Published in June 1976, *Healer* garnered decent reviews. I shall now tell you what I did to insert my name into the public consciousness and have my book read by the masses:

Nothing.

Why should I do anything, I thought, when the publisher would soon be mounting a huge publicity blitz? (I hadn't checked this out with the publisher. I just assumed.)

As I said: Naïve doesn't cut it. How about *dumb*?

....

The important word there is manage — time management, to be precise.

....

So for weeks and months I scanned *The New York Times Book Review*, waiting for the full-page ads trumpeting the arrival of *Healer*. I searched the Best Sellers list every Sunday for my title. I went to bookstores and most often couldn't find a single copy of my book. Had they sold out? If so, why weren't they restocking?

Finally I gathered the courage to ask the manager of a Doubleday Bookstore — owned by Doubleday, my publisher — why he of all people wasn't carrying my book. He looked up *Healer* on his microfiche (no store computers in those days) and informed me that it was out of print.

Out of print? It had been published in June and this was only November! There had to be some mistake!

I staggered home and called Sharon, who patiently explained that as soon as the libraries have their copies and paperback rights have been sold (Jim Frenkel at Dell picked up *Healer* almost as soon as it was published), Doubleday remainders most of its science fiction books. I'd be getting a letter soon allowing me to buy leftover copies for pennies on the dollar.

Welcome to the wonderful world of big-time publishing.

I'm older and (somewhat) wiser now, and as of this writing, I'm putting the finishing touches on my thirty-fifth book.

Thirty-five books (counting the two anthologies I edited) in thirty years, and practicing medicine full time during twenty of them. How did I manage that?

Good question. The important word there is *manage* — time management, to be precise. Early on I found the prospect of writing a five-hundred-page novel daunting. It seemed impossible. No way I can write five hundred pages!

But I can write three.

And tomorrow I can write three more.

In operant terms, writing a novel is a long task with a reward not only distant, but not even assured. So we must find incremental rewards along the way. Writing a few good pages a day can be their own reward. And if today's aren't as good as you'd like, tomorrow's will be.

So, I've found that a minimum of three first-draft, double-spaced pages per day does the trick. That's twenty-one per week. At this rate you've got over 540 pages in six months. That's around 120,000 words — a decent-sized novel.

In writing those three pages per day, avoid tinkering with them. This stalls you by fooling you into thinking you're still writing. You're not. The story is not advancing and you're losing momentum. Get the words down on today's three pages and then leave them alone and tomorrow go on to the next three pages. The time to fix and hone them is after you've finished that all-important first draft. You'll know your characters better by then and can go back and make meaningful edits and additions.

When I was practicing full time I'd use my commute and lunch break to compose my next pages so that I'd be primed when I sat down at the keyboard.

And here's a key point: Turn off your damn iPods and radios! Stop wasting valuable time listening to other people's words. You're a writer. When you're driving or walking around you should be working on your words—the words you want to tell other people.

The key is writing every day—*every* day—to maintain the narrative flow. Even a few days off will slow your momentum, and it can take time to bring your narrative back up to speed.

Three pages a day … keep making those increments … keep moving those grains of sand. Call it your Daily Duty.

Sometimes those three pages fly by; sometimes they move with the speed of an arthritic escargot. On a bad day—that means I'm stuck deciding whose scene it is or how to present a twist in the plot, or being dragged from the keyboard by things like trips to NYC to see my agent or my editor or to research a location—I'll barely make those three pages. Other days I'm done in an hour, but I keep going (remember, the three pages are a *minimum*).

An outline makes the Daily Duty considerably easier.s

And here's a key point: Turn off your damn iPods and radios!

I know, I know; you hear authors say they never outline, that an outline stifles a work of fiction, acts like a straitjacket on creativity. I've heard a number of respected writers say, "I simply take a few characters, drop them into a situation or environment, and off we go." Or something to that effect.

I admit I've stuck a character into a situation and winged it, but only in short fiction. I cannot imagine doing it for an entire novel.

I've heard another well-known author say that the stories are out there, floating around, waiting to be told, and all you have to do is snag one and get it down on paper.

Who's he kidding?

Snagging a story out of the air? No, can't say as I've had the pleasure. Haven't dug up any in my backyard, either. I'm one of those poor slobs who has to sit down and make something out of nothing.

And to do that right, I've found I need an outline.

It's probably my nature to outline. I mean, I'm not a guy who gets in a car and just drives. I always have a destination in mind. And I don't shop—I *buy*. I don't go to a store just to browse the aisles (unless it's a bookstore)—I go with a purchase in mind. I'm a hunter, not a gatherer.

Add to that my many years as a part-time writer and it's obvious how outlining had to become an integral part of my writing process.

Or maybe it's not so obvious. Let me explain.

I think it's safe to say that the vast majority of the world's writers don't do it full time. It simply doesn't pay enough. They need a day job to feed their writing jones. For a part-timer, writing time is a scarce and precious commodity, so you want to make the most of every second. You can't afford the luxury of writing yourself into a corner, or down a blind alley or dead-end street.

Years ago I was talking to Rick McCammon and he casually mentioned that he'd just tossed out three hundred pages of a novel because he'd lost interest in it. I had to find a seat. Three hundred pages … at the time, that was almost four months' output for me. Obviously Rick was a full-timer. And quick with the keys. He could afford that. For me it would be a catastrophe.

That's why I've always outlined my books: to avoid dead ends and blind alleys, to avert the horror of dumping hard-earned pages into the wastebasket. Also I want to know in advance if the story is worth telling, if it's going to stand up to lengthy treatment, and most of all: Can I bring it to a satisfying conclusion?

That—the satisfying conclusion part—is, I believe, the best reason for an outline. Count how many novels have done this to you: You're sailing along, digging the prose and the plot and the characters when, about three-quarters of the way through, you start to notice it falling apart, eventually concluding not with a satisfying bang, not even with a whimper. It doesn't really end, it just seems … to … dribble … away ….

I'll lay you odds of a hundred, no, a *thousand* to one, that book was written by an I-simply-take-a-few-characters-drop-them-into-a-situation-or-environment-and-off-we-go writer. He had a great idea and started his story without knowing how to end it. He figured when the time came, he'd know. Well, he didn't.

That's not to say that it can't be done. Some of my favorite authors have never used an outline, and their stories tie up beautifully. I envy them that ability.

But I can't work that way. If I'm not sure I can end a story, I don't start it. I feel I owe the reader a good ending. Not necessarily a happy one, not necessarily a neat tying-up of every loose string, but at the very least a catharsis, a release of all the narrative tension I've been building. If I don't do that, I've failed you. I haven't done my job, and you haven't received your money's worth.

I see an outline as a narrative road map. It's how I get from here to there. I often have key scenes and set pieces written in my head before I put word one on paper. (*The Tomb*, the entire novel, evolved from a single set piece: the battle on Jack's rooftop.) Outlining allows me to situate those key scenes where they'll have maximum impact on the story and the reader, allows me to build toward them so that they feel as if they *belong*.

Even if I weren't an outliner, I'd have had to become one for the Repairman Jack novels. As a rule I involve him in multiple plotlines and parallel story threads that often crisscross. The sequence of events and their relative timing have to be carefully worked out in advance. I'll often outline the threads separately, then mesh them. Sometimes this is so complex that I have to cut up the separate outlines into their respective scenes and lay them out side by side on the floor. Then I interweave them so that all the fuses are lit when the lines intersect.

An outline is not simply a road map; it's a sort of safety net too. I'll be writing along and all of a sudden I find myself stuck. Things aren't meshing the way they're supposed to. I don't write with the outline in front of me, so I pull it out and often find that I solved that very problem months ago. I'd simply forgotten.

Once the outline is done, I print it out and stick it in a drawer for a couple of weeks. I'll often send it to my agent and editor to see if they notice any major inconsistencies or lapses in logic. By the time I expose it to the light again, my subconscious has been gnawing on it. I see places where characters and situations need to be shored up or pared down, where the order of scenes has to be rearranged. I make changes and additions, usually by hand.

I've learned to leave the outline loose, keep it a simple ordering of events with just enough elaboration to clarify motives and justify actions. If you overdetail it you can wind up with a depressing sense of authorial *déjà vu*—a feeling that you've already written this book. You've got to leave room to surprise yourself.

And surprises are inevitable.

Tropical Storm Elvis in my novel *Gateways* is a good example. On one of my research sorties to Florida, my plane's flight path was adjusted to the west because Tropical Storm Edouard was churning up the Atlantic off Daytona. I made a mental note to have Jack's flight do the same, and thought it would be fun to call the storm "Elvis." That was all Elvis was supposed to be: a passing mention.

The storm wasn't even in the outline, but Elvis wound up a major player in the final draft.

So, once the road map is done, I begin the trip. I start with chapter one and go from there. That works best for me. I have those aforementioned key scenes and set pieces already visualized, and I'm itching to get to them, but I hold off. A good friend who's a successful author writes his books out of order. His rationale: When he's ready to write a scene, he writes it. All well and good if that works for you, but I use those scenes as carrots to keep me grinding through the areas I haven't worked out. I find it best to let events unfold in order. That way I can monitor motivation and causality as I go along, making sure each scene builds from the last and reaches for the next.

Along the way I inevitably find areas where what worked well in outline won't hold up in fully fleshed text. So I make adjustments and deviate from the map.

Sometimes I've taken so many unplanned turns that a pre-visualized set piece has to be drastically altered to make it fit. If I'd written it in advance I'd have to tear it down and rewrite it. Wasted time. Wasted effort. I hate waste.

The upshot is that the novel almost always winds up in the place I intended, but hardly ever gets there via the intended path.

That's it. As I said, it works for me—has for thirty years. Might work for you too.

How Do I Become a
TV Writer If I Don't Have
Any Contacts?

LEE GOLDBERG

Those who haven't read his series featuring Monk or his *Diagnosis Murder* books have probably seen Lee Goldberg's work as a screenwriter on *Monk*, *Diagnosis Murder*, *Missing*, *Baywatch*, and a host of other television shows. He's also written several stand-alone novels including *The Walk*, *My Gun Has Bullets*, and *The Man with the Iron-On Badge*, as well as a terrific book on screenwriting titled *Successful Television Writing*. Visit Lee's Web site at www.leegoldberg.com.

....

I get this question a lot ... but it's disingenuous, since I'm a TV writer/producer and whoever is asking me that is *really* asking me to either read their script or to invite them in to pitch. So, theoretically, they already know somebody in the business.

They're luckier than I was when I got started. I didn't know anybody in the TV industry. But I got in. How did I do it? Everybody's story is unique, as this book certainly proves. Most of those stories, however, probably share one common element: You have to put yourself in the right place to get your lucky break. And it's easier than you think.

The first thing you have to do is learn your craft. Take classes, preferably taught by people who have had some success as TV writers. There's no point taking a class from anyone who is not an experienced TV writer.

You'd think that would be common sense, but you'd be astonished how many TV courses are taught by people who don't know the first thing about writing for television or who, through a fluke, sold a story to *Manimal* twenty years ago and think that qualifies them to take your hundred bucks. Even more surprising is how many desperate people shell out money to take courses from instructors who should be taking TV writing courses themselves.

There's another reason to take a TV writing course besides learning the basics of the craft. If you're the least bit likeable, you'll make a few friends among the other classmates. This is good, because you'll have other people you can show your work to. This is also good because somebody in the class may sell his or her first script before you do … and suddenly you'll have a friend in the business.

A writer we hired on staff on the first season of *Missing* was in a Santa Monica screenwriters group … and was the first member of her class to get a paying writing gig. Now her friends in the class suddenly had a friend on a network TV show who could share her knowledge, give them practical advice, and even recommend them to her new agent and the writer/producers she was working with. Many of my own writer/producer friends today are writers I knew back when I was in college, when we were all dreaming of breaking into TV some day.

Another route is to try and get a job as a writer/producer's assistant on an hour-long drama. Not only will you get a meager salary, but you will see how a show works from the inside. You'll read lots of scripts and revisions and, simply by observation, get a graduate course in TV writing. More important, you'll establish relationships with the writers on the show and the freelancers who come through the door. Many of today's top TV producers were writer/producer assistants once. All of the assistants I've had have gone on to become working TV writers themselves … and not because I gave them a script assignment or recommended them for one. I didn't do either.

The first step towards getting in to pitch a TV producer for an episodic writing assignment is to write an episodic teleplay on spec. By that, I mean a pick a show and write an episode for it.

Although there are some producers who prefer to read screenplays, most showrunners, agents, and network executives want to read an episodic teleplay. Even if your spec feature script has acceptable levels of dialogue, characterization, and structure, people thinking of hiring you will still wonder, "Yes, but can he handle *my* characters? Does he understand the four-act structure?" An original piece can demonstrate that you have a strong voice, but it doesn't show whether or not you blend that voice with ours. Can you write what we need without losing whatever it is that makes you unique? That's why we need to see your talents applied to a TV episode. To someone else's characters. To someone else's voice.

How do you pick a show to spec? Easy. Pick a show you like. Odds are, if you're thinking about trying to become a TV writer, you already know what show you want to spec—you just don't know you know. It's the one you watch every week, and when it's over, you find yourself thinking: *That was pretty good, but wouldn't it be cool if….*

Don't worry about what's hot and what's not—choose a show you feel a connection to, one that you "get." With some exceptions:

1. Try to stay away from syndicated or basic cable science fiction shows like *Andromeda* or *Stargate.* Not because they aren't good shows, but because most showrunners and network executives don't watch them. They wouldn't know whether an *Angela's Eyes* or *Wildfire* spec was any good because they've never seen the shows.

2. Also try to stay away from first-year shows, unless they are big hits. Otherwise, by the time you finish your spec, the show could be cancelled already … and your script will be useless. No one is going to read a spec for a show that was cancelled after thirteen episodes … or twenty-two.

Many writers feel compelled to write a *Sopranos* or *The Shield* simply because they're "hot" shows. That's great if you have some kind of feel for the shows—but if you don't, you're not going to write a good *Sopranos* no matter how fine a writer you are.

What shows do you look forward to? Which world would you like to live in? Which characters would be happiest living in your brain for a few weeks? *That's* the show to write.

What you're going to be writing is a typical episode. It's not your job to write the show you think it should be; it's your job to write the best possible version of the show that *is*. You need to prove that you can mimic the style and feeling of a show while still letting your unique voice and vision shine through.

Let me underscore this again. You want to write a typical episode. You don't want to write a "mythology" episode that delves into the deep backstory at the heart of the series. If it's a show that derives much of its conflict from the sexual tension between two characters, you don't write the episode where they sleep together. If it's a show about people lost in space or on an island, don't write the episode where they find their way home or get rescued. If it's a show about a fugitive on the run for a crime he didn't commit, don't write the episode where he proves his innocence. (And don't ever, ever, ever write a spec "cross-over" with characters from another series, movie, book, or animated cartoon).

What you're trying to prove with your spec is:

1. You're not illiterate. You know how to write.
2. You know how to write a script in the proper format.
3. You know how to structure a scene.
4. You know how to structure an act.
5. You know how to tell a story.
6. You understand the four act structure.
7. You can craft a story that serves the franchise of the show (i.e., a story that could only be told within the conceptual framework of that particular series).
8. You can capture the voices of the characters.
9. You can capture the storytelling style of the show.

What you *aren't* trying to prove is how clever you are, or how much better you'd be writing the show than the people who are already writing it. Your goal is to write an entertaining, tight, *typical* episode of the show that illustrates your professional skills ... not your amazing style and unique voice. While TV producers are interested in your voice, what they really want to hear is how well you capture *their* voice. Your job as a TV writer to is channel the showrunner's vision, not your own.

And as soon as you finish writing that terrific spec, start on another for a different series, preferably one that's the opposite of what you've just written (for example, a procedural and a melodrama). Because the first thing a TV producer will ask after reading your spec is ...

Do you have another spec he can read?

The Secret to Getting Published

RAY WHITE

The Publication Blues

I've queried and networked, till blue in the face
Submitted, submitted all over the place
Read my rejections (and some made me cuss)
"Great concept," "well written"—"just not right for us."

Then what, I would ask, does it take to succeed?
If "great concept," "well written" won't get me a read
Persistence, it seems, in the face of rejection
Is the only sure path that leads to selection.

The odds are quite simple—you will or you won't
Those who will, do—and those who don't, won't.

— RAY WHITE

There is, of course, no secret way to get published. No hidden key, no insider information, no shortcut. There is no way to skip over these mandatory steps: First learn to write; then go out and sell it.

Certainly you can short-circuit the system by self-publishing. You won't have to study the market, write tedious query letters, or get rejected by agents and editors. You won't even have to be any good at writing.

But self-published means you have to do everything yourself. Choose the printer, design the cover, sell the book, store the printed copies ... and pay for it all yourself.

Self-publishing is when you pay for the books. Getting published is when someone else pays.

If you want to *get* published you have to be good, you have to be determined, and you have to attract the attention of an agent or an editor at a publishing house. To do that you need only two things: luck and persistence.

Persistence is sending letters again and again, ignoring the rejections, sending more letters, and so on, until somebody caves and takes your book. **Luck** is buying a lottery ticket. Luck is your Uncle Phil being the manager of a large publishing house, or your cousin's babysitter being the daughter of a top literary agent.

The Pros and Cons of Luck

The plus side of luck is that it does happen. You could send out a single query letter and get an immediate response: "Loved your book. Want to publish it. Where do I send the money?" Your manuscript might be just what they're looking for that day. If they turn down books because it's not what they're seeking, then sometimes they have to take a book because it *is* exactly what they need.

After all, somebody always wins the pot in a poker game. As a buddy of mine, who plays poker professionally, said, "Over the course of an evening, skill will determine the winner. But on any particular hand luck can beat skill." And despite Hollywood insanity, movies do get made. New authors do get published every year. Lottery tickets always pay off for someone. The problem with the luck strategy is that *your* lottery number isn't likely to come up, which leads us to ...

The Pros and Cons of Persistence

The plus side of persistence is that persistence is as close to a sure thing as possible in this business.

Persistence is sending out a new query every time you get a rejection. And while you're doing it you can think, "Take that!" There's no guarantee you're going to win, and it costs some time and money and hope and faith. But it feels great when an agent says yes. Euphoria.

Two sides of the same coin:

Persistence is doing the same thing over and over until it works.

Insanity is doing the same thing over and over and expecting different results.

Persistence is like door-to-door sales or telemarketing: a game of numbers. You can improve your odds by doing it a lot. In sales there's a rule of thumb: it takes one hundred nos to get a single yes. Any time a telemarketer or a door-to-door salesman gets a phone or door slammed in their face they are expected to feel a bit closer to success.

Call—slam!—"Oh, goody; I'm one step closer to my goal." A motivational speaker once said, after being told about a writer who received another three rejection letters, "*Congratulations!* You are now three steps closer to your goal!"

Which Is Better: Persistence or Luck?

Neither. Persistence is the king. Luck has to happen. The secret to success—in anything—is both. Read the stories throughout this book of how other writers made it. You'll find that there are many more instances of people who wouldn't give up than there are of happy coincidence. Many more. But all of the writers had to have that moment of being in the right place at the right time.

If luck were all, we'd just wait by the phone for it to ring. If persistence were all, the nags would rule the world.

In both cases, luck and persistence, you have to actually go out and *do something*. Nobody is likely to come to your door and ask politely, "Excuse me, I'm a literary agent. Is there a writer here?" Even Publisher's Clearing House won't send Ed McMahon and the Dream Team out to your house unless you stick the envelope in the mail.

All lottery winners had to buy a ticket. All gamblers had to go to the casino. All published writers had to write something—*and send it out!*

You have to send query letters or go to conferences and talk to people and keep doing these things even when you'd rather just go home and write another book. Since you have to go out and do something, the question becomes *what*? Writers conferences? Query letters? A compelling Web site?

The plan is the answer to the question, "What am I going to do when I get up tomorrow?"

Are you going to send query letters? How many? To whom? Are you going to send directly to editors that accept unagented writers, or will you target agents?

Whatever your plan, it's time to get busy and get on with making things happen.

Your Goal: To Get an Agent or Publisher

Right? You're not reading this book to learn how to write; you're doing so to get published. To do that you have to meet, and get accepted by, an agent or an editor. So here's what you do.

1. WRITE SOMETHING.

2. EDIT IT, GET CRITIQUES, AND RE-EDIT IT.

3. CREATE A "HOW TO GET PUBLISHED PLAN."
    a. Query letters to agents
        (1) Mass mailing or one at a time to a specific agent? In either case, find contact information
            (a) Writer's Market books
            (b) Online
    b. Direct to publishers
        (1) Research who to send to
            (most don't accept without agent)
            (a) Writer's Market books
            (b) Online

(c) Meet agents in person

    1. At conventions

    2. If they ask for sample chapters/synopsis, go to step 6.c (Keep Sending)

4. WRITE A QUERY LETTER, INCLUDING

a. A terrific title

b. A one-sentence hook

c. Author bio

d. A one-paragraph synopsis

e. The SASE

5. MAIL CAMPAIGN

a. Who do you mail to?

    (1) Find agents in *Writer's Market* or *Jeff Herman's Guide to Book Publishers, Editors & Literary Agents*

    (2) Search online

b. Multiple submissions — how many are you sending out?

    (1) Mail or e-mail (their choice)

    (2) How do you keep track? (Suggestion: the log in/log out)

6. RESULTS

a. Receive a "Dear Author" letter or the dreaded no response at all

    (1) Rewrite your query letter and send it out again.

b. The agent sends a personal note

    (1) Keep sending

c. The agent requests three sample chapters and a brief synopsis

    (1) Write a terrific 2–3 page synopsis

    (2) Send the chapters and synopsis

    (3) Log them in and wait

    (4) And wait. And wait

        (a) Get another rejection and go back to step 6.b.1 (Keep Sending), or

      (b) The agent likes them and you're requested to send
          a complete manuscript
          1. Follow the rules for sending a manuscript
          2. Get a call from the agent/editor saying "Yes!"

That's the entire plan. Certainly there are other ways. We used a very effective query letter and sent it to every agent we could find and that led to this book being published.

But overall, the tried and true method of getting an agent who will represent you and get your book in the door of a publisher seems to be the best route.

I Didn't Know Any Better

GAYLE LYNDS

New York Times best-seller Gayle Lynds is the award-winning author of eight international espionage novels, including *The Last Spymaster* (described by *Library Journal* and the *Chicago Tribune* as one of the finest thrillers of the year), *The Coil*, *Masquerade*, and *Mesmerized*, which are published in some twenty countries. Her books have been *People* magazine's "Page Turner of the Week" and "Beach Book of the Week." A member of the Association for Intelligence Operatives, Gayle is cofounder and co-president (with David Morrell) of International Thriller Writers, Inc., and is listed in *Who's Who in the World*. Born in Nebraska, raised in Iowa, she now lives in Southern California. Visit her at www.GayleLynds.com.

I gnorance is bliss, or so we're told. Personally, I find ignorance is also destiny. I didn't know I wasn't supposed to write international thrillers. No one told me. Who would've thought? I loved them. My girlfriends and guy friends loved them. Everywhere I looked, from beaches to boardrooms, from sweaty locker rooms to jam-packed economy classes, adults and teens of all sexual persuasions, skin colors, ages, religions, accents, and percentages of body fat devoured books by Ludlum and Le Carre, Forsyth and Follett.

Let me back up here. A few years before, I hadn't realized something else: I wasn't supposed to cover what those of us in the trade called *hard news*. I was a kid reporter for the *Arizona Republic*, a fine old rag with a reputedly progressive outlook about gender equality.

Alongside the men, women "manned" the city room, with specific assignments like the weather and vegetable gardens — not my cup of cyanide, I thought.

I had an advantage — I was a newbie, and, hence, a general-assignment reporter in supposedly a brand-new era. As far as I was concerned, that was a license to write, and the world itself was my beat. Thus, when riots erupted in downtown Phoenix, I asked, then begged (when I want something, I don't mind a little public humiliation) to go out to cover the mean streets. But as my male pals rushed off to fulfill the public's need to know, the city editor explained the work was too dangerous for a girl, and he gave me a another assignment — obituaries.

Writing obits is considered an art form by some. I told myself that. I really tried to like it. I worked to convince myself it was enough to know I was doing a service. Plus, if I just threw in some multisyllabic words, extended my sentences until each was a paragraph long, and used "darkling" a few times, I'd be the Faulkner of Phoenix.

Right. All I could think of was Dante's *Inferno*. I was in hell.

Sometimes you get what you want not because it's right or fair or even smart, but because you just don't know any better.

For those in the know, the obit desk is the classic punishment in a city room. I could see no escape. Then a young guy arrived — a new hire, general assignment reporter, hungry to learn. Fueled by desperation, I took him to lunch — hot tacos washed down by a multitude of icy margaritas, emphasis on the margaritas. We talked about the future and his dream of becoming a first-rate reporter. Of course, to achieve that, he really needed to experience all the city room had to offer. Unfortunately, he couldn't take over obits. Too bad. I had that juicy assignment.

He couldn't believe I liked it. But at that moment, writing obituaries became to me the most fascinating, most rewarding, most career-enhancing job ever. I was reluctant to switch with him, of course. Still, I let him talk me into it.

Sometimes you get what you want not because it's right or fair or even smart, but because you just don't know any better. The city editor threw up his hands then threw in the towel. As it turned out, the forces of society's progress had become evident even to a knuckle-dragger like him. My goal had been escape, but my reward was far greater: After a lecture and several deep belly-growls of disapproval, he sent me out to cover the tail end of the riots. I returned tired, happy, and with news stories. Both of us had done our jobs—at last.

Thus in 1996 when my first novel, *Masquerade*, was published, I knew international thrillers—or spy novels, if you prefer—had been the domain of male authors for decades. Still, women read them. In fact, women were such big fans that they not only accounted for a significant percentage of sales, but they also introduced them to their boyfriends, husbands, and sons. Since I loved spy novels, that's what I wanted to write. As I said, ignorance is destiny. It didn't occur to me I wasn't supposed to.

But it occurred to others. When *Masquerade* was published, one prominent magazine claimed I was "aping" my male betters. I would've preferred "chimpanzeeing" since they apparently have a higher facility for language. A couple of men who reviewed for large publications were more graphic—telling me in person that they'd never review my books because I was in effect cutting off the private parts of male authors.

I had a brief vision of winged penises sailing through the air, making a sexy, whooshing sound.

I explained that I suspected guys' "private parts" were fastened on a lot better than that, but the boys were drinking—martinis, it was happy hour—and thought I was being typically illogical.

Then there was the time a publisher tried to get me to rewrite one of my books as a romance before it was published. I had to fly to New York to explain that fans of the novels I was coauthoring with Robert Ludlum probably would want to try my books, but if they didn't find what they expected with this new one, they'd be unlikely to bother to buy another, thus hurting the publisher's bottom line.

Also, my dust jackets were less than helpful. One sported a woman in a black bodysuit, aiming a very lethal-looking pistol—and wearing spike heels so high they probably made their first appearance in a comic book. Another showed a couple running ... well, more like trotting (gotta catch the doggie before he lands in the neighbor's doo-doo)—and holding hands as if they'd just discovered love. And those were the two *best* covers. You may have noticed that the dust jackets of spy thrillers written by men have little in common with the ones I just described.

To say I was being marginalized is an understatement. My sales plummeted. I have no idea why I didn't quit. Stubbornness, perhaps. Or maybe it was simply that I am so besotted by the work, by the joy of words and ideas, by high adventure and low politics, by secrecy and smart skullduggery, by the imperative to try to make some sort of sense of our confounding universe ... that as long as I can crawl to a computer or a quill pen, I will write.

And, too, if I'd given up, I would've missed a lot of fun.

Finally, senior editor Keith Kahla of St. Martin's found my work, liked it a lot, and took me on. A brilliant editor and publisher, he's helped to repackage my books in such a way that they speak to large numbers of readers. Another change was in the times—because of 9/11, readers' desire for international political fiction was re-ignited. Then in 2004 I cofounded and was elected co-president (with David Morrell) of International Thriller Writers, Inc., which has become a force in the industry (who could've predicted that would happen?).

Recently, the Military Writers Society of America awarded my new book, *The Last Spymaster*, its Novel of the Year prize. Do they care that I'm female? Obviously not. Then the erudite Peter Cannon of *Publishers Weekly* compiled a list of fifteen top spy novels: Right after number seven—Ken Follett's classic *The Eye of the Needle*—appeared my debut novel, *Masquerade*. What a wonderful honor. *BookPage* claims, "Lynds has joined the deified ranks of spy thriller authors like Robert Ludlum and John le Carre." With Ludlum, I created the Covert-One series, and one of the novels I wrote for it, *The Hades Factor*, was a CBS miniseries in April 2006. Today I'm not only listed in *Who's Who in America*, but *Who's Who in the World*.

Staying the course is hard, especially when it seems as if everything is going wrong. Our only solace as writers is in the work itself, and perhaps also in a penchant for blissful ignorance that allows us to gamble, to risk, to keep going where others would tote up the odds and stop. But these are the sweetest victories of all, and with a soupçon of luck, our destiny.

Getting Started
Getting Published

GREG BEAR

Upon meeting Greg Bear for the first time, Isaac Asimov looked at his name tag with a surprised expression and said, "So you're Greg Bear. I'm glad you weren't around when I was getting started." Now that's a compliment! Greg is one of the lucky few who knew he wanted to be a writer from a very early age. The author of *Eon, Darwin's Radio*, and some thirty other superb works of fiction and nonfiction, Greg has won two Hugo Awards and five Nebula Awards for his work. For more information (and for excellent tips on writing), visit his Web site at www.gregbear.com.

....

My story is simple enough: I've been writing since I was seven or eight years old and began submitting stories to magazines when I was twelve. (My mother submitted a cartoon of mine to the *Saturday Evening Post* when I was eleven, and it received a very nice rejection letter ... .) By the time I was fifteen, I was corresponding with editor and writer Robert A.W. Lowndes about the "blood and gore" factor inherent in the cover design for his new magazine, *The Magazine of Horror*—suggesting he tone it down a little and go upscale. I submitted my own logo design along with the letter, and he graciously replied but stuck with the blood and gore. (Later, Lowndes would publish an early Stephen King story between those very same garish, gory covers.)

A few months later, I submitted a short story to another of Lowndes's magazines, *Famous Science Fiction*, and lo and behold, the blessed gentleman purchased that item, promising to pay the munificent sum of ten dollars on publication!

A year later, my story came out, and some high school buddies and I made a trek to Readerama, a book and magazine emporium in Grossmont Shopping Center in San Diego, California. There I bought a copy of my first professional appearance in print. Some of my high school English teachers found it difficult to believe they were trying to tutor a writer with such high literary accomplishments. (I was almost refused entrance into the Advanced English program, because my test essay discussed *Dune* rather than some more acceptable title, like *Moby Dick*.)

It took me four more years to sell another story, but in that time period I began writing novels and going to conventions and making many important contacts, which have served me well to this day. So — thanks to Doc Lowndes for his support!

I found my first agent while collaborating with Alan Brennert on a potential *Star Trek* script in the 1970s. The script did not sell, but I did hook up with Richard Curtis (an agent), who then negotiated the deal for my first novel, *Hegira*, which had already been accepted by Jim Frenkel at Dell Publishing.

I've been with Richard ever since — and it was Jim Frenkel who later bought *Eon* after a number of other publishers had rejected it.

There's a Word for a Writer Who Never Gives Up ... Published

J.A. KONRATH

Readers first meet Lieutenant Jacqueline (Jack) Daniels in *Whiskey Sour* where she is hunted by one of the most twisted serial killers ever encountered in fiction. While her tough cop persona doesn't suffer in *Bloody Mary* or *Rusty Nail*, J.A. Konrath makes her ever more human and sympathetic in each novel. He also delivers the goods with a tongue-in-cheek sense of humor that leaves his readers chuckling and seriously looking forward to getting *Dirty Martini*. J.A., or Joe, as his friends call him, has put together a great Web site full of terrific writing tips for unpublished and struggling writers. Visit it at www.jakonrath.com

After my sixth novel failed to sell, I knew it was time to get serious. My Rejection Book was filled to bursting, bong slips divided into *agent* and *editor* categories. Close to five hundred of them. With the baby's first birthday approaching and a new house recently purchased, my friends and family were beginning to wonder when I was going to give up this "hobby" and get a real job working nine to five.

I made my living waiting tables. The flexible schedule allowed me plenty of time to write. My girlfriend (who later became my wife) worked in the same restaurant, and I would often trade shifts with her if the muse was in overdrive. She'd always been supportive, even when we were dating and I had my *bad agent experience*.

Rewind to three years earlier. I was fresh out of college, where I majored in television. I'd switched my major to TV from film, because I heard it was too hard to get a job in film.

I found out it was just as hard to get a job in television. Though I had good grades, and a killer show reel, I'd graduated in the middle of a huge recession and was going up for entry-level positions against people with years of experience.

I tried my best, failed, and then wondered what the heck my education was good for, other than teaching me how to make my own beer bongs and how to add watermelon Jolly Ranchers to a bottle of vodka for some wicked sweet shooters.

Since writing is what I wanted to pursue in both film and TV, and since I had a love of books and had already written dozens of short stories, I decided to take the plunge and write a mystery novel.

It took a few months. When I finished, I picked up a *Writer's Market* book, picked out six agents, and sent them copies of the book, figuring it was only a matter of time until one of them called me.

Believe it or not, one did.

He was a respected, well-known agent with some big-name clients, and I immediately signed on the dotted line. I drove to New York to meet him soon after, and he took me to a five-star restaurant and filled my head with promises of fame and riches while I fought a losing battle of matching him martini for martini.

Life was good.

When I came back home, I considered quitting my job. After all, the sale would come quick, and the money would roll in.

A week passes. A month. Three months.

I call my superstar agent and get an assistant who explains that sometimes it takes a while to sell a book.

That hadn't been what Mr. Bigshot told me over Grey Goose, but I still trusted the guy.

Six months pass. A year. By this time, I've written a sequel to the first book, and I send it to Mr. Bigshot.

A few weeks pass, and I call him to see if he's read the new book.

His assistant explains that he's really busy.

Another six months go by. Finally, I call up Mr. Bigshot and insist on speaking to him personally. The assistant won't allow it. So I insist on getting a list of all the publishing houses that have rejected my book.

The assistant sends me a list. A list of two houses.

In nineteen months, he'd shown my book to two editors.

Even though I was ignorant about New York publishing, I knew this was bad. There were dozens of publishing houses who bought mysteries. Only going to two of them proved this guy wasn't doing a thing for me.

I fired him, deciding to look for a new agent. After all, he was easy to get. All I had to do was buy the latest *Writer's Market*, pick out a few more agents, and wait for them to call.

No one called. I tried every agent in New York and couldn't get anyone interested in my series. This lead to a bout of depression. My girlfriend offered to cheer my up by buying me a unique gift. A tattoo.

"That's very white-trash of you, honey," I told her.

But she explained that she had 100 percent faith that I'd someday be published, and a tattoo would inspire me to keep trying.

Well, we went to Jade Dragon in Chicago, and I had them put a little frowny face on my right shoulder.

But now, after six unpublished novels, all the frowny face did was depress me even more.

Should I continue pursuing the dream of becoming a published author? Or should I do the responsible thing and get a well-paying office job?

"You aren't allowed to give up," my girlfriend/now-my-wife told me. "You're a writer, whether you get paid for it or not."

She was right. I'd be miserable doing anything else.

So I decided to write a blockbuster.

My previous approach to writing was very free-form and unstructured. I'd write when I felt like it, about whatever I felt like. My growing pile of form letter rejections was testament to how well this worked for me. I needed to regroup.

The term "high-concept" is often bandied around Hollywood, used to describe movies that have strong, central hooks. Blockbuster novels have hooks as well. "Shark kills swimmers on New York beach." "Little girl is possessed by the devil." "Science learns to clone dinosaurs." "FBI trainee interviews a captured serial killer." I wanted to write something like that, something that could be described in a brief sentence but still perfectly conveyed the story idea.

Coming up with a catchy hook on which to base ninety thousand words was easier said than done. I took a break from writing to brainstorm. How could I put a new spin on an old concept? What topic could capture the public's imagination?

I decided on something with universal appeal. The hook: Satan is being held and studied in a secret government laboratory.

It would be a cross between *Jurassic Park* and *The Exorcist*. A thriller that pits cutting-edge technology against thousands of years of theology. Plus, it had the biggest monster of them all: an eight-foot-tall, cloven-hoofed Beelzebub, complete with bat wings, horns, and a predilection for eating live sheep.

To do the story justice, I knew I had to research the hell out of it, so to speak. When I had a confident grasp of the science and religion involved, I worked on developing characters who would interact with the demon, and then a story line that would do the concept proud.

A year later, my techno-thriller *Origin* was completed.

Now what was I supposed to do with it?

I went back to my Rejection Book to review my previous queries and was surprised to see how poor they were. The letters fell into two distinct categories: egocentric and desperate. Rather than succinctly pitch my novels, I had been begging for them to be read or stating how rich I'd make the publisher once they bought me.

Plus, I was shocked to see typos and poor grammar, not only in the queries, but in the sample chapters I'd submitted.

For *Origin*, I needed a different approach. I decided to do the same thing publishers do to sell books. Namely, an ad campaign.

Rather than a standard query letter and sample chapters, I put together a four-page package. The first page was a two-paragraph excerpt from the novel, when the hero first sees Satan sitting in a gigantic Plexiglas cage. The second page was styled like back-jacket copy, describing the story and the hook in a few sentences. The third page was an author bio, with black-and-white photo. The final page was a simple note stating that the book was seeking representation, and my phone number.

I went back to my Rejection Book to review my previous queries and was surprised to see how poor they were. The letters fell into two distinct categories: egocentric and desperate.

No SASE or return address. I didn't even personalize the note.

I made one hundred twenty submission packages and sent one to every agent in the Writer's Digest *Guide to Literary Agents*.

I sent these on a Thursday.

By Tuesday, I had five agent phone calls, all demanding to see the book.

I was in shock. Usually, an agent response took between three and ten weeks. Now I had them fighting over me. What should I do?

This time, I wanted to hire an agent who would work for me. I wanted to be involved in every aspect of the submission process. My next agent would keep me informed, be my biggest advocate, and help me build a career.

After several phone interviews with ultimately twelve agents, I decided on Todd Keithley from Jane Dystel Literary Management. Todd was my age, had a specific plan to market me, and most of all, loved the book.

There was rewriting. And more rewriting. And more rewriting.

Todd generated a buzz in New York about the book and went out to the top fifteen publishers with an expiration date on the manuscript.

It was very exciting, and a thrill to be a part of it.

The rejections were the hardest of my life.

On the plus side, many editors said wonderful things about me and my book. I got many compliments and, finally, confirmation from the publishing world that I indeed had talent.

But *Origin* was ultimately rejected because it slipped through the genre cracks. Editors didn't know how to market it. Was it horror? SF? Techno-thriller? Comedy? Where did this book fit on the shelves?

To compound the injury, Todd then left the agency to pursue a law practice in Maryland.

I was devastated.

Luckily, his boss saw potential in me. Before Todd bid his final adieu, I received a phone call from Jane Dystel who succinctly asked, "What else have you got?"

I did have something else, another high-concept idea that came to me while writing *Origin*. I pitched it over the phone to Jane.

"Write it," she advised.

I did.

Another year passed, research and writing. When I finished, I gave Jane the same kind of ad campaign I'd designed for *Origin*.

Jane loved it. She generated a buzz and went out to seventeen publishing houses.

The rejections mirrored those received by *Origin*. What kind of book was this? Was it a thriller or a comedy?

But one publisher liked it. There was a problem, however. The book was a hundred thirty thousand words.

"Can you cut thirty thousand?"

I said I could. The effort was one of the most frustrating—and at the same time rewarding—episodes in my writing career. Because I didn't want to affect the story, I delegated myself to trimming the fat.

And there was fat. A lot of it.

When I finished, the editor read the revision and said, "Cut another ten thousand words."

Now there was no choice; I had to cut story. It was very difficult to do. I was forced to confront my novel and determine what was essential to the plot and what could be left out without disturbing the narrative flow.

But I did it. And it improved the book, a lot.

The editor read this version and said, "You know, I think I like your concept more than your execution of the concept. Can you start over from the beginning?"

Jane stepped in before I popped a blood vessel.

"We'll move on to the next book, Joe."

For my third book with the agency, I decided to make sure I wrote in a specific, distinct, defined genre: the medical thriller. Also, because editors seemed puzzled by the amount of humor I was putting in my books, I completely cut out the jokes.

After another year of writing and research, I gave the results to Jane.

She *hated* it, and refused to represent it. Jane liked my sense of humor, and a novel without jokes had no spark.

Back to square one.

Again, I took time away from writing to brainstorm. I liked Jane a lot, as a person and as an agent, but I didn't think she'd keep me on as a client if I kept giving her books she couldn't sell.

My last three books were failures, but they were important failures. They taught me how to rewrite. They taught me that I needed to use humor. They taught me that techno-thrillers and medical thrillers weren't working for me.

So what genre was left? What would be the best vehicle for my sense of humor?

I went downstairs and began perusing my library. A pattern emerged. Janet Evanovich. Robert B. Parker. Lawrence Block. Robert Crais. Donald Westlake.

All my life I loved mysteries. My favorites were series characters, especially ones that were funny.

Why hadn't I thought of that before? This was a genre I knew and loved, and something that would allow me to zing the one-liners and have fun.

I created Violent Crimes Lieutenant Jack Daniels of the Chicago PD. I used every convention popular in successful mysteries; a flawed but funny female hero, a recurring cast of oddball characters, a catchy title that instantly identified the series, a spring-loaded plot.

A few months later, I gave *Whiskey Sour* to Jane, along with proposals for the second and third books in the series, *Bloody Mary* and *Rusty Nail*.

Jane loved it.

She helped me tweak the concept, and after two requisite rewrites, she went out with the book.

In the meantime, I started work on another high-concept novel, so when *Whiskey Sour* got rejected, I'd have something else to pitch to Jane.

But the damnedest thing happened. A few days after Jane submitted the book, she gave me a call.

"We have an offer. It's for six figures."

She named a number. I jumped around my house like a wind-up toy.

"That's great! We're accepting it, right?"

"No. Another editor is interested. I think I can get more. In the meantime, Leslie Wells at Hyperion wants to talk to you. Is tomorrow morning good for you?"

Leslie was a hero of mine, having edited two of my favorite authors, Ridley Pearson and Robert Crais. The thought of working with her awed me.

But what should I say? How should I act?

"Just be yourself," Jane advised. "I think you'll like each other."

Leslie and I instantly hit it off. She loved my book, but more importantly, she had great plans for the series, and great ideas on how to make *Whiskey Sour* even better.

I got off the phone hoping Hyperion would wind up with the book.

The call came two days later.

"Joe? Jane Dystel. Are you sitting down? Hyperion made an offer."

After ten books, twelve years, 460 rejections, my dream had finally come true.

My wife took me out to celebrate. But we didn't go out to eat. We didn't go to a concert, or a show, or to France.

We went to a tattoo parlor.

Now, on my left shoulder, there's a smiley face.

To match the other smiley face I wear all the time.

Above Movies

JOHN GILSTRAP

In seven days John Gilstrap went from unpublished novelist to millionaire ... an inspiring story if there ever was one. Read his books—*Nathan's Run* (one of the most gripping adventures ever written), *At All Costs, Even Steven, Scott Free,* and *Six Minutes to Freedom*—to learn how it's done from a master. In addition to being a *New York Times* bestselling author, John is generous in his efforts to help aspiring writers, so check out his Web site at www.johngilstrap.com. The following article is taken with permission from that site.

Two days after I sold the North American hardcover rights for *Nathan's Run*, and my head was still spinning from the equivalent to hitting the lottery, I got an amazing phone call from my literary agent. The conversation went something like this:

"Hi, John, this is Molly. I was wondering if you had anything special planned for this evening."

"Well, this is Friday, so we usually do pizza and a movie. Why?"

"Funny you should mention movies. The bidding's getting pretty hot in Hollywood for the movie rights. Last time I heard, seven studios were involved. I think the deal will probably close tonight, and I'd like you to stick near the phone for a while, if that's not too much trouble."

You've got to remember now that just two days before, I was teaching classes on the handling and storage of hazardous wastes. I was an engineer, for God's sake, living in Woodbridge, Virginia; not exactly the center of the media universe. After mulling the question for about one one-thousandth of a second, I said something cool and aloof like, "What, are you kidding??? Of course I can stick near the phone! Oh, my God, a movie??"

The bidding was indeed furious, and after a few intervening phone calls—during which I found out for the first time that I had a Hollywood agent (my literary agent saw to that)—Matthew (the Hollywood guy) called at around ten o'clock that night to tell me that Disney had an offer on the table for more money than I had ever seen, cumulatively, in my entire life, and that we had ten minutes to make a decision.

"There's a decision to make?" I gasped.

"Well, yeah," said Matt. "In fact I'm advising you not to take it. At least not yet. We haven't heard from Warner Bros. Besides we have ten minutes...actually about eight-and-a-half minutes."

Disney's ten minutes were not approximate; their offer was good for precisely nine minutes and sixty seconds.

In fact, while we sat on the phone chatting—okay, he was chatting, and I was hyperventilating—Matt had to drop off the line every minute on the minute to take another call from the Mouse House, advising him that his client had exactly seven minutes to make up his mind. Six minutes ... five minutes.

When we got down to under three minutes, I started to crack. "Let's just take the offer," I begged. "I mean, I can't... ."

"Wait," Matt said. "I've got Warner Bros. on the other line."

He was gone for all of fifteen seconds.

"Warner just beat the offer from Disney," Matt announced. "Now, with your permission, I'd like to just play them against each other, unless you have a preference for producers... ."

Confession: At that point in my life, I didn't know what a producer did, let alone why I should prefer one over the other. I told him to use his best judgment.

Warner Bros. won, and I went to bed that night high as a kite, and reasonably certain that I was the only person in all of Woodbridge who'd closed a movie deal that night.

Oh, how quickly a life can change!

Nathan's Run Redux

Two years after I'd sold the movie rights to *Nathan's Run*, there'd still been no forward progress on the movie. Script problems, they said. Insurmountable ones, in fact. Matt the movie agent called with the bad news in August 1997: Warner Bros. was putting *Nathan's Run* in turn-around, the first in a complex series of steps that generally lead to a movie's death.

All because of script problems. I told Matt that the previous script-writers were missing the point of the story, that I could do better, if only given the chance.

Important Hollywood Lesson: Be careful what you say.

"Hmm," said Matt. "Do you think you could do it by next week?" The word "sure" escaped my lips before the filter in my brain had a chance to stop it. Sure I could write a screenplay in a week. Why should I let a little detail like never having seen a screenplay—let alone write one—stand in my way?

Bravado, baby. If you're gonna be a dog, be a big dog, that's what I always say.

So, I dashed out to my local bookstore and picked up a copy of William Goldman's book, *Adventures in the Screen Trade*, and read it cover to cover in a day. In it, he's got the complete script for *Butch Cassidy and the Sundance Kid*, and when I finished it, I actually thought I had a handle on this screenwriting thing, so I started writing. Three days later, I had a completed script for *Nathan's Run*.

Matt loved it. The executives at Warner Bros. loved it—enough to pull it out of turn-around and back into active development. But best of all, I had a decent writing sample for my agent to shop around Hollywood, in search of additional screenwriting work.

Oh, and where does the *Nathan's Run* movie project rest now, you ask? It's back in turn-around ... .

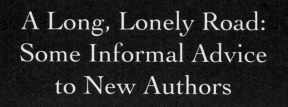

A Long, Lonely Road: Some Informal Advice to New Authors

DAVID BRIN

Fans of post-apocalyptic thrillers will find in David Brin's *The Postman* one of the best. (The movie starring Kevin Costner wasn't bad either.) But of course he's best known for his science fiction, most notably *The Uplift Saga*, *Second Foundation*, and the Out of Time series. David also writes illuminating nonfiction, proving that a writer of such talent and insight just can't be pigeonholed. All thinking beings should visit and explore his fascinating Web site at www.davidbrin.com, but be prepared—it's easy to spend hours there. And writers won't want to miss articles like the one below, reprinted with his generous permission.

Writing is a worthy calling—one that can, at times, achieve great heights that ennoble the human race.

Actually, I believe writing was the first truly verifiable and effective form of magic. Think of how it must have impressed people in ancient times! To look at marks, pressed into fired clay, and know that they convey the words of scribes and kings long dead—it must have seemed fantastic. Knowledge, wisdom, and art could finally accumulate, and death was cheated one part of its sting.

Still, let me admit and avow that writing was not my own first choice of a career. True, I came from a family of writers. It was in my blood. But I wanted something else—to be a scientist. And by the fates, I became one.

I also had this hobby, though—writing stories—and it provided a lot of satisfaction. I always figured that I'd scribble a few stories a year, maybe a novel now and then, while striving to become the best researcher and teacher I could be.

Don't mistake this for modesty! It's just that I perceive science—the disciplined pursuit of truth—to be a higher calling than spinning imaginative tales, no matter how vivid, innovative, or even deeply moving those tales may turn out to be.

I know this seems an unconventional view—certainly my fellow scientists tell me so, as they often express an envy that I find bemusing. As for the artists and writers I know, they seem almost universally convinced that they stand at the pinnacle of human undertakings. Doesn't society put out endless propaganda proclaiming that entertainers are beings close to gods?

Ever notice how this propaganda is feverishly spread by the very people who benefit from the image?

Don't you believe it. They are getting the whole thing backwards.

Oh, don't get me wrong; art is a core element to being human. We need it, from our brains all the way down to the heart and gut. Art is the original "magic." Even when we're starving—especially when we're starving—we can find nourishment at the level of the subjective, just by using our imaginations. As author Tom Robbins aptly put it, "Science gives man what he needs, but magic gives him what he wants." I'll grant all that. But don't listen when they tell you the other half—that art and artists are rare.

Have you ever noticed that no human civilization ever suffered from a deficit of artistic expression? Art fizzes from our very pores! How many people do you know who lavish time and money on an artistic hobby? Some of them are quite good, yet remain stuck way down the pyramid that treats the top figures like deities.

Imagine this. If all of the professional actors and entertainers died tomorrow, how many days before they were all replaced? Whether high or low, empathic or vile—art seems to pour from Homo Sapiens, almost as if it were a product of our metabolism, a natural part of ingesting and excreting. No, sorry. Art may be essential and deeply human, but it ain't rare.

What's rare is honesty. A willingness to look past all the fancy things we want to believe, peering instead at what may actually be true. And while every civilization had subjective arts, in copious supply, only one culture ever had the guts to seek objective truth through science.

As a child, despite my talents and background, it was science that struck me as truly grand and romantically noble — a team effort in which egotism took a second seat to the main goal. The goal of getting around all the pretty lies we tell ourselves. I strove hard to be part of it.

But what can you do? Choose your talents? No way. Eventually, as my beloved hobby burgeoned, threatening to take over, I found myself forced to admit that science is hard! I am much better at art — making up vivid stories — than I ever was at laboring honestly to discover new truths.

At least, that's what civilization seems to be saying. My fellow citizens pay me better to write novels than they ever did to work in a lab.

Oh, I still like to do occasional forays into science. Some articles are posted in my nonfiction section. See also my nonfiction book — *The Transparent Society: Will Technology Force Us to Choose Between Freedom and Privacy?*

Still, the jury came back to say I do something else much better. It's silly to complain that your gifts are different than you'd like. Putting stylish cynicism aside, these two elements enrich each other. The rigor of science combines with the "what-if" freedom of imagination.

Anyway, I believe it behooves a person to help pass success on to those who follow. So, after writing the same answers, over and over, to many letters I received from would-be writers, I decided to put it all together here. Call it a small trove of advice. Mine it for whatever wisdom you may find here … bearing in mind that no profession is more idiosyncratic than writing! In other words, don't just take my word for anything. Collect every piece of wisdom you can find, then do it your own way!

Despite all of the raging ego trips, writing is much like any other profession. There's a lot to learn—dialogue, setting, characterization, plus all the arty nuances that critics consider so much more important than plot. The process can be grueling. Still, there is a bit of luck; you can have fun creating amateur stuff along the way! Later, you may even find some of that early stuff is worth taking out of the drawer again and hacking into presentable shape.

If I spoke dismissively of critics, that doesn't mean I put down criticism! At its core, criticism is the only antidote that human beings have discovered against error. It is the chief method that a skilled person can use to become "even better." The key to discovering correctable errors before you commit a work to press.

But criticism hurts! A deep and pervasive flaw in human character makes all of us resistant to the one thing that can help us to do better. The only solution? Learn to grow up. To hold your head high, develop a thick skin, and take it.

If a reader didn't like your work, that may be a matter of taste. But if she did not understand the work—or was bored—that's your fault as a writer, pure and simple.

The first ten pages of any work are crucial. They are what busy editors see when they rip open your envelope—snatched irritably from a huge pile that came in that morning.

Oh, you must learn to take feedback with many grains of salt. Many of the people you ask for feedback will be foolish or distracted or simply mistaken. Be very wary of taking advice *how* to solve a problem. You are the creator; finding solutions is your business. Still, other people will be very helpful in pointing out that there is a problem in a passage.

The fundamental rule: if more than one reader is bored or confused by a given passage, you did not do your job right. Find ways to tighten and improve that scene.

Make the book hard to put down—in order to feed the cat, go to work, go to bed. Your aim is to make the reader appear at work or school tomorrow disheveled and groggy from sleep deprivation, with all of their loved ones angry over book-induced neglect! If you induce this condition in your customers, they will buy your next book. That is the sadomasochistic truth.

Back to criticism. Look at the acknowledgments page at the back of every book I publish. There are at least thirty names listed, sometimes more—names of people to whom I circulated early drafts.

Yes, this is at the extreme end among writers. Many circulate manuscripts early in their careers, then stop doing so, telling themselves, "I am a professional now, so I don't need feedback."

Baloney! If you are a daring writer, you will always be poking away at new things, and exploring new ground. Testing your limits. That means making both wonderful discoveries and awful mistakes. So? Refine the discoveries and solve the mistakes! It helps to have more eyes—the outsider perspective—to notice thing that your own eyes will miss.

Anyway, it works for me.

Writing is about half skills that you can learn. The remaining half—as in all the arts—can only arise from something ineffable called talent. For example, it helps to have an ear for human dialogue. Or to perceive the quirky variations in human personality and to empathize with other types of people—including both victims and villains—well enough to portray their thoughts and motives. (See my note below about "point of view"). Sure, a lot of hard work and practice can compensate for areas of deficient talent, but only up to a point.

In other words, no matter how dedicated and hardworking you are, success at writing may not be in the cards. Talents are gifts that we in this generation cannot yet manipulate or artificially expand. So don't beat yourself up if you discover that part lacking. Keep searching until you find your gift.

But, assuming you do have at least the minimum mix of talent, ambition, and will, let me now offer a few tidbits of advice — pragmatic steps that might improve your chances of success.

The first ten pages of any work are crucial. They are what busy editors see when they rip open your envelope — snatched irritably from a huge pile that came in that morning. Editors must decide in minutes, perhaps moments, whether you deserve closer attention than all the other aspiring authors in the day's slush pile. If your first few pages sing out professionalism and skill — grabbing the reader with a vivid story right away — the editor may get excited. Even if the next chapter disappoints, she'll at least write you a nice letter.

Alas, she won't even read those first ten pages if the first page isn't great! And that means the first paragraph has to be better still. And the opening line must be the best of all.

Don't put a plot summary at the beginning. Plunge right into the story! Hook 'em with your characters. Then follow chapter one with a good outline.

There are at least a dozen elements needed in a good novel, from characterization to plot to ideas to empathy to snappy dialogue and rapid scene setting, all the way to riveting action … and so on. I've seen writers who were great at half of these things, but horrid at the rest. Editors call these writers "tragic." Sometimes they mutter about wishing to construct a Frankenstein author, out of bits and pieces of several who just missed the cut, because of one or two glaring deficits.

Only rarely will an editor actually tell you these lacks or faults. It's up to you to find them. You can only do this by workshopping.

Have you workshopped your creative efforts? Find a group of bright neo-writers who are at about your level of accomplishment and learn from the tough give-and-take that arises! Local workshops can be hard to find, but try asking at a bookstore that caters to the local writing crowd. Or take the "writing course" at your local community college. Teachers of such courses often know only a little. But there you will at least get to meet other local writers. If you "click" with a few, you can exchange numbers and form your own workshop, after class ends.

Another advantage of taking a course — the weekly assignment. Say it's ten pages. That weekly quota may provide an extra impetus, the discipline you need to keep producing. Ten pages a week for ten weeks? That's a hundred pages, partner. Think about that.

Avoid overusing flowery language. Especially adjectives! This is a common snare for young writers, who fool themselves into thinking that more is better, or that obscurity is proof of intelligence.

I used to tell my students they should justify every adjective they put in their works. Write spare descriptions, erring in favor of tight, terse prose, especially in first draft. Your aim is to tell a story that people can't put down! Later, when you've earned the right, you can add a few adjectival descriptions, like sprinkles on a cake. Make each one a deliberate professional choice, not a crutch.

Learn control over point of view, or POV. This is one of the hardest aspects of writing to teach or to grasp. Some students never get it at all.

Through which set of eyes does the reader view the story?

Is your POV omniscient? (The reader knows everything, including stuff the main character doesn't.)

Does the POV ride your character's shoulder? (The reader sees what the character sees, but doesn't share character's inner thoughts.)

Or is it somewhere in between? In most modern stories we tend to ride inside the character's head, sharing his/her knowledge and surface thoughts, without either delving too deeply or learning things that the protagonist doesn't know.

Decide which it will be. Then stick with your choice. Oh, and it's generally best to limit point of view to one character at a time. Choose one person to be the POV character of each chapter — or the entire book.

Think *people*! as Kingsley Amis said:

These cardboard spacemen aren't enough

Nor alien monsters sketched in rough

Character's the essential stuff.

Here's a nifty little trick. When puzzled over how to do something — dialogue, for example — *retype* a favorite conversation that was written by a writer you admire. The same can hold for other elements of style, like setting, characterization and point of view. Find a truly great example and retype it.

Don't shortcut by simply rereading the scene! You will notice more by retyping than by looking. This is because a skilled writer is performing a "magical incantation" using words to create feelings and sensations and impressions in the reader's mind. If you simply reread a passage, especially one written by an expert, the incantation will take effect! You'll feel, know, empathize, cry … and you will *not* pay close attention to how the author did it!

So don't cheat. Actually retype the scene, letter by letter. The words will pass through a different part of your brain. You'll say, "Oh! That's why he put a comma there!"

Don't be a "creative writing major" in school. That educational specialization offers no correlation with success or sales. A minor in writing is fine, but you are better off studying some subject that has to do with civilization and the world. Moreover, by gaining experience in some worthy profession you'll actually have something worth writing about.

If you really are a writer, you will write. Nothing can stop you.

A final piece of advice: Beware the dangers of ego! For some, this manifests as a frantic need to see oneself as great.

Oh, it's fine to believe in yourself. It takes some impudent gall to claim that other people ought to pay you to read your scribblings! By all means, stoke yourself enough to believe that.

But if you listen too much to the voice saying "Be great, *be great!*" it'll just get in your way. Worse, it can raise expectations that will turn any moderate degree of success into something bitter. I've seen this happen, too many times. A pity, when any success at all should bring you joy.

Others have the opposite problem: egos that too readily let themselves be quashed by all the fire-snorting fellows stomping around. These people tend (understandably) to keep their creativity more private. That makes it hard for them to seek critical feedback, the grist for self-improvement. At either extreme, ego can be more curse than blessing.

But if you keep it under control, you'll be able to say: "I have some talents that I can develop. If I apply myself, I should be able to write stories that others may want to read! So give me a little room now. I'm closing the door and sitting down to write. Don't anyone bother me for an hour!"

Whatever you do, keep writing. Put passion into it!

If you do all these things, will success follow?

For a majority, a fine hobby may result. In the internet age, as hobbies thrive and self-publication becomes increasingly respectable, that may be a noteworthy level of accomplishment in its own right. Many amateur creators are gathering readers and fans out there, numbering in hundreds or thousands.

In a few cases, some combination of talent, skill, and hard work will lift you higher on the pyramid of your chosen art form. An occasional professional short story sale? A first novel? One per decade? Per year?

A series of luscious and wonderful surprises may come as success drags you (kicking and screaming?) away from your day job. It can be a great feeling, especially if you keep your ambition and effort high and expectations low.

Enjoying craftsmanship is what it's really all about. So have fun writing. Take your time. Be a useful person along the way — and it may all come true, in time.

Good luck!

Write Two Novels

John Gobbell is the James Michener of naval thrillers. His WWII novels are truly the Tin Can Navy at its best. His books—including *The Brutus Lie, The Last Lieutenant, A Code for Tomorrow, When Duty Whispers Low, The Neptune Strategy,* and his latest, *A Call to Colors*—are rich with the details of the day, and his characters simply glow with authenticity. Lovers of history, the U.S. Navy, or rousing sea battles should visit John's Web site at www.johnjgobbell.com and check out his books.

irst, getting published is difficult, to say in the least. One should get used to rejection is an understatement. The best thing I can say about rejection letters is to save them. Once they become inconsistent with each other, then you know you have something. In other words, when the rejection letters stop saying things like "poor narrative" or "character development lacking" and say something like "not right for our list" or "we can't move on this at this time," then you know you have something. So keep trying. Perhaps the best advice I had was, "You must write two novels to get one published." And that's what I did. The first one crashed and burned. But the second one, *The Brutus Lie*, made it.

Becoming a Published Author

JOHN LESCROART

John Lescroart (pronounced less-kwah) has been producing outstanding thrillers since 1981, when *Sunburn* appeared. His other novels are *Son of Holmes, Rasputin's Revenge, Dead Irish, The VIG, Hard Evidence, The 13th Juror, A Certain Justice, Guilt, The Mercy Rule, Nothing But the Truth, The Hearing, The Oath, The First Law, The Second Chair, The Motive, The Hunt Club,* and *The Suspect.* Many of them are part of his excellent Dismas Hardy series. For more about John's novels *and* his delightful music, visit his Web site at www.johnlescroart.com.

In 1978, a novel of mine entitled *Sunburn* won the San Francisco Foundation's Joseph Henry Jackson Award for Best Novel by a California Author. Needless to say, this was an incredible thrill, especially when I learned that there were 280 other entrants, including *Interview with a Vampire*. I figured that as a novelist I was at last on my way.

Three years later, however, I was still unpublished, living in a furnished one-bedroom apartment in San Francisco, divorced, writing another book that no one would read, working days as a legal secretary at the Bank of America. At the same time, my brother Mike went to a high school basketball game in Berkeley and ran into an ex-girlfriend of mine named Margie Close. She asked what I was up to, and Mike told her that I was basically a loser—a description I wouldn't have disagreed with too strongly, by the way—but that I had at least won this dumb literary award a few years back.

Margie, a mother of three babies living in Los Angeles (she'd been in Berkeley visiting her parents), and with no connection whatever to the publishing business, asked Mike if he thought I'd let her read the manuscript. Since the demand wasn't exactly high, I was delighted to send it to her. Much to my surprise and delight, she liked the book very much and asked why it wasn't published. I told her that I'd sent it to New York and every publisher there had rejected it. So did every agent, for that matter. So Margie then asked if I'd mind if she tried to get it published. I didn't.

She checked the yellow pages for "Book Publishers" and found Pinnacle Books—a legitimate "New York" publishing house (now Kensington Press) that had a Los Angeles office less than a mile from Margie's house.

So she pushed her baby carriage down to Century City and handed the manuscript of **Sunburn** over the front desk to the secretary, saying it was a good book that had won this prize and maybe Pinnacle should publish it.

The very next day, they bought the book for two thousand dollars.

I realize that this is not how everyone gets published for the first time. But the real message is that this series of extremely unlikely events did happen, and the result, now nearly thirty years later, is a wonderful career of eighteen novels (and counting). We've all got to start somewhere, and there isn't simply one way, or even ten ways. There's the way it happens for each of us—that's all. Even when it seems impossible. The key is not to lose faith, to keep writing, and to keep believing in yourself and your work. And who knows, someday your sibling might run into your old sweetheart … .

Tough Cookies

CASSIE MILES

Kay Bergstrom, also known as Cassie Miles, has published over sixty novels of romance and suspense, mostly for Harlequin Intrigue. She's been recognized with several awards, including the 2003 Rocky Mountain Fiction Writer of the Year, and has taught writing in grade schools and at the college level.

A long time ago—when my publicity photo was new and my now-adult daughters were babies—I spent a bit of time as a breast-feeding, bread-baking, stay-at-home mom. Naturally, my thoughts turned to mayhem and murder.

Armed with a couple of completed mystery manuscripts and a handful of rejections, I tried networking and happened to meet a local agent. She was a large woman in a flowing caftan. I knew at once that we had something in common: a love of chocolate.

Rather than mail my manuscript, I loaded the kids into the car and drove to the address listed on her business card. On her doorstep, I left my carefully typed pages along with two dozen homemade chocolate chip cookies.

She called. Loved the cookies. Wasn't crazy about the book. This agent was smart enough to notice something about my work that I hadn't seen: except for the brutally murdered corpse and the heinous bad guy, everybody lived happily ever after. She suggested I try the burgeoning field of romance.

"Can you write fast?" she asked.

"Hey, I'm a mom. I can write a book with one hand and change a diaper with the other while balancing the checkbook and singing the 'Rubber Ducky' song from *Sesame Street*."

After I read several romances, I was motivated. My stay-at-home time was running out, and there was a definite need for income. Fueled by cookies of my own, I wrote on a sugar high.

My first book was titled *Tongue-Tied*. It was about a politician with a stutter who went to a speech therapist. When she kissed him, he was fluent.

Harlequin bought that book and many, many more.

Happy ending.

The Mild-Mannered
Professor With the Bloody-
Minded Visions

DAVID MORRELL

David Morrell is the author of twenty-eight novels, many *New York Times* bestsellers. *First Blood* gave us Rambo and is widely regarded as the first modern action/ adventure book. Among his best-known works are *The Brotherhood of the Rose* (which became a highly rated TV miniseries starring Robert Mitchum), *The Fifth Profession, The League of Night and Fog, The Covenant of the Flame, Assumed Identity, Testament, The Totem, Fireflies, Desperate Measures*, and *Extreme Denial*. Check out his site at www.davidmorrell.net. The following essay is excerpted from his book *Lessons From a Lifetime of Writing: A Novelist Looks at His Craft*.

"Write what you know about," is a common rule in creative writing classes. It sounds like good advice, but what does it mean? In the first half of the twentieth century, writers in America were often expected to go into the world, gain a wealth of experience, and put a fictionalized version of their experiences on the page. Jack London wrote about his adventures in Alaska. Hemingway went to World War I. Steinbeck traveled with depression-ravaged "Okies"... .

I think it would be beneficial for fiction-writing teachers to tell their students, "Get out of here. Travel. Join the Peace Corps. Fight forest fires. Experience as much as you can. Write about it. If you have trouble with technique, come back a couple of years from now, and we'll talk. Class dismissed."

I like this advice because one of the occupational hazards of being writers is that all the time we're sitting at our desks, laboring over stories, life passes us by. To keep things fresh, I long ago decided that between projects I ought to find stimulating new things to do, activities that would be fascinating to learn and (not incidentally) useful in a book. On a simple level, that means taking advantage of vacations to research locales, seeking out a new, interesting place each time. I've been to the Mexican resort of Cancun and to the Mayan ruins nearby, for example. Loved the experience, used it in the novel *Assumed Identity*... .

On another level, research means immersing yourself in your subject matter. Back in the early seventies, I began making notes for my second novel, *Testament*, realizing that many scenes would depict wilderness survival. The trouble is, everything I knew about the subject came from movies. A library junkie, I decided that I'd better read some books about staying alive in the wilderness, but after going through several, I got the unsettling feeling that the writers of those books were basing their information on other books. They weren't giving me a vivid sense of what it was like to be in the dangerous situations I wanted to depict.

I decided I needed "hands-on experience" so I enrolled in the National Outdoor Leadership School and drove to Lander, Wyoming, where... .

For the next thirty-five days, along with twenty-nine other students, I carried a sixty-pound backpack through the Wind River mountains. We learned about camping without a trace, crossing wild streams, living off the land, navigating with a compass and contour map, rock climbing, rappelling, surviving blizzards (it was June, but we had seven days of fierce snow), digging snow caves, avoiding hypothermia, dealing with altitude sickness and so on.

I lost twenty-five pounds during the course and came back with invaluable first-hand knowledge that made the survival scenes in *Testament* seem authentic. All these years later, my NOLS training shows up in my novels.

It's worth emphasizing that the experience wasn't only good for my fiction—it was good for *me*. Instead of being limited by writing only about what I already knew, I decided to write books about subjects that I wanted to learn, using the opportunity for research to make my life fuller. I developed a pattern—do the reading, conduct the interviews, the get hands-on experience.

James Thurber once wrote a story about a character named Walter Mitty, an ordinary man with adventure-filled fantasies. Every writer can be like Mitty, with the advantage that in dramatizing the products of our imagination we're able, via our research, to live our fantasies.

Writing the (Ugh) Synopsis

RAY WHITE

Duane and I flipped a coin, and I lost. I think that word, "lost," pretty much sums up every writer's feeling about doing a synopsis. You need one. You know you do. Every agent wants to see one, and, next to your hook and query letter, it's the most important piece of writing in your submission. But does anyone know how to write a synopsis?

No one even seems to know where to begin.

The books we read mostly said "take your book a chapter at a time and reduce each to a short paragraph, but keep the emotion and motivation. Oh, and make it entertaining" (which, near as we can tell, translates as "keep your unique voice"). These books all offered tips on synopsis writing, and we are passing the best of them on to you.

Actually the best time to begin a synopsis is while you are writing your manuscript, not after. I keep a pad of paper on my computer desk, and on it I note the high points of each chapter as they occur. It's also a really good way for me to keep track of subplots I want to follow up on later. I call it my "memo pad" approach, and it works for me.

Unfortunately you didn't know about it when you wrote your novel, so now you have to read your whole book again and jot this stuff down as you go. By the time you are done you will have what amounts to a reverse outline. An added benefit of this work is that sometimes while you are busy distilling thirty-page chapters into a paragraph you'll come up with a better one-line hook for your novel than you had before.

Of course, if you're the kind of writer who outlines your work before you write it, then you are ahead in the synopsis sweepstakes because you already have the skeleton of your story. Now all you have to do is make it compelling.

A good trick is to pretend you are writing a long jacket blurb. Blurbs must be exciting and intriguing. The purpose of a blurb is to get a reader to buy your book. The purpose of your synopsis is to get an agent to take you on or an editor to buy your book. Same thing. A synopsis is a sales tool, and therefore it must be sexy. It must read like you write and convey a sense of your style, because if an agent doesn't like your synopsis, she probably won't bother to read your sample chapters. In the final analysis, your synopsis will sell your book — or not — so put your very best effort into it.

There are two main ways to begin. The one I favor is to start with your hook. Sure, you already put it in your cover letter, but so what? It's a great line that conveys your great concept in an intriguing way, so it bears repeating. If possible, relate your hook to your main character immediately because the second way to begin a synopsis is to … .

Start with your main character, leave the bit players out, and describe the conflict. If your setting is critical to understanding why things happen the way they do — civilization has been destroyed, it's 1957 Chicago, or your main guy is stranded on Planet X where the inhabitants are man-eating bloodworms — then include it. Otherwise leave it out.

Be sure to put motivation in, because the reasons your characters do things is what makes a reader relate to them, and if you can do that in a synopsis you will convince an agent your writing is good. Every single word must convince first an agent, then an editor, and then an editorial review board to place a bet on you.

But is that it? Of course not. There are lots of other little details.

Every book we read agreed on the use omniscient voice — so of course I'm using first person to tell you how, but it's good advice. In fact, omniscient voice is the only way to pull off a readable, or even halfway entertaining, synopsis. You don't have room for dialogue or to bounce back and forth between third-person limited viewpoints. Also, use present tense to lend a sense of immediacy.

The appropriate length is usually found in the agent's submission guidelines. Most only want a page or two, though some will accept ten. That's another point. You need different synopses for different purposes. Many writing contests require one that is eight or more pages long, so when you're writing one, write two—of different lengths.

And that brings us to the issue of page count. Again, an agent's Web site or info sheet in *Writer's Market* will often tell you both the number of pages they will accept *and* whether to single-space. The how-to books and the authors who contributed to this book disagree on whether to double- or single-space a synopsis. Those in favor of double-spacing say it's because such writing is easier to read and therefore will be more favorably regarded by agents. Those who say to single-space claim you need to do so because you get more words on a page that way and that it makes for a very clear differentiation between the writing in your synopsis and that of your manuscript.

I'm with the double-space school of thought, because I think single-spacing will make it less likely your synopsis will be read. All the agents and editors I've talked to are protective of their eyesight, and I want my synopsis read, but here's another twist: *Writer's Digest* recommends that authors single space a one or two-page synopsis, but double space any that are longer.

Finally, be sure to cover your entire plot. Answer all questions; don't leave an editor or agent hanging. They want all the issues resolved, and they want to see how you got there.

The real skinny on synopsis writing is there is no magic formula, just lots of difficult practice; then run it past your critique group for feedback and start over. Keep at it—there's that persistence thing again—and eventually you will produce a readable synopsis. It's hard, no one disputes that, but hey, if this were easy, anyone could be a writer and all writers would get published.

With a Little Help From My Friends

KATHI KAMEN GOLDMARK

Kathi Kamen Goldmark is the author of *And My Shoes Keep Walking Back to You*, a novel published by Chronicle Books. She is coauthor of *The Great Rock & Roll Joke Book* and a contributor to several collections of essays, including *Mid-Life Confidential: The Rock Bottom Remainders Tour America With Three Chords and an Attitude*. With her partner, Sam Barry, she writes a monthly column in *BookPage* called "The Author Enablers." Kathi is the founder and a member of the Rock Bottom Remainders, president and janitor of "Don't Quit Your Day Job" Records, author liaison for Book Group Expo, and producer of the coast-to-coast radio show *West Coast Live*. She likes to think she is ready for anything.

....

I t was my very first public reading ever, from a work in progress: a collection to which I'd contributed, slated for release a few months down the road, containing my first published essay. After years in the publishing business I knew what to expect: a few acquaintances and my aunt Trudy gathered in the back of a dingy bookstore. I figured I'd have to shout over the air conditioner and cappuccino machine, that the event would be a mere blip on the screen at the 1993 Miami Book Fair.

So you can imagine my surprise when I pulled up in front of the venue and saw my name, along with three of my coauthors, on a theatre marquis:

>   Stephen King
>   Dave Barry

Ridley Pearson
Kathi Kamen Goldmark

And I bet you can imagine the ice-cold terror creeping up my spine as I realized the theatre held two thousand seats, nearly every one of them filled. The crowd may not have been there to see me, but I was still going to have to read in front of aunt Trudy and 1,999 other people—and as the rookie I was first up to bat.

Rewind the tape a few months, to other terror-filled moments, hunched over my IBM Selectric II, banging out my recollections of instigating "Stephen King and Dave Barry's" rock band. This had all started when I'd recruited over a dozen well-known authors, aka the Rock Bottom Remainders, to play one set of bad rock & roll with me at a book convention. The adventure had snowballed, and I'd picked up major support from most of the authors' publishers and a few musical equipment companies. Then I'd hired rock legend Al Kooper to be musical director and managed to interest Van Halen's tour manager in the project. He provided a ten-block luxury tour bus ride from our hotel to the Cowboy Boogie bar in Anaheim, California, and back again. This ride, more than any other event, sparked enthusiasm for a follow-up tour, ultimately financed by a book proposal sold to Stephen King's publisher at a fraction of his usual price, with everyone in the band agreeing to contribute a chapter.

"Everyone" didn't include me, though, right? I had done my part. I would be credited with pulling together one of the world's worst rock bands and generously honored in the book, and that seemed perfectly appropriate. It turned out, though, that my bandmates wouldn't hear of such nonsense.

"Um, didn't you make me wear those ugly boxer shorts? Didn't you make me sing that stupid song? Didn't you make me miss my deadline? Didn't you send me off to do that 6:00 A.M. interview?" they cried. "You, my dear, are writing a chapter. After all, you're the only one who knows the whole story."

So there I was hunched over that typewriter, staring at blank white pages, paralyzed by the horror of having to create my first published writing for an anthology that would also include the likes of Roy Blount Jr., Stephen King, Barbara Kingsolver, and Dave Barry. Actually, it *would* include those very people. I'd write a tentative sentence or two, interrupted by the phone and a conversation along these lines:

Me: Hello.
Amy Tan: Hi, can I read you a paragraph to fact-check?
Me: Sure, go ahead.
Amy Tan: [perfect gem of exquisite prose]
Me: Um, I think that might have been in Atlanta, not Philly.
Amy Tan: Oh! Okay, thanks.

I'd pull my own pathetic effort out of the typewriter (this was before everyone in the world had a computer), crumple it up, and aim for the wastebasket—usually missing my target by several inches.

When I finally sent in my first draft, I got an irate call from band-mate and editor-elect Dave Marsh.

"Don't you know what five thousand words means?" he growled. "You sent me twenty single-spaced pages; that's way too long! No editor can write notes on single-spaced pages. Everyone knows that."

I didn't know that.

Slowly and painfully, I shortened the chapter. I left out a lot of the background stuff, trying to imagine what readers would really care about—not my years as a high-school folksinger or my wild life as the drummer's girlfriend in Steely Dan, it turned out; not my complex and sometimes troubled relationships with my husband and son—I was expected to tell one simple story, the story of starting the band. After many revisions and countless excruciating conversations with Dave, I completed an appropriate essay, submitted only a few days past our group deadline, on the way to that "work-in-progress" reading at the Miami Book Fair.

Standing in the wings, I heard myself introduced and walked across the huge empty stage to the podium. There were a *lot* of people out there, and my voice shook slightly as I began my chapter. But once I got going I found myself editing long-winded passages on the spot, omitting whole sentences that would have slowed the story's momentum. I finished to polite applause, leaving the rest of the evening to the headliners—the folks everyone had really come to see. When the second the show was over, I dashed to the nearest phone (this was also before everyone in the world had a cell phone) and called New York.

"I need one more week," I cried. "I have to edit my chapter again."

"Hmmph, okay ..." was Dave Marsh's thoughtful answer.

I shortened and tightened some more, eliminating everything I had *not* said onstage. This time, though, I enjoyed playing with my own words, remembering the joy of creating a remarkable occurrence, proud of having invented something that would become a small part of literary history. I ended up writing an essay that was published alongside those of my illustrious and vastly more experienced coauthors, in a book that I actually saw on the shelves of bookstores.

I learned a few things that night in Miami:

1. Reading your work out loud is an essential part of the process. *Always* read your work out loud, even if it's just to the dog.
2. Writing can be fun, joyful, and exciting.
3. Raw terror is sometimes good for you.
4. Remember to walk the dog after you read to him. Trust me.

The biggest surprise of all: When it was over, I found I missed writing. I was hooked.

Shortly after *Mid-Life Confidential: The Rock Bottom Remainders Tour America With Three Chords and an Attitude* was published, Dave Marsh and I collaborated on a rock & roll joke book. My first novel was published a couple of years after that. I'm now working on a new novel, am the coauthor of a monthly column in *BookPage*, and have contributed to several non-fiction anthologies. There's no doubt about it: I'm a writer now. If you asked me how that happened (as the editors of this book actually did), I'd have trouble coming up with a simple answer, but it really did happen.

And the Rock Bottom Remainders have been performing together for fifteen years, longer than the Beatles.

The Wall of Shame and Tom Clancy

KYLE MILLS

Kyle Mills is the bestselling author of *Rising Phoenix, Fade, Smoke Screen, Sphere of Influence, Free Fall, Storming Heaven, Burn Factor*, and *The Second Horseman*. His books featuring FBI agent Mark Beamon are exciting, fast-paced, fun, and realistic—as only someone with Kyle's excellent FBI and DEA contacts can make them. Visit him at www.kylemills.com.

....

After I finished the manuscript for *Rising Phoenix*, I took the obvious path of buying a copy of the *Guide to Literary Agents* and sending off query letters. I had no writing credits at all and, outside of my recently completed novel, had never written anything longer than a term paper.

My success was limited, to say the least.

I put up a bulletin board that I called The Wall of Shame and started sticking my rejections to it in order of how interesting they were.

As I recall, my favorite was one where the agent had just stamped "NO" on my letter and sent it back to me in the envelope I'd provided.

Eventually, the board got so heavy it ripped off the wall. I wish that was a joke, but it's not.

Enter my father, who is pretty good friends with Tom Clancy and had met his editor a few times. He sent a copy of my manuscript to that editor, who promptly sent me back a thoughtful two-page letter on why he didn't like it. I made a few of the revisions he recommended, but honestly didn't agree with a lot of his suggestions. I'm not sure why I bothered, though, since I couldn't even get an agent to leaf through the first few pages of the thing.

I started sending out query letters again.

My father is not one to be easily discouraged and gave my manuscript to Tom to pass on to his agent. As I recall, Tom was moving at the time and the manuscript got misplaced for a while.

I had kind of forgotten about it when, months later, I got a call from a fast-talking New Yorker who identified himself as Tom Clancy's agent, said he'd read my manuscript, loved it, and was going to get it published. My initial reaction was that someone was playing a joke on me. I called my father, who told me it was for real and that Tom had called him just that morning, really excited that his agent had liked my book. Predictably, two days later, one of the agents I'd sent a query to requested my manuscript. Feast or famine.

From then on things went surprisingly quickly. I seem to remember *Rising Phoenix* being turned down by ten or so of the editors who looked at it, but two made offers. My luck continued to hold when a big book slated for publication at the publisher I signed with wasn't finished in time, and I got the slot.

In the end, *Rising Phoenix* went on to be a national best-seller, and I went on to make writing a sometimes very strange career.

So, what's the moral to my story?

Contacts work great, but persistence is a good substitute. And just because most of the editors who read your book don't like it, that doesn't mean it won't become a bestseller.

Finally, keep your sense of humor—you're going to need it if you decide to make writing a career.

How Nymphos and Vampires Got Me Published

MARIO ACEVEDO

Mario Acevedo channels the voices in his head for the Felix Gomez vampire detective series. A former helicopter pilot, infantry officer, art teacher, and retired intergalactic jewel thief, Mario currently lives and writes in Denver, Colorado. Visit his Web site at www.marioacevedo.com to learn about *The Nymphos of Rocky Flats* and how it's the only vampire novel in history to require a Department of Energy clearance.

O ne night I got struck by lightning. I wandered home in a trance, smoke drifting from my hair, and sat at the keyboard. The Muse whispered—no she crooned—into my ear. The ideas and words shot from my fingertips, raced through the computer circuits, and danced on the screen. I was powerless to stop the inspiration.

Pretty good story, huh? And a big, fat lie. After all, I do write fiction.

This is what really happened. For seventeen years I marched through a blizzard of rejection letters. I had notions of writing serious literary tomes heavy with political relevance. I'd write and polish one manuscript, send it off, and start on another one.

My critique partners said, "Mario, you're not as smart as you are a smart-ass. Use that in your writing." And so I wrote *The Nymphos of Rocky Flats*.

Where did the inspiration for that story come from? I worked at Rocky Flats and wondered what could be the most ridiculous premise I could pull out of my ... I mean, the air. A vampire detective investigates an outbreak of nymphomania at the Rocky Flats nuclear weapons plant. Practically a ready-made story pitch. Then I had to flesh out the story. Why was the protagonist a vampire? What was his world like? Who were the villains? Since the story involved nymphos, there had to be a love interest.

Once I had the manuscript ready, to gird myself for the grueling slog through Rejection Land, I attended the Colorado Gold Writers Conference. I sat in a query letter workshop presented by the literary agent Scott Hoffman. In his lecture about what makes a good query letter, Scott mentioned that he had represented a novel about zombies.

"Well," I thought, "if Scott can work with zombies, then he can surely do vampires."

After his presentation, I accompanied Scott to the hotel elevator. I told him how much I enjoyed his talk and asked if he would like to hear my story idea. He did, so I gave him the fifteen-second elevator pitch … in the elevator. Scott offered his business card and told me to keep in touch. Afterwards I sent him an e-mail reminding him of our introduction and asked if he was still interested in reading my manuscript. That led to his representing me and selling my story as part of a three-book deal with Rayo HarperCollins.

It happened because I paid my dues for almost two decades learning what I had to know about getting published. And I got lucky.

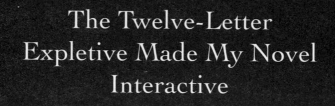

The Twelve-Letter Expletive Made My Novel Interactive

PATRICK McMANUS

Patrick McManus is the author of several books including his first full-length novel, *The Blight Way,* and several side-splitting *New York Times* bestselling short story collections: *The Night the Bear Ate Goombaw; Never Cry "Arp!!"; The Grasshopper Trap; Real Ponies Don't Go Oink; Into the Twilight, Endlessly Grousing; The Bear in the Attic; A Fine and Pleasant Misery; They Shoot Canoes, Don't They?; Rubber Legs and White Tail-Hairs;* and *How I Got This Way,* to name a few. Patrick can be reached through his Web site at www.mcmanusbooks.com.

The main problem that faced me in starting to write my first mystery novel, *The Blight Way,* was that I knew absolutely nothing about writing a mystery novel. Over the years I had read quite a few, but, not at the moment intending to write one, I hadn't paid much attention to how the novel was written. So I read several current novels and found them to have extremely graphic sexual scenes and to be sprinkled with obscenities, not that there is anything wrong with that, as Jerry Seinfeld might say.

Over the forty years that I have been writing short humor pieces, however, I have acquired a terrific audience of readers, many of which consist of families that include children. I didn't want to write a book that would offend them. The first decision I made was to leave out any sexual scenes, explicit or implicit, pretty much like the old-fashion mystery novels. I did want my characters to be realistic enough to occasionally express themselves with obscenities, but I left the obscenities out and put in only the number of letters in the particular obscenity. This in part was intended as a send-up of some of the current mysteries. It also made the novel interactive in the sense that the readers had to insert their own obscenities, if they so desired them.

There was no problem making the transition from humor to mystery novel, because writing the mystery was so much easier.

Much of my other research was basic. For example, I didn't know how long to make my mystery. I found that the ones I read ran to about sixty thousand words, so that's how long I made mine. I learned that the protagonist often has a sidekick with whom to carry on a dialogue, and to satisfy this requirement I added the seventy-five-year-old father of my sheriff character. I noticed that one of my favorite mystery writers, Peter Bowen, uses a lot of dialogue in his novels, so I put in a lot of dialogue. Most of the humor in my novel arises from the fairly comic personalities of the characters.

It seems to me that readers of mysteries read them primarily for the story, so I tried not to let the humor interfere with the mystery itself. The humor becomes sort of a bonus to the story.

In the mysteries I studied, I found that the writers are constantly telling the reader what clothes the characters are wearing. I found this detail to be tedious but I went ahead and dressed most of my characters. The reason for this, tedious as it is, seems to be that it gives the reader a more complete visual image of the character. They also feed their characters quite often and tell the reader what each character is eating. So, tedious as I found this to be also, I did the same thing.

One of the things I learned on my own is that it is necessary to keep a list of the character's names, his relationship to other characters, his age, his hair color, his weight and height, etc. Fictional people may resemble real people but they can change their appearance in a fraction of a second. A girl who is blonde on page 10 may show up as a brunette on page 105, if you aren't careful.

Another big problem of writing mysteries, I've found, is keeping track of the passage of time. How long does a particular event require ...

say, driving from one town to another? If you aren't careful, you'll discover that the driver had to be doing about three hundred miles an hour. This may not be a problem for the experienced writer of mysteries, but it was a problem for me.

In a how-to-write book I once read, I learned that it is important not to let dialogue occur in a vacuum, by which I mean that while your characters are discussing something you should from time to time insert some physical detail, such as the lighting of a cigarette, the scratching of the head, a yawn, something.

The best thing I learned in writing this novel is simply to be guided by your instincts and write what you want, not what you think an editor or publisher might want. The first publisher my agent sent *The Blight Way* to turned it down because it was "too soft for today's mystery market." The second publisher, Simon & Schuster, bought it.

I tried for two years to get my first book published and to get an agent, with no luck.

I and my family went off to Mexico where I had a teaching job for the spring quarter. A couple of days after we arrived, Henry Holt and Company called and said it was taking the book. The next day another publisher called and said it wanted the book. The next day an agent, Ollie Swan, called and said he wanted to represent me.

So the way I got an agent was to get a publisher first.

(Ollie Swan, by the way, was famous, and over time we became good friends. When he died *The New York Times* gave him a half-page obit. He was a super agent.)

Bondage Paraphernalia

RAYMOND BENSON

Between 1996 and 2002 Raymond Benson wrote six original James Bond 007 novels, three film novelizations, and three short stories—all published worldwide. The *James Bond Bedside Companion* was published in 1984 and was nominated for an Edgar. As "David Michaels," Raymond was the author of the *New York Times* bestsellers *Tom Clancy's Splinter Cell* and *Tom Clancy's Splinter Cell: Operation Barracuda*. Raymond's recent original thrillers are *Face Blind*, *Evil Hours*, and *Sweetie's Diamonds*. Go to www.raymondbenson.com for more details.

....

For seven wild years I had the privilege and honor to be appointed official scribe of the James Bond 007 novels. The Bond literary copyright holders, Glidrose Publications Limited (now Ian Fleming Publications Limited), commissioned me to continue in the footsteps of 007's creator, Ian Fleming, and the subsequent continuation novel authors, Kingsley Amis (who wrote as Robert Markham) and John Gardner. Seeing that I was a genuine Bond fan-geek since the early sixties when Sean Connery was considered the *only* 007 imaginable, it was a dream job come true.

So how does one go about writing a James Bond thriller? Answer— the same way an author would go about writing *any* thriller. The tricks are to have a compelling hero, a particularly nasty and clever villain, a plot that twists and turns and threatens not only our hero but Civilization As We Know It, exotic locales that Normal People only fantasize about visiting, and the essential dollops of sex and violence to make it slightly more interesting. Since the hero was already provided to me, the biggest challenge was to come up with a suitable villain and his dastardly scheme. There have been over twenty Bond films and over thirty Bond novels, so doing this was easier said than done.

Required by my employers to provide an outline, I quickly learned that this was an invaluable tool for any writer. My outlines are not really outlines of the A, B, and C type—instead they are prose treatments broken out in block paragraphs. Each paragraph represents a chapter in which I spell out all the important *stuff* that needs to happen in that chapter. Believe me—it's much less painful to move around, edit, chop out, and add paragraphs in a fifteen-page treatment than it is to mutilate dozens of pages of a manuscript. The treatment ultimately becomes the blueprint for the novel, giving me a clear structure and flowchart from which to write.

Once the outline was approved, I then made a point to travel to the various so-called exotic locations for research. I did this on my own dime. I realize many authors can't afford to travel to, say, Japan, for three weeks. I couldn't either. The money came out of my advance; hence I never seemed to have the kind of money one might *think* the "Bond-writer" would make. At any rate, I felt it was important to "write what you know," so I purposefully walked the walk—I stayed in Bond's hotels, ate Bond's food, drank his horrible martinis, mapped out his chases, and viewed the world through 007's eyes. The only things I didn't do were bed his women or kill anyone.

Another important component of the research, at least for Bond, was learning about things technical—weaponry, bombs, machines, submarines, airplanes, boats, trains, cars, diamonds, gold, and gadgetry. The paraphernalia of Bondage. I found that the best way to do this was to talk to experts in those particular fields. You'd be surprised how many people open up to Someone Who Is Writing a Novel.

Armed with my treatment and a ton of research in the form of notes and photographs, I set about writing the book.

Required by my employers to provide an outline, I quickly learned that this was an invaluable tool for any writer.

I like to write a *scene* a day. Whether this scene is twenty pages or only two, it must have a beginning, middle, and end. Sometimes this is an entire chapter. I superficially correct the day's work to make sure there are no glaring grammatical or spelling errors, and then I repeat the process the following day. I believe it's important to get through the first draft quickly because this creates the fast pace that is essential in any thriller. End chapters with a cliffhanger, make action scenes as detailed and *visceral* as possible, and never lose sight of story propulsion. Once the first draft is finished, only then do I go back and carefully edit, revise, delete, add, and sometimes spit on my work. After a third our fourth draft, then it's time to show it to my employers for more wonderful suggestions and notes.

I basically learned how to write novels by creating adventures for one of the world's most popular fictional icons, which was a sobering and humbling experience. Since escaping from Bondage, I still use these tools of the trade in writing my own, non-Bond suspense novels. Now the process is routine. I find that I don't vary my methods much. It's a job.

But it's a job I love.

Seven Ways to Avoid the Risk of Being Published

GILLIAN ROBERTS

Gillian Roberts won the Anthony Award for Best First Mystery for *Caught Dead in Philadelphia*. She is also the author of *Philly Stakes, I'd Rather Be in Philadelphia, With Friends Like These..., A Hole in Juan, In the Dead of Summer, The Mummer's Curse, The Bluest Blood, Adam and Evil, Helen Hath No Fury, Claire and Present Danger*, and *Till the End of Tom*, among others. Beginning with *Caught Dead in Philadelphia*, Gillian Roberts's schoolteacher, Amanda Pepper, has been at the center of fourteen City of Brotherly Love crimes for two decades (the most recent and final installment was *All's Well That Ends*). Gillian is also the author of two books featuring Northern California PIs Emma Howe and Billie August, another that advises others on how to enjoy a life of crime (*You Can Write a Mystery*), and, writing under her actual name, Judith Greber, four novels in which people sometimes die, but nobody sleuths. She can be reached at her Web site at www.gillianroberts.com.

....

T hese have proven 100 percent reliable through extensive testing by millions and are guaranteed to work.

1. Say—believe, even—that you'll write "someday," but not right now. There will surely come a time when the kids are grown up, your job is less taxing, your social life less hectic, your responsibilities minimal and you'll find yourself wondering what to do with the endless stretch of time ahead of you. And that day, FedEx will deliver not only a full-blown plot, but the craft with which to bring it to life.

Ignore the fact that writing's a lifelong apprenticeship and that the page you write today teaches you how to make the page you write tomorrow better than it otherwise would be.

2. Don't write until/unless you feel inspired. The Muse will arrive to save the day right after Prince Charming charges down your street on a white horse and rescues you from the doldrums.

3. Don't finish anything that isn't going along splendidly. Why bother? If the going's hard, it must mean it isn't worthwhile.

Surely other people's first drafts pour out of them and are instantly glorious. Surely nobody else writing a long work hits a wall somewhere in the middle of it.

Besides ... you've got this other idea. A better one and surely it'll be easier and ... .

If you do not want to risk being published, make a habit of deciding the idea was stupid in the first place and move on to the next project.

4. Constantly question whether you are good enough. This has many splendid variations, enough to keep anyone from making it into print. Compare yourself (negatively, of course) to the best-selling, prize-winning work you're reading. There's always an obligatory jerk who'll say: "So. Are you writing the Great American Novel, or what?" How to answer? What if it's only a semi-great American novel? Oh, Lord, is a middling American novel permitted?

Encourage all worrisome thoughts about whether your idea is new enough, let alone good enough. Ignore the fact that there are no new ideas, only new voices and approaches to giving life to those ideas.

Worry about what people will think/say about what you're writing and/or of the audacity of your thinking you could do it in the first place. Will this upset your mother, annoy your English teacher, embarrass your minister?

5. Don't show your work to anybody before submitting it, because who needs criticism? Don't you already feel bad enough about your skills, ideas, possibilities? Besides, what do they know, anyway? Might as well send it directly to the professionals.

Don't waste time on nit-picking things like spelling, grammar, and format. That's why publishing houses have copyeditors.

6. Don't study any of the many fine resources for finding the right agent or editor. Why waste time? You're going to make money for that agent, so who cares if she says she only wants the first chapter? Your tenth chapter is brilliant, so send it, instead—no—send the entire manuscript. She'll love it—unless she's an idiot.

7. Rejected? Give up. Take to your bed. Never write again.

Ignore these rules at your own hazard. Publication parties and book signings can be exhausting!

How did I get published? I was too insecure to follow my own rules, so after much hair-pulling instead of quitting, I persisted, and revised, and collected rejections, and kept on writing until, apparently, I wore them down.

Finding a Literary Agent

STEVE ALTEN

The following is taken almost verbatim and with permission from Steve Alten's excellent and informative Web site at www.stevealten.com. His writing tips section is superb; writers especially should visit the site. The author of *MEG: A Novel of Deep Terror*, *MEG: Primal Waters*, *The Trench*, *The Lock*, *Domain*, *Resurrection*, *Goliath*, and soon *The Shell Game*, Steve is a master of chilling suspense.

Okay, you've poured your heart into a manuscript, edited your work, dazzled your loved ones, and you had at least one other pair of eyes read your work to give you some feedback. Now you want to make the jump from writing a book to getting it published. You'll need two things:

1. An agent.
2. Thick skin.

Publishers are inundated with manuscripts every day. In order to get your work looked at, you'll need representation. A literary agent's job is to bring your work to publishers and get it read. But first you have to find an agent.

After I finished the original manuscript for my first novel, *MEG* (originally titled *White Death*), I purchased a book entitled *How to Get Published*. Like many of you, I had no "ins" or distant relatives in the business; I was starting out from scratch. The book contained a list of literary agents, each firm describing the genres they were most interested in (fiction, nonfiction, romance, etc.) and instructions on how to contact them.

As a first step, almost every agent asks for a two-page query letter describing your story. They do *not* want the manuscript unless they are interested in your story. Agents also ask you to provide a SASE (self-addressed stamped envelope) ... to make it easier to reject you. Ouch.

This is where the tough skin comes in. You are about to enter a field where rejection is the norm. If you can't *persevere* through this phase, you won't make it. That's why you need goals. Because now more than ever, you need to remind yourself what your goal is and how badly you want to achieve it. Remember, if it were easy, then everyone would be doing it.

Having been in sales, my philosophy was simple: I was going to send a two-page query letter to every literary agent that handled fiction. First I developed my two-page query letter. Extremely important: Make sure you compose a letter that *Sells Your Story*. Next, I started with the As and went through the Zs. Mailed those puppies out and prayed ... *Enter Rejection*. Of the sixty-five letters I sent, I received twenty-eight responses on a 3" x 5" card with my name scrawled in pencil (usually misspelled) that basically said *Thanks But We Have Enough Clients*. I received four letters from agents who asked to see the first three to five chapters. The other agents? I never heard back from them. Of the four agents who asked to see chapters, only one was interested in working with me. One out of sixty-five! But I only needed one, right? Ken Atchity in Los Angeles believed *White Death* would make a great book and movie, but first the manuscript needed a ton of editing. Ken describes it like this:

Editing is like cutting a fish: First you chop off its head and tail, then you get to the meat.

Ken also felt:

1. My manuscript took too long to get to the action.
2. There was no central hero.
3. The book droned on too much about science.

Ken made me an offer. He would assign a member of his editing team to work with me, but I had to pay the editor's fees. The cost: six thousand dollars. Gulp. I was broke, supporting (barely) a family of five. Now a man who I had never met wanted more money than I had earned in the last six months to edit a book that still might never be published. And no, he wasn't about to do the work, then collect later. No other agents were interested. What to do?

At some point you too may come to this fork in the road. I can't advise you here. You have to weigh your priorities. Me, I was miserable in my job as a door-to-door salesman. I had to make a change. I had to believe that I was going to make it.

I have also always believed that goals cannot be achieved without sacrifice. I preached this to my basketball players when I was coaching. Now it was time to put my money where my mouth was.

Sacrifice #1: I had worked nights and weekends to finish the book.

Sacrifice #2: I owned a '71 Malibu convertible my father had bought me when I was seventeen. I realized it was time to sell it. With that money, and money I borrowed from loved ones, I paid for AEI's editing fees.

Ken's editor, David Angsten, taught me a lot about pacing. He'd edit a few chapters, even create new scenes, then I'd go in and edit his work. After a while, I understood where he was going and took over. Six months later, a new story: *MEG: A Novel of Deep Terror* was created. Ken was happy but not satisfied. He had me hire another editor, Ed Stackler, to do a line edit. Ed did a terrific job with *MEG*. He really tightened the writing and taught me a lot.

Some of you may be wondering if all these editors were necessary. For some of you they might be; for others, no. To me, these were my first real teachers. I knew I had a great story to tell, and I knew I could write action, but I was inexperienced. A few basics I learned:

1. Format: Manuscripts should be double-spaced in a twelve-point font. Seems like a little thing, but no one had ever taught me that.

2. Every story needs a central protagonist (hero) and antagonist (villain). I had lumped a team of people to catch the Megalodon.

3. Jump into the action ASAP. My first chapter with the MEG vs. T-Rex helped sell the story, but then I drifted a bit. By cutting out the fat, I streamlined the action.

Finally, the manuscript was finished. It had taken me from August 1, 1995, to January 15 to write *White Death*, then February 1 through September 10 to edit it into *MEG*. Since January, I had been working as a sales manager at a local meat company. The owner had promoted me to general manager so he could retire and I could referee battles between his son and stepsons. My job was to unite the family to manage the business. Guess I united the family a bit too well.

On Friday, September 13, 1996, I went to my J.O.B. (Just Over Broke) and learned I had been fired. I thanked the family and went home, convinced it was the best thing that could have happened.

That weekend, Ken sent *MEG* and a one-page treatment for a second book (eventually the story that would become *Domain*) to the biggest publishing houses in the country. *MEG* had a decided advantage over other manuscripts. Months earlier, Ken and producer Warren Zide had secured a deal with Hollywood Pictures (Disney) to option *MEG* as a movie. Although I hadn't been paid yet, things looked promising.

A two-day bidding war yielded a huge two-book deal with Bantam-Doubleday. By setting a goal to become a writer, I had changed my life for the better.

Just Put Your Butt in the Chair

STEPHEN WHITE

Readers who love gut-twisting suspense should read any of Stephen White's fifteen best-selling novels featuring psychiatrist Dr. Alan Gregory. Whether a patient has died and left behind an incriminating diary (*Privileged Information*) or the Death Angels are coming (*Kill Me*) Stephen keeps his readers hearts pounding. His novels earn that rare accolade, "If only this were longer!" Find out why at his Web site, www.authorstephenwhite.com.

M ost novelists, I suppose, acknowledge to themselves that they might be writing a book at a time in the process somewhere *before* they've accumulated 125 manuscript pages. Not me.

Most novelists, I suppose, consider the possibility, even the fantasy, that the pile of pages they've written might someday be published *prior* to the moment that they type the last word on the final page of the first draft. Not me.

It was with some great surprise that I came to believe the story I had written back in 1989—that's what I was calling the completed 450-page document, the "story"—might be worthy of a publisher's attention.

My surprise left me in a quandary. I had never been part of a writers' group, never attended a writers conference, didn't know any published authors (at least any non-academic ones), and had never read a word about the process of getting from here (a manuscript) to there (a published book). To learn the machinations, I did what people of my generation did in the dark days before the Internet—I searched for a book to teach me how to find a publisher.

My quest began in the remote, comfortable corner of the third floor of the third-generation Tattered Cover in Cherry Creek. For those of you unfamiliar with bookstore Meccas, that's the Bookstore (with a capital *B*) that for many years filled an old department store on First Avenue in Denver, Colorado. In that third-floor nook, two six-foot-wide, eight-foot-tall pine bookcases came together at a right angle below a simple cardboard placard that read, "Writing."

I bought books. I learned about literary agents and query letters and slush piles.

I learned about the odds I was facing. They were, shall we say, long. One author estimated the number of new manuscripts written each year to be in excess of 100,000. The number of first novels published annually by major houses?

Three to four hundred.

I had taken two graduate courses in statistics. I didn't like my chances.

From the various options for finding a publisher outlined in the books I was reading, I selected all of the above.

I distributed manuscripts to family, friends, friends of friends, relative strangers, and total strangers hoping that someone would read my trifle, adore it, and that that someone would know someone else in New York's publishing community who would stand up and yell "Bravo" to announce my imminent arrival on the literary scene.

I wrote and rewrote and rewrote again a query letter and began sending it to prospective agents along with sample chapters of my manuscript.

I approached directly all the publishing houses that the books I was reading indicated would accept manuscripts unagented.

What did I get for my efforts?

I used up a year, most of my enthusiasm, and a lot of money. I collected many rejections along the way. Most of the rejections came from agents. I was turned down by the top agents in the industry, and by a few agents that were less illustrious. Some of the rejections I received were cursory. Some were thoughtful. Some of the thoughtful ones were encouraging. Some of the thoughtful ones were, shall we say, unkind.

Only one publishing house replied to my over-the-transom submissions. The one responded with a form letter. The gist?

My manuscript had found its way into the slush pile.

So ... the end result, after a year, was that I had not succeeded in getting the entire manuscript read even once by either an editor or a literary agent. (A couple of agents' assistants were forced to wade through it, apparently. Not happily, by all reports.)

The odds of getting your first novel published are binary. You will, or you won't.

The closest I came to a complete reading was about halfway through the year. It turned out that a good friend's wife's mother's new husband's daughter-in-law was a literary agent. She received a copy of my manuscript as a disguised mitzvah after a Passover seder in New York City. After reading enough of my manuscript to be convinced of her opinion, she replied (reverse the order above to understand the routing) that it wasn't her kind of work.

A year of concerted effort complete, I prepared to box up my efforts, find a shelf in a closet, and acknowledge that although I hadn't succeeded in becoming a published writer, I'd thoroughly enjoyed (most of) the process of writing my (unpublished) novel.

Then ... one of my oldest brother's good friends (and her husband) read a copy of the manuscript and liked it. They, it turned out, had an old college friend who was an assistant editor at Viking. They sent the manuscript on to him with their recommendation. A month passed. I heard through my brother that the old college friend had liked it but was only acquiring nonfiction and had sent it "upstairs" for further consideration. I admit to some growing cynicism at that stage of the process, and I was convinced that what was "upstairs" at Viking was the mailroom.

On April 2, 1990, I received a call from a very kind man. He said, "My name is Al Silverman. I'm the publisher of Viking Penguin, and we would like to buy your book." After he and I dealt with my bewilderment (it was the day after April Fools', after all), he got around to asking for the name of my agent so he could negotiate a deal. I told him with some trepidation that I didn't have an agent, fearing that fact might scuttle my chances. I even admitted that I hadn't been able to get one. Al laughed a gentle, compassionate laugh. He said, "You'll be able to get one now."

Al was right about that, as he was right about so many things to come.

Remember those odds I was discussing?

The last unagented novel purchased by Viking prior to *Privileged Information* was *Ordinary People* in 1979. To the best of my knowledge they have not bought one since.

What's the lesson?

The odds of getting your first novel published are binary. You will, or you won't.

What's the best strategy for becoming a one and not a zero? I don't know, but I suggest not waiting around to be discovered. Do something to get read. Then do it again. And again. What does that mean?

Every day, put your butt in the chair and write the best stuff you can write. Nothing is more important. Once the writing is done each day, do something that will help you put your work into a reader's hands. You are not going to get two readers until you get one. Readers beget readers.

Very few writers will ever get "discovered." Fewer still will get anointed. Very few. For the rest of us, success boils down to some difficult-to-decipher amalgam of craft and determination.

And a little luck. Luck is good.

Plan of Attack

TROY COOK

Troy Cook is the award-winning author of *47 Rules of Highly Effective Bank Robbers*, a "Killer Pick" by the Independent Mystery Bookstore Association (IMBA). He's also one of the hardest working writers in the business—setting up book signings and readings at book clubs and attending conferences as a panelist to promote and sell his books. Every author does this, but Troy does it more frequently and successfully than most. Visit www.troycook.net for sample chapters and reviews, as well as a preview of his next book.

A jolt of adrenalin surged through my body the day I decided to write a novel. I love creating stories, and writing novels was something I knew I had to do. At the same time the notion was terrifying.

The statistics are daunting, proclaiming a failure rate of 98 percent for authors attempting to get published. And those are the lucky ones that actually finish their novels in the first place.

What I needed was a plan to storm the gates of the giant publishing houses.

So I started working on my own version of the Pincer movement as if I were going to war—developing the nuts and bolts of the Troy Cook Plan of Attack. I know that sounds a little lofty, but this was a difficult proposition and it needed a forceful, cohesive plan to pull it off.

Step One: Write a novel worthy of being read by others. Not easy, but something I felt I could do if I studied the craft well. So that's what I did—study. I read books on writing, even took a class. In the latter stages a writing critique group was also helpful. Fortunately, I'd had some previous writing experience in the film industry, which made things a little easier. I'm glossing over this step as if it's an easy one when I think this is actually the hardest step to accomplish. But it's easier to explain the path to successful publication than the craft of writing.

Step Two: Get connected. And I don't mean to the Mafia. From past experience, those kind of connections can be helpful at times, but with publishing, not so much. What I needed were connections to the publishing industry.

So I started going to mystery conventions around the country in an effort to meet agents, reviewers, fellow authors, and potential fans. And I didn't just attend; I broke free of my somewhat reserved demeanor and made friends. This is difficult for a lot of authors, but this may have contributed to the "buzz" eventually generated about my debut novel. Either way, it's how I found my first agent and reviewers that actually reviewed my novel. I also met many friendly and helpful authors that had been in the same situation I was in and were eager to help, as well as some great readers and potential fans.

Step Three: Convince publishers that they should publish my book. But how to accomplish that task? Even with an agent that wasn't easily achieved. I thought about bribing, sneaking, or kidnapping my way into the publishing arena, but even though I love to write about that kind of thing I am not actually capable of committing any of those acts.

I believe we all make fewer mistakes if we draw on our previous experience, so I decided to use the knowledge I'd learned in painting houses and directing movies to help with this daunting task. Painting houses? Sure, why not. When I owned a house-painting business one of my major jobs was selling, convincing others to believe in my company. It was something I'd never done for a living and wasn't altogether comfortable with. But when you have to feed your family you get good at it really fast. And this is what I learned about selling: basically, just because *I* knew I would provide a good service for the potential customer, that did me no good whatsoever if *they* didn't know it.

It's the same thing with a book idea; you have to make publishers believe that your story is one that *needs* to be published, that it's a wise decision.

It's the same with directing movies—if you want to direct you have to be good at pitching movie ideas to producers. From what I'd learned about publishing it seemed to have a very similar structure to the movie business. So I decided to borrow a tactic from the film industry: the hook.

If you've got a good hook for your story, you're in, baby!

In practical terms, that means that you have to be able to pitch your story idea in thirty seconds, ideally with one sentence. If you can get it down to one sentence that makes them want to buy it, you're golden. In the film business they call it "High Concept."

....

You have to make publishers believe that your story is one that *needs* to be published, that it's a wise decision.

....

There are a couple reasons why it's a good idea to work on your hook until you've got it perfected. Some say that film executives are so busy that they'll only pay attention for a maximum of thirty seconds. If you haven't hooked them in that amount of time you can forget it. In my experience, that was often the case. But the other reason is that if a story can be told in thirty seconds then it's a story they can sell easily because it gives them a way to hook the audience in today's fast-paced world.

Editors and agents in the publishing biz are very similar to movie execs—incredibly busy with little time to spare, and they want stories with a universal hook. Here's the one I came up with, one that I spent months reworking while I was writing my novel: What if your father raised you to be a bank robber? Instead of Barbie & Ken, you played with Smith & Wesson? And now you're twenty-two and ready to flee the nest, but your homicidal pop won't let you go?

Interesting, right? While the story isn't for everyone, the concept is a real grabber, and it forced agents and editors to pay attention. And if you make them pay attention, then they actually read your novel. And if they read your novel, they might just publish it.

Of course, then you have to force them to keep you in print. But what you do *after* you get published is another story entirely.

A Gripping Title and a Short, Catchy Tag Line

DUANE LINDSAY

Imagine yourself watching television. You hit the button for the listings and what do you see? Two hundred eighty-three listings, not counting the premium movie channels. What are you going to watch? How can you *possibly* decide?

This is the problem that faces agents. Yes, they are actively looking for new books—exactly like you're trying to find something to watch while eating dinner. (*Law and Order?* Nah, it's a repeat.)

A thousand query letters come through their mail slot every month, similar in format, alike in quantity to your TV listing guide. (*CSI Omaha?* Uh-uh; not in the mood.)

The agent gives the most cursory glance at the heading of one letter (*Deal or No Deal?*—maybe, but you keep looking) before moving on to the next. Shuffle. (Click.) And the next. Shuffle. (Click.) And the next.

Suddenly she stops, captured by the title in one letter (you stop, finger poised a centimeter above the remote button). Is this interesting? Is this something new, exciting?

She reads further (you press the information button) and sees that the subject is mystery. She likes mysteries. Reading further, she sees the tag line, a quick plot summary (you read the television short description). You both nod.

She considers the author biography. (You check out the actors. Nobody you know, but it was written by the guys who directed *Friends*.

You liked *Friends*.) She sees that the author—you!—won prizes for best new novel of the year.

The agent places your letter in the to-be-answered pile where she will write a personal note and request three sample chapters and a short synopsis. (You press OK and settle back to watch the start of this new series.)

Deciders

So, what made her pause over that letter?

Well, consider what made you pause at that show. Was it the title? Certainly, since that's what immediately caught your eye. Was it the brief description, or the stars, or the rating, or the subject? Consider that on another evening you might not be in the mood for a mystery but want a nice romantic comedy instead. You might press next and move on.

The show is still as good (or bad, to strain the television analogy) but not what you have in mind at this particular moment. Tough luck, too bad, and better luck next time.

There are a lot of proposed books out there seeking a home, just as there are a lot of shows you haven't seen. All of them are vying for that two- to six-second window of opportunity to get your attention in the hopes that you'll read further.

What Got Her Attention?

As I said, your query letter is the equivalent of the TV listing. It has to attract the agent's attention.

There are only three things that will attract that attention: the title, the tag line, and the subject. Four if you count your name, but we're assuming here that, since you're an unpublished writer, your name doesn't mean much to the agent.

Unless you're Paris Hilton or somebody similarly talent-challenged but media-rich, saying, "My name is … [*insert name here*]" isn't going to sell your book.

So: title, tag line, subject. That's all you've got to make an impression. If other writers follow the rules (most do), the agent gets a whole lot of the same-looking business letter. One page (maybe two), single-spaced, Times New Roman type, twelve-point, addressed professionally to the agent by name. They have to actually read the letter to see why it's different than the others. Since they have so many, they don't spend a lot of time with each one.

In an ordinary business letter, the subject (the subject line in an e-mail) is just above the salutation, as in:

> Date
>
> Bud Smith Literary Agency
> 500 Main Street, Suite 105
> Pittsburg, CA 94307
>
> Re: *The Grifter's Daughter* (Even a Bad Girl Can Be Good)
>
> Dear Mr. Smith,

Notice how the title *and* the tag line got into the salutation? Even if Mr. Smith doesn't read much farther, you got your title into his brain.

So pick a title that sums up your book, is catchy (perhaps a variation on a common phrase) or a combination of two unlike metaphors. Something that makes it jump out at you. For instance:

Drinks: *Bloody Mary; Whiskey Sour; Rusty Nail* by J.A. Konrath
Numbers: *One for the Money, Two for the Dough* by Janet Evanovich
Letters: *A is for Alibi; B is for Burglar; C is for Corpse* by Sue Grafton
Colors: *The Green Ripper* by John D. McDonald

How about using a play on words?

A Hole in Juan; Adam and Evil by Gillian Roberts
False Profits; Cover Your Assets by Patricia Smiley
Holmes on the Range by Steve Hockensmith
Tongue Fu by Sam Horn

Simple titles often work wonders:

The Stand by Stephen King
Jurassic Park by Michael Crichton
Jaws by Peter Benchley

Then there's the just plain bizarre:

The Flaming Luau of Death by Jerrilyn Farmer
Duncan Delaney and the Cadillac of Doom by A.L. Haskett
The Island of the Sequined Love Nun by Christopher Moore

A tag line is a catchy phrase that expands or explains the title or the subject of the book, for example: *The Stupidest Angel (A Heartwarming Tale of Christmas Terror)* by Christopher Moore. A good tag line makes you want to read further. It's usually difficult to come up with.

One caveat: Don't count on your publisher to keep your brilliant title—once marketing gets a hold of your book they will decide what it's called. But then once you have a publisher you've solved your how to get published problem, haven't you?

Bucking the Cross-Genre Issue: M.J. Rose Interview

M.J. Rose's edgy, steamy, and sizzling writing style holds the attention of men as well as women. She is the author of nine novels and a contributor to *Writer's Digest, Poets & Writers, Oprah Magazine, The Readerville Journal,* and *Pages.* M.J. is also the co-author with Doug Clegg of *Buzz Your Book.* Check out M.J.'s books and blogs at www.mjrose.com. M.J. also runs AuthorBuzz (www.authorbuzz.com), the first marketing service for writers that puts them in touch with readers, book-sellers, and libraries.

....

I understand getting published was a bit of an adventure for you because your first novel crossed too many genres.

Yes, *Lip Service* was turned down by several publishers even though more than one editor loved it. It wasn't erotic enough to be an erotic novel, mysterious enough to be a mystery, or romantic enough to fit in the romance section, so the marketing departments didn't know how to place it.

My agent and the positive feedback from the editors convinced me there was a readership for my book, so after putting up with the frustration of having it rejected by people who liked it, I finally decided to self-publish.

It sounds like that was a difficult decision.

It was. I'd put a lot of hard work into producing the manuscript and finding an agent and the editors had been so encouraging ...

well, I fought against self-publishing until I felt I'd exhausted the traditional avenues.

So, how did you market your book?
I set up a Web site where readers could download *Lip Service* for $9.95 and began to seriously market it on the Internet.

And this was when?
Late in 1998.

And how did that work out?
After selling more than 2,500 copies (in both electronic and trade paper format), *Lip Service* became the first e-book and the first self-published novel chosen by the Literary Guild/Doubleday Book Club as well as being the first e-book to go on to be published by a mainstream New York publishing house.

Which led Time *magazine to call you the "poster girl of e-publishing" and to you being profiled in* Forbes, The New York Times, Business 2.0, Working Woman, Newsweek, Poets & Writers *and other publications, both in the U.S. and abroad.*
Yes, but I honestly believe no one should try self-publishing unless they've done the work involved with getting an agent and had enough positive feedback on their book to know there is a market for it.

Still, your self-publishing success led to appearances on Today, Fox News *and* The Newshour with Jim Lehrer?
Yes, it was great publicity.

But you don't recommend this approach to others?
Of course not. I had years of advertising and marketing expertise and several helpful contacts. My advertising career taught me how to network effectively and generate buzz.

But even that success didn't spell the end of your cross-genre problems did it?
Certainly not. After four novels, and still not breaking out, my agent suggested that my continuing to write cross-genre books might not

be serving me well. The covers weren't good—didn't communicate what the books were about, since they were about too many things—and the reviewers kept saying for a mystery it's not a mystery, for an erotic book it's not all that erotic, and on and on.

My agent suggested I pick one of the genres I was crossing and stick with it. Either literary, or commercial, or suspense, or erotic but not all of them. I tried and tried and finally came up with Dr. Morgan Snow. A sex therapist who because of doctor/patient confidentiality would be perfect for a main character in a suspense novel.

"So let's call it suspense," I said. She smiled. Somehow I'd managed to keep every single genre I wanted to write and still come up with a way for publishers, booksellers, and reviewers to fit me in somewhere. And I managed to keep my integrity and continue to write exactly what I wanted.

Five Rules

HALLIE EPHRON

Hallie Ephron is the co-author with Donald Davidoff (together they write as G.H. Ephron) of five Dr. Peter Zak mysteries: *Amnesia, Addiction, Delusion, Obsessed*, and *Guilt*. Each of these novels explores an intriguing aspect of psychology, charting the borderland between the mind and the brain. This series has won starred reviews from Kirkus, as well as praise from *Publisher's Weekly* and newspaper reviewers across the country. Hallie reviews crime fiction for *The Boston Globe* and won the Ellen Nehr Award for excellence in mystery reviewing. She is also the author of *Writing and Selling Your Mystery Novel: How to Knock 'Em Dead with Style*, one of the best how-to books around. Visit her Web site at www.hallieephron.com.

....

I had the good fortune of working with a coauthor on my first published novel. Writing together was great fun, firing ideas back and forth, taking turns as cheerleader. And when selling the novel turned out to be much harder, I had someone with whom to share the angst—and there was plenty to share on the way to publication.

Looking back after six books and having helped many authors find their way to publication, I've discovered a few rules of survival for desperate unpublished writers.

Rule 1: Do not send your work out before it's ready for prime time. Over and over, I see new writers querying agents too early. They have partially completed manuscripts or work that hasn't been exposed to multiple readers and polished to lapidary perfection. My coauthor

(Donald Davidoff) and I spent a full year writing the first Dr. Peter Zak mystery, *Amnesia*, then another year revising. We asked readers who were not related to either of us to give us their unvarnished reactions. And along the way, we hired a tactful and insightful freelance editor who suggested ways to tweak the novel so characters were richer and story more believable, surprising, and fast-paced.

Rule 2: Do not query twenty-four agents at once unless you want to mortgage your child's college tuition to Kinko's and UPS. To find an agent, we followed the basic process that's outlined in the many guides to the publishing business. We came up with a list of literary agents that we had reason to believe would respond to our novel—agents who represented authors in the genre, agents of friends, friends of relatives, and so on. One Monday morning I mailed twenty-four query packets that each included the opening chapter, a synopsis, and a cover letter. By Friday we had seventeen agents requesting the manuscript. You do the math: three hundred-page manuscript times eight cents a page plus shipping times seventeen. Ouch.

Rule 3: Just because an editor says you should change the gender of your protagonist doesn't mean you should do it. Finding an agent was painful; finding a publisher was sheer torture. First round, our agent sent our book to a half dozen editors. Among the rejections we received, some editors offered comments and suggestions. One wondered if we shouldn't have made our main character a woman. We groaned. Our character and the stories we were telling were based on my coauthor's experiences working in a psychiatric hospital, evaluating defendants in prison, and testifying in court. Don's experiences are what they are in part because of his male-ness. But the editor's comment made us scratch our collective head. Maybe there was something wrong with Peter. My writing group came up with the answer. Every time our male protagonist faced conflict, he apologized his way out of it. As the psychologist in my writing group pointed out: *men don't apologize.* I realized that I'd written a character who reacted to conflict the way I do. De-wussification was in order, not sex change. We roughened Peter's edges, making him a tad ruder when the situation called for it, more willing to argue, get in someone's face, even throw a punch or two.

Rule 4: Success may be around the corner; if you give up, you'll never know. Out the manuscript went again to the next tier of publishers. No takers. More revisions. More rejections. It was at around this time — I remember I was officially on "revision twenty-six" — that my coauthor, unflagging until then, began to cave and suggested maybe we should throw in the towel. But we hung in there and eked out one more revision. It went out again and, this time, found a home with editor Kelley Ragland at St Martin's.

Rule 5: Don't quit your day job. We accepted a two-book contract and immediately took ourselves and our spouses out to dinner and blew a hole in our as-yet-uncollected advance.

Don't Try This at Home

K.J.A. WISHNIA

K.J.A. Wishnia was born in Hanover, New Hampshire, to a roving band of traveling academics. He has lived and worked in Scotland, France, and Ecuador, been chased by riot police on two continents, and teaches writing, literature, and other deviant forms of thought at Suffolk Community College on Long Island. The novels in his Edgar Award-nominated series include *23 Shades of Black*, *Soft Money*, *The Glass Factory*, *Red House*, and *Blood Lake*. His short stories have appeared in *Alfred Hitchcock's Mystery Magazine*, *Ellery Queen's Mystery Magazine*, *Murder in Vegas*, and *Queens Noir*. His Web site is www.kjawishnia.com.

I'm in this book because my first novel, *23 Shades of Black*, was rejected by agents and editors for years before I gave up on the idea of commercial publication, self-published it, and was nominated for the Edgar and the Anthony Awards for crime fiction.

My novels have made "Best Mystery of the Year" lists in *Booklist*, *Library Journal*, and *The Washington Post*, and I've been compared to Ken Bruen, Raymond Chandler, Sue Grafton, Graham Greene, Dashiell Hammett, Marcia Muller, Sara Paretsky—aah, you get the idea.

So I wasn't sitting on a dog here, people. And some of those rejections were just ... what's the word? Oh, yeah: stupid.

One agent wanted me to change the ending—not to make it more logical, or hard-hitting, or any other advice that I might actually have listened to, but to give it a run-of-the-mill ending where the hero unambiguously wins the day and Justice Is Served. That didn't fit my vision of the novel, or why I chose to write crime fiction in the first place.

I did my homework, too, only querying agents and editors who had published authors whose work was in the same subgenre as mine (mostly hardboiled crime fiction with a feisty female detective). I never sent out a blind or unsolicited manuscript.

Another time, an editor at a major New York publishing house told me that they loved the book, loved the gritty realism, loved the tough female protagonist. There was just one problem: "Cut the politics," she said. Now, I'll admit there were a few spots where my character gets on a soapbox and gives a speech. So, trying to be accommodating, I said, "I know just what you're talking about. I'll cut those passages." And she said, "It isn't a matter of a few passages. It's pretty much every sentence."

You love the book, but you want me to change every sentence? What on earth does that mean? Here's a clue: my character is an Ecuadorian immigrant who views American society from a unique perspective as a partially assimilated outsider. They wanted me to gut the novel of all social content and produce—you guessed it—a run-of-the-mill book that any idiot could have written.

So I said, "You don't mean cut the politics, you mean *change* the politics." Didn't go over well.

This went on for *nine years*. Not that I was sitting by the phone the whole time. I got a doctorate in Comparative Literature, wrote the first drafts of my second and third novels, and kept polishing *23 Shades of Black* until the last round of queries, when I resolved to publish it myself. I learned how to do this at the Small Press Center in Manhattan.

I typeset it using desktop publishing, bought a 600-dpi laser printer, and (here's the key) paid a company to make about a dozen ARCs, which I sent out to all the usual pre-publication review sources.

This is when [cue fanfare] fate stepped in: *Booklist* gave it a rave, I was able to put their blurb on the cover, and submit the book to the Edgar Awards committee, even though it was clearly a small-press book. (As of this writing, the Edgar Awards judges will not consider self-published books, but I didn't know that at the time.)

The award nominations led to a three-book contract with Dutton/ NAL, then a two-book contract with St. Martin's Press and numerous short stories in anthologies and magazines. There are now five novels in what the Minneapolis *Star Tribune* called "one of the most distinctive series in crime fiction." So it worked out. Which is good, because I was ready to break into a publisher's offices and start taking hostages.

Only sharp, original stuff lasts, but it usually has a much smaller share of the market—which means the big guys will drop you quickly and you'll be out-of-print again, unless you go with a smaller press.

I'd like to leave you with a few thoughts. First, as I mentioned, dozens of agents and editors passed on a manuscript that went on to get nominated for two awards and optioned by HBO.

Second, not much has changed. Even though they say they're always looking for something fresh, exciting, and different, the bottom-liners for big presses still want authors who churn out derivative, formulaic crap that might get you a book contract but will probably soon be out-of-print because there's nothing to distinguish it from all the other stuff crowding the shelves.

Only sharp, original stuff lasts, but it usually has a much smaller share of the market—which means the big guys will drop you quickly and you'll be out-of-print again, unless you go with a smaller press. I'm beginning to think that, unless you are one of the very lucky few, this is the only way to go with anything truly distinctive.

Don't try this at home. I broke in by being bold and outrageous, but self-publishing may not be the answer for you. (I managed it, but it's a hard trick to pull off.) My advice is: Be yourself, write in your own voice, and if you keep at it and don't sell your soul, you'll find your audience.

Dayenu

KEITH RAFFEL

Keith Raffel has been a construction worker, historian, congressional staffer, candidate for elective office, professional gambler, marketing executive, and founder of an Internet software company. With the 2006 publication of *Dot Dead: A Silicon Valley Mystery*, he embarked on another career—as an author—where he finds the psychic (if not the monetary) rewards high. Bookreporter.com deemed *Dot Dead* "without question the most impressive mystery debut of the year," while the *San Jose Mercury News* called it a "pleasure" and *Library Journal* called it a "well-plotted mystery" where "you can't go wrong." Check out www.keithraffel.com to see what he's up to now.

P lenty of writers in this volume will advise you to never give up. To work hard and never take success for granted. Sure, sure. Listen to those folks and follow their advice. But listen to this, too:

Before you've saved the first chapter on your laptop, define what success in writing means to you.

I have a friend who wrote a novel—a whole book—during November, which is National Novel Writing Month. Her family, neighbors, and friends all rooted for her day by day. By the last week she was making do with three hours of sleep per night. Her fingers practically fell off from all the typing, but she got it done. Has her manuscript been published? No. Was it a success? You bet! She set out to write a novel in thirty days and did it. Full stop. She met her goal and anything after that was going to be a bonus.

Before telling you about the trap I found myself in, I would like to make a confession. I have career ADD. I don't mean to make light of those who really suffer from Attention Deficit Disorder, but let me explain. I've been a carpenter, a history graduate student, a writing teacher, a congressional staffer, a candidate for elective office, a full-time gambler (I was a much better horseplayer than politician), a high-tech marketer, an entrepreneur, and now finally I find myself a writer (or, as my friends remind me, a published author). I undertake each of these new careers with the single-minded goal of making it a success. In some of these endeavors, success is easy to define. As a horseplayer, I made enough money to support myself. Success. As a candidate for office, I lost. Now I know that the journey is supposed to be more important than the destination, but losing that election was like jumping out of a plane without a parachute. It doesn't matter how wonderful the trip down was; the landing overshadowed it. Splat! Not a success.

So anyway, my career as a writer started by taking a course at the University of California Extension. I wrote two chapters and received an A. Did that make my writing venture a success? No, I don't think so. Completion of the manuscript kept getting delayed by this and that—having a kid, starting a company; you know, those kinds of interruptions. Well, I did finally finish that blasted manuscript after seven or eight years. A success now? No, not for me.

I was turned down more times than the bedsheets in a fancy hotel room, but eventually I did find a capable, hardworking agent.

But then we had to find a publisher. More rejection, then four publishers said yes, almost simultaneously. Success now? Not in my mind. The reviews that appeared were terrific, but somehow the three *Times*—New York, Los Angeles, and the weekly newsmagazine—all overlooked it. Damn.

The book made it onto the bestseller lists of a few bookstores and of the daily newspaper in Boulder, Colorado. Was that enough? No, not to this maladjusted fellow. Why not the *San Francisco Chronicle?* I asked myself. Because I did not define success up front, whatever happened would not satisfy me. Hell, if *Dot Dead* had made it to number one on *The New York Times* bestseller list, I would have been measuring its sales figures against those of *The Da Vinci Code*. I couldn't help myself. That's how I am. Like a steeplechaser, as I jumped over one fence, I was thinking ahead to the next one.

I have another colleague who was flying high indeed. She couldn't get her first book published in the U.S. For her second book she got a big deal agent, and her book showed up on the bestseller list of a major metropolitan newspaper. She had lunch with a friend—of the toxic variety—who sweetly inquired if she expected to make the *New York Times* list, too. My colleague was thrown into a bout of depression when she should have been enjoying one of the apogees of life on this earth.

So here's my advice: Define success early. If getting that damn manuscript done, if just writing those seventy-five thousand words is the goal, then celebrate when you have accomplished it. Plenty of people run marathons. Their objective may not be to win. It's to finish. Or to do a personal best. Or to break four hours. Decide before the race. Otherwise you can run twenty minutes faster than you ever have and still be disappointed.

Every spring Jews around the world celebrate Passover and sing a wonderful song called "Dayenu." Dayenu means something like "that would have been enough" or "it would have sufficed." So when the verse goes "If God had brought the Israelites out of Egypt [and done nothing more]", the response is "Dayenu!" A later verse says "If God had split the sea for the Israelites [and done nothing more]"; the response once again is "Dayenu!" The entire litany of the Exodus is recounted, and each step is met with a shouted "Dayenu!" I think that's the right way to look at writing.

Decide up front what will be enough and when you've accomplished it, shout "Dayenu!"

Whether it's getting the manuscript completed or getting published or getting on *The New York Times* bestseller list, decide before you start rapping on the computer keys what's going to be enough. If you don't decide up front, you may never be satisfied and just run around like a caged squirrel on an exercise wheel. When you reach the goal you set, shout "Dayenu." If you reach another milestone, shout "Dayenu" again. I wish I'd played it that way.

At Book Expo America, I had a long line of people waiting for me to sign bound galleys of my book. I kept asking people why they were waiting in line for an author whom they did not know, who had written a book they had not read. Truth be told though, I felt like a rock star for thirty minutes. I had a taste, just a tiny taste, of celebrity and learned what a high it could produce. (The Rolling Stones might need fifty thousand screaming fans to get the high; I needed only 150 polite, patient mystery readers.) I should have shouted "Dayenu" then and there. I didn't. Don't make the same mistake. Set your writing goal up front and remember to sing out "Dayenu!" when you reach it.

Send the Damn Thing Out

JACK BLUDIS

Jack Bludis has published more than forty novels and over four hundred short stories in several genres using various pseudonyms. His latest novel, *Shadow of the Dahlia*, set in the Hollywood during the time of the infamous "Black Dahlia" murder, received a Shamus nomination. His story "Munchies" was nominated for both a Shamus and an Anthony. Jack has lived in Baltimore most of his life but travels often, particularly to New York City and Southern California. Visit his Web site at www.jackbludis.com. Jack Bludis tends to get right to the point. When asked how he got published, this was his reply.

M y story is simple and probably uninspiring. I kept writing until I got published. I'll keep getting published until I make a living at it.

There is no magic formula—just persistence and send the damn thing out.

Photographed in
President Reagan's Office

STEPHEN COONTS

Stephen Coonts is the author of *Flight of the Intruder*, *Under Siege*, *Final Flight*, *Cuba*, *America*, *Liberty*, *Fortunes of War*, *The Red Horsemen*, *The Intruders*, *Liars and Thieves*, *Hong Kong*, *The Minotaur* and his latest thriller, *Traitor*, all of which are great reads, exciting, entertaining, and insightful. No one does better flying sequences than Steve, which makes sense because he is a former naval aviator who flew A-6s during the Vietnam War. Steve's writing talents aren't limited to thrillers. He has authored a couple of first-rate science fiction books, *Saucer* and *Saucer: The Conquest*, and several captivating anthologies on flying and war. His nonfiction work, *The Cannibal Queen*, was genuinely inspiring and *The Garden of Eden* (released under the pen name Eve Adams) very funny. For more on Steve and his books visit his Web site at www.coonts.com. The following was taken from his site, with permission.

A lifelong reader of true flying stories, I realized during the Vietnam War that the naval aviation combat adventure would make a hell of a story if it were properly written. I was too busy living it at the time to try to write it, but the seed was planted. After the war, when I was a flight instructor on A-6 Intruder aircraft at NAS Whidbey Island, Washington, I began trying to write flying scenes, to capture the feeling of flying a carrier-based jet in combat. Writing in the evening on a portable typewriter on the dining room table after the kids were in bed, I created Jake Grafton and his squadron-mates, and worked out the basics of the flying scenes that I wanted to use. These scenes were not yet a novel because I didn't have a plot, but I pounded away diligently and wore out a typewriter trying to figure out how to put the reader into the cockpit and take him flying. In 1975 and 1976 when I was an assistant catapult officer aboard USS *Nimitz*, I bought another portable typewriter and kept writing.

During the spring and summer of 1977, after I was out of the navy and driving a taxicab in Denver, I rewrote some more and looked into creative writing courses that would, I hoped, help me acquire the craft necessary to complete the novel. Alas, I had neither the time nor the money for writing classes.

Law school and life as a neophyte attorney further delayed the writing. About 1982 or 1983 I dreamed up a plot for the novel, but I didn't have the spare time to devote to it. It wasn't until 1984, after I was divorced, that I finally had the time to work seriously on this novel. I never thought it would be published, but I wanted to write it, to complete it. At that time in my life I needed to fulfill a dream, and I needed something to keep my mind off my personal and legal troubles. My secretary at the oil company where I worked, Sandra Hyer, taught me to use the word processor, so in the evenings and on weekends and holidays, I sat at her desk and pounded the keys.

The story of the pilot who tried too hard, who flew an unauthorized mission and was caught at it, was simply a framework for the flying stories that had been percolating through my head for years. Most of the flying stories were true or based on missions that were flown by me or guys I knew. One, however, the best one, was pure fiction: the story of an A-l Skyraider pilot, shot down and trapped in the cockpit of his shattered plane, who asked his friend to kill him. I had carried that tale around in my head since 1974 and wanted to work it into this flying story somehow. An A-l would not have been used over North Vietnam this late in the war, so the action had to occur in Laos. I bent the plot of the tale around so that this story would fit. Shot up over Hanoi, Jake and his bomber/navigator, Tiger Cole, go to Laos to eject instead of heading out to sea, which is what they logically should have done. Not a single reviewer or fan called me on this plot twist.

The A-1 pilot's tale actually made the story stronger because this event could be Jake's catharsis. After listening to the pilot's pleas on the radio to his airborne wingman, Jake realizes the truth that all good soldiers know: the important thing is how you live, not whether you live or die. Jake overcomes his fear and goes to rescue Tiger Cole, or die with him.

After I finished the first draft of the manuscript working nights and weekends, I was ready to try to find a publisher. The book was rejected by thirty-four publishers before the Naval Institute Press, which was looking for another novel after publishing Tom Clancy's *The Hunt for Red October*, accepted it. I was amazed. After all those years thinking about it and writing at it, I never really believed my little flying story would see the light of day. The Press insisted I re-write the thing one more time, then we edited the hell out of it. Eventually they decided to send it to the printer. I was so sick of the tale by that time I would have willingly trashed it and returned their advance, five thousand dollars, if I hadn't already spent the money.

Flight of the Intruder was published in September 1986 and found some fans inside the U.S. Naval Institute, and the book worked its way up the chain of command—until that fateful day lightning struck and it was photographed on President Reagan's desk for an article in *Fortune Magazine* on "Reagan, the Manager," one of the September 1986 issues. The USNI had the wit to trumpet that event to the four corners of the earth, publicity that certainly helped put the book before the American public where it hit just the right note.

It spent twenty-eight weeks on the *New York Times* bestseller list in hardcover.

Write a *Bit* of a Novel

SIMON LEVACK

Simon Levack's series of historical thrillers, featuring a resourceful slave in Aztec Mexico, have been praised by critics for their gripping, suspenseful storylines, richly detailed background, and black humor. *Demon of the Air*, the first, won the Crime Writers' Association's Debut Dagger Award, and *Publishers Weekly* said, "Historical novels ... don't get much better." It is published in the U.S. by St Martin's Minotaur. Also in the series to date are *Shadow of the Lords* and *City of Spies*, as well as some short stories. A former lawyer, Simon Levack lives in London, England, with his family. His Web site is www.simonlevack.com.

T his is how I got published. I'm not sure how much you can learn from it: In the end I suspect the only way to succeed at anything is just to keep doing it until it works. People tell me I must be clever to write books and get them published, or I must work terribly hard. I tell them no, like all the other writers I know, I spend most of my time staring out of the window. I'm just too bloody-minded to know when to quit. That seems to be the secret. But anyway, this is how I did it.

I'd been writing for as long as I could remember. As a child, I wrote stories to amuse myself. Then I found out there were things called magazines, so I tried writing for those instead, because they had money and I didn't. Unfortunately the editors all seem to have missed the point, or maybe there was a mix-up in the post room, as they kept sending me back the stuff I sent them instead of the checks I was expecting.

I didn't get despondent. Instead, I wrote poetry. I reasoned that no one ever reads poetry by living writers anyway, and if my poems are rejected after I'm dead, I'm unlikely to care. Oddly enough my poems did better than my stories, but "better" is a relative term, and they didn't make me any money.

Then I hit on the idea of writing novels. It seems obvious that you should start with short stories and then wean yourself onto the hard stuff, but it isn't necessarily so. Short fiction is so unforgiving: a bad paragraph or even a bad line can blight a five thousand-word story, but several bad pages in a row can pass unnoticed in novel, if the rest is good enough. And why invent a whole plot and cast of characters twenty times over when once will do? Finally, it turns out books are easier to sell. Thinking about it, it was so simple, so obvious; it was like an epiphany.

Of course, the novels didn't sell either.

I might have given up then. If the publishing industry hadn't got the message by now, maybe they never would. However, it was at this point that I finally stumbled on the winning formula.

Don't write a short story. Don't write a novel. Write a *bit* of a novel and just leave it there.

I found out that the Crime Writers' Association ran a competition called the Debut Dagger Award. They gave it (and still do) for the best first chapter of an unpublished novel, word limit three thousand words. I thought any fool could write three thousand words; I could do it in a couple of evenings. I didn't have an unpublished novel, but that didn't seem to matter. What I did have was an idea that I thought would work and for sure had not been done before—an Aztec detective. So I dashed off my entry, trimmed it down to the required length (the First and Only Rule of Competitions: Read the Rules), sent it off, and forgot about it. As you'll have guessed by now, I won.

The prize was two hundred fifty British pounds, a couple of nights in a nice hotel courtesy of the CWA, a gala dinner, and (this was the good part) a lot of attention from agents and publishers.

The agent who signed me up was named Lisanne Radice. She wanted to sell my book. As I still hadn't actually written one, that was when the hard work started. Still, I got there eventually: it took about eighteen months to finish, but I made enough out of it to quit the day job, at least for a while, and sold two more on the strength of it.

Which all sounds good, but here's the bit you can maybe learn from. I was given my prize at the gala dinner. The Master of Ceremonies was Robert Barnard, who had earlier warned all speakers that they were expected to talk for three minutes, no more. When I got up I said I wouldn't need anything like three minutes.

"*You* don't have three minutes," he hissed at me. "*You've* got *a few words!*"

Success is sweet. Enjoy it.

Don't expect anyone else to be impressed.

The Write Stuff

STEVE HOCKENSMITH

Steve Hockensmith is the author of 3.5 mystery novels. (Two, *Holmes on the Range* and *On the Wrong Track*, have been published so far.) He blogs at www.stevehockensmith.com and writes a column about genre TV shows and movies for *Alfred Hitchcock's Mystery Magazine*. The father of 2.0 small children, he is frequently sleep-deprived, but only occasionally cranky about it.

A few years back, I attended a panel at an annual mystery convention that was called something like "We're Real Authors Now— Nyah Nyah Nyah!" It featured three or four writers (let's split the difference and say 3.5) talking about their recently published debut novels. Now, when I say I "attended" the panel, I mean in the audience. This was three or four years (let's split the difference and say 3.5) before my own debut novel, *Holmes on the Range*, was published by St. Martin's Minotaur. So I didn't have a microphone before me that day—just 3.5 years of struggle and self-doubt.

Toward the end of the panel, when the moderator asked if there were any questions from the audience, I didn't have the guts to stand up and ask what I really wanted to know, which was, "How the hell did you do it? How did you get from out here to up there? How how *how*?!?" And it's a good thing I didn't, since I would've been escorted from the building by goons in blue blazers if I had.

But someone with guts *did* ask the question, albeit sanely. And the answers just about drove me nuts.

"Oh, my cousin's a literary agent," said Panelist Number One. "I just sent it to her."

"One of my frat brothers is an editor at Bantam Dell," said Panelist Number Two. "I just sent it to him."

"Panelist Number Two's frat brother is my cousin," said Panelist Number Three. "I just sent it to him, too."

"I own Harper Collins," said Panelist Number Three Point Five. "I didn't even have to send it to anybody."

Of course, I've exaggerated here for comedic effect. Panelist Number Three didn't actually refer to Panelist Number Two as "Panelist Number Two." He called him "Blake." Other than that, this anecdote is 100 percent true! (Truthiness margin of error: 51 percent.)

Being a regular Joe—a fellow whose cousins work in IT, a fellow with no high-powered frat brothers (or low-powered ones, for that matter), a fellow who is not Rupert Murdoch—I did what any other regular Joe would do: I killed every one of the panelists with my bare hands. (Truthiness margin of error: 99.9 percent.)

I'd learned nothing from the panel that would help me get published—except perhaps "Be born lucky," and it was way too late for that. So, as I so often do, I turned for guidance to the only other place I knew to look: the bumper stickers and t-shirts of the 1970s. There I found words to live by—and I'm not talking about "If the van's a-rockin', don't come a-knockin'." Though that *is* sound advice, if you stop to think about it.

Actually, my new creed was "Keep on Truckin'", and it served me well.

Of course, I didn't turn to *literal* truckin'. That hasn't worked as a back door into the entertainment industry since C. W. "Convoy" Mc-Call, and look what happened to him.

No, I'm talking about writing here. I wrote and wrote some more. "If the keyboard's a-clackin'," I'd tell folks, "don't come a-distractin' [me with non-writin' stuff]."

Eventually, an agent came to *me*. She wasn't a cousin (of mine, anyway). She wasn't a frat brother (or sorority sister ... of mine, anyway). And she certainly wasn't Rupert Murdoch (as far as *anybody* was concerned).

But she was a pro, and she'd seen one of my short stories in a magazine and she wanted to know if I'd written a novel. And as it turned out, I had indeed. So I sent it to her.

And she said no.

I'd learned nothing from the panel that would help me get published — except perhaps "Be born lucky," and it was way too late for that.

Or "not quite," to be more exact. So I rewrote and rewrote and rewrote some more until the poor woman no longer had the stomach (or the printer cartridges) for another rejection. She said yes.

Not long after that, I had a three-book deal — I was going to be a published author. Which is why this year I found myself on a mystery convention panel called "Holy Shit! I Sold My Novel! (Now What?)." (Yes, that was the actual title. Truthiness margin of error: .01 percent. If you're offended, just be glad they didn't use the original name — "Holy *Censored* Shit! I *Censored* Sold My *Censored* Novel! (Now What the *Censored* Do I Do?")

The panel consisted of four (yes, definitely four) writers talking about their recently published debut novels. And I waited and waited and waited for someone in the audience to ask me The Question: How the hell did you do it? But no one did ... so I'm telling you now.

Take heed, struggling, unagented, pre-published writers of America. The next time you get a rejection letter or your critique group hates your story or your cousin tells you for the one thousanth time that she only represents upmarket nonfiction and you've got to stop sending her that damn *Babylon 5* novel, just remember what the t-shirt said.

"I'M WITH STUPID."

Oh, and keep on truckin' while you're at it.

"No One Wants to Read This Crap!"

SUE ANN JAFFARIAN

Like her character Odelia Grey, Sue Ann Jaffarian is a middle-aged, plus-sized paralegal. She lives and works in Los Angeles and writes mysteries and general fiction, as well as short stories. In addition to writing, Sue Ann is sought after as a motivational and humorous speaker. She is a member of Mystery Writers of America and very active in the Los Angeles Chapter of Sisters In Crime, an international nonprofit organization dedicated to the mystery genre. Visit Sue Ann at www.sueannjaffarian.com.

L ike Dr. Martin Luther King, I had a dream. That dream was not to be a tall, thin, wealthy blond surrounded by hunky cabana boys. (That's my fantasy, a totally different thing altogether.) No, I was one of those unfortunate creatures who dreamed of being a published author. I say "unfortunate" because, considering the climate of publishing, and with plastic surgery being what it is, I might have had a better chance at the tall, thin, blond fantasy.

Before I started writing mysteries, I wrote two general fiction novels that were represented by a New York agent (hereinafter known as the wicked witch of the east — "WWE" — so as not to be confused with my current agent, the good witch of the south — "GWS"). While WWE did get my first novels read by numerous top publishing houses, they were never bought, in spite of some pretty good rejection letters. It was a case of "close, but no cigar." Meanwhile, WWE suggested that I try my hand at writing mysteries. Since I had read very few mysteries up to that point, I was totally aghast at the thought—but I do love a challenge.

By trade, I am a corporate paralegal just like my protagonist, Odelia Grey, so I decided to address the task as I would a project at work. So off to the bookstore I went, returning with armfuls of bestselling and award-winning mysteries by women. I read until my eyes bugged out, making a chart along the way on a yellow legal pad. In one column I listed what I liked about a particular book, in the other what I didn't like. When I was through reading, I developed what I hoped would be my own unique style and applied it to the novel I was currently working on, a dark comedy about weight prejudice entitled *The Back of the Bus*. Many months later and with much excitement and fanfare, the completed manuscript with a new title of *Too Big to Miss* was shipped off to WWE. A few days later WWE called me.

"No one wants to read this crap."

Yep, that's what she said to me. In addition, she called it "prurient" and said she would be embarrassed to represent it. How's that for helpful words of encouragement?

Okay, I confess, immediately following the call I cried my eyes out for about two hours, then I picked myself up, dusted my big ass off, applied fresh makeup, and went in search of other opinions. I gathered up a half dozen people who were big readers—acquaintances of all ages and backgrounds I knew would be straight with me about the quality of the book—and handed each of them a manuscript. Within a week, every one of them encouraged me to move ahead with *Too Big to Miss*.

So I did.

First, I got rid of old baggage—I terminated my relationship with WWE. Next, I went in search of a new agent. When one didn't materialize, I considered self-publishing. I was determined to get my book out to the public, come hell or high water. After researching the various self-publishing venues, I decided on iUniverse. A few months later, I was holding the published version of *Too Big to Miss* in my hands—New York be damned!

Okay, call me stupid, but I actually thought that once I was published, bookstores would roll out the red carpet for me for book signings.

Imagine my surprise and disappointment when I encountered prejudice, bold-faced rudeness, and straight-out rejection when they realized I was self-published. (To be fair, I must note here that often bookstores cannot handle self-published or print-on-demand books because of return issues, and many were very gracious and professional when advising me of their company's policy. It's simply unfortunate that many others did not even attempt to be professional.) But did I give up and retreat into a pint of Ben and Jerry's? No! I had already vanquished WWE; a dozen flying monkeys were nothing. Bring 'em on!

Armed once again with a pen and my trusty yellow legal pad, I set down a marketing plan for my self-published baby. It was obvious I would have to reach readers directly if I wanted people to know about and read *Too Big to Miss*, so the first thing I did was identify specific niches that I felt would be most interested in reading my book. Then I set about reaching them directly by various means, including the use of the Internet, press releases, and direct personal mailings.

I also made a point of establishing good relationships with a couple of independent bookstores that believed in my book and who had toll-free and/or online ordering and steered readers specifically to those stores or to Internet booksellers. It was time-consuming and tedious, but it worked.

....

Okay, call me stupid, but I actually thought that once I was published, bookstores would roll out the red carpet for me for book signings.

....

Next, I set about contacting specific large groups about speaking appearances and soon found myself a guest speaker or keynote speaker at several conferences and events across the nation, something I still do as much as possible.

While a few of my marketing ideas did not work, most did, and soon word of mouth was selling *Too Big to Miss* across the nation. It even snagged a couple of accolades, including Honorable Mention in the *Writer's Digest* International Self-Published Book Awards, and appeared on several library and online reviewer's favorite reads lists. In no time people were asking for the next book. Another book? Gulp! What if I'm a one-hit wonder? Which is exactly what worried me and exactly why two years after *Too Big to Miss* came out I self-published *The Curse of the Holy Pail*.

In hindsight, I probably should have approached agents and traditional publishers at this point. After all, I had sales figures and reviews to prove *Too Big to Miss* was not a failure. But the words *no one wants to read this crap* still clung to me like barnyard stink and mired my self-confidence.

So once again I applied my tried-and-true grassroots marketing strategy, and *The Curse of the Holy Pail* sold even faster than the previous book. At this point I knew that if I was serious about being a professional writer, I would have to leave self-publishing behind. So even though I had already written the first couple of chapters in the third Odelia Grey mystery, I shelved it and set out to find an agent. This time around I was determined to find an agent who saw my vision, and find her I did—enter GWS. In time GWS found my current publisher, Midnight Ink, who also saw my vision. After heavy rewrites, Midnight Ink republished both *Too Big to Miss* and *The Curse of the Holy Pail* and purchased the third Odelia Grey mystery. The Midnight Ink edition of *Too Big to Miss* was published almost five years to the day after the iUniverse edition was released, and received extensive praise from reviewers and readers alike.

Three months after its Midnight Ink release, *Too Big to Miss* was optioned for television.

Not bad for *crap*.

Getting to Know Literary Agents and Editors

DUANE LINDSAY

Editors are the gatekeepers of the publisher's checkbook. It is their job to select books to present to the editorial board of the publisher, with an eye toward getting that book published. Editors turn down many more books than they *ever* approve. The number of rejections is in the 95 to 99 percent range. They get a lot of submissions ,and there are a small number of slots to fill.

Agents are screening devices for editors. Good agents know what editors are looking for and can open doors closed to the public. They also demonstrate to the editor that somebody likes your work and is willing to champion it, at their own time and expense.

Given how hard it is to get an editor to read your work—most publishers no longer accept unagented submittals—it's a good idea to get an agent to shop your book for you. But how? There are only three ways: You can write to them using a query letter, you can meet them at conferences, or you can run into them (not literally) in the grocery store.

Method three is probably best and certainly the least expensive—bumping into them at the local market. But how many agents do you know personally (we averaged around none), and where do they shop? Hard to meet them socially, too: like doctors, agents are constantly bombarded by people with favors to ask.

Method two is to meet them at writers conferences. Pay money and get a one-on-one meeting with the editor/agent of your choice. With luck and a good presentation you could walk away with a personal invitation to send that person your sample chapters and synopsis, along with that golden phrase *Requested Material* written right on the envelope. This tells the person opening the mail that you are not part of the great wave of hopefuls fated for the slush pile. You are wanted.

Method one? Send a query letter into that vast stream of other letters bound for an agent's office. If you follow the rules, your letter is like all the others: black ink on white paper, same format—like a penguin in a penguin parade, you all look alike.

You aren't all alike, of course, and there's the problem. The agent receives hundreds of letters a month, thousands a year, all asking the same thing. Your special task is to *look* the same and *be* different.

That's the system we've got. Go to a conference for a face-to-face (expensive) or line up in the queue. Though we don't recommend these methods, some writers try standing out from the crowd by doing a special/unusual package such as using pink stationery or green ink, or sending agents a box of chocolates. That might get the attention of some agents, but it will certainly irritate most of them.

The best way to increase your chances is to be better informed than other writers sending queries. You can buy a copy of *Guide to Literary Agents* and *Jeff Herman's Guide to Book Publishers, Editors & Literary Agents*. In these books, both highly recommended, you'll find tons of relevant information about agents and editors. Who they are, where they are, what they like, whether they want what you're selling, submission guidelines, their Web sites, if they accept new authors at all—everything you need to know. Follow up by going online. Read what they have to say about the books they represent. Arm yourself with information to improve your chances.

So Far and No Further

Many (most) of the books and Web sites we studied recommended that you research an agent personally. Some even go as far as suggesting your opening line in your query letter be a personal connection. Did you go to the same school? Does the agent like peanut butter and celery sandwiches? Amazing; so do you! And so on.

We disagree. There is enough to do just to get the letter out the door, so there's no profit in delaying in order to find some obscure nugget of information that might (probably won't) attract a tiny bit of interest. As we discuss later, it is important to research an agent to find a solid business connection—she's looking for YA mysteries and that's just what you have— but trying to find some obscure personal connection is a waste of time.

Remember, it's better to get fifty good query letters sent now than one perfect letter sent later, if at all. Like editing, you can take this research way too far, chaining yourself to a degree of finicky perfection that's neither needed nor effective. Eventually you have to say, "Here's what I'm sending; it's good enough."

By all means, go through the books and collect the raw data. Make a list of all the agents in the book who accept *anything* from unpublished writers. Go online and rate your list into the best, the medium, and the I'll-get-to-it. Find out which agents prefer e-mail submissions and which prefer hard mail. Hard mail lets you do a more elegant letter. It also costs more (postage to send it, plus that pesky SASE) and takes longer to get a response. E-mail is cheaper and allows you to get rejected faster by more agents—truly a technological miracle.

Now start an assembly line. Assuming you've written the best query letter ever, address it to the first agent on your list. If you have anything personal to say—like you met them at a conference or you actually *did* go to the same school— by all means, lead with that. Otherwise, time is money. Finish the letter, print it (or e-mail it), and go to the next one.

You've just planted anywhere from a dozen to a hundred seeds. Now comes the hard part. Sit back and see if they grow.

The Most Powerful Force Is Luck

THOMAS PERRY

Author of *The Butcher's Boy*, *Sleeping Dogs,* and eleven other novels including *Vanishing Act*, *The Face-Changers*, and *Shadow Woman* from the acclaimed Jane Whitefield series, Thomas Perry's writing is riveting and compelling. Go to his Web site at www.thomasperryauthor.com and get into some of the very best thrillers around.

My first publication was not a novel. It wasn't even a piece of fiction. It was a poem I submitted to a university literary magazine when I was in college. Encouraged, I wrote another for a different campus literary magazine, then a third. At that point my advisor, a wise English professor who was a poet and had taught fiction writing to a number of well-known writers, told me to stop. He said my stories were good, but my poetry was not. So I stopped writing bad poetry and began an undergraduate novel that was no better. But the novel helped me learn some things about constructing a long narrative and gave me some practice.

I never stopped writing. I went to graduate school and got a Ph.D. in English, worked as a commercial fisherman because I was sick of being indoors, then became a university administrator, but I still wrote. After a couple of early slip-ups I learned that no good can come of telling anyone you're a writer, so I kept it to myself.

My ideas for stories were getting bigger. I wrote a couple of book-length manuscripts. I became used to the idea that I was writing because I loved it and learned to concentrate on the quality of what I wrote rather than on publication. Then, when I was thirty-three years old, for the first time I finished a manuscript that seemed to me might be of interest to people who weren't related to me. It was a book about a professional killer, and I called it *The Butcher's Boy.* I was sure it was no worse than many things that had been published, but I didn't know what to do with it.

Very soon after that, I happened to see a magazine article on the subject. It was a journalist's attempt to prove that getting a book published without connections had become impossible. To prove his point, the journalist selected a book that the publishing world had declared to be excellent. I believe it was Wallace Stegner's *The Spectator Bird*, which had won that year's National Book Award (I wish I still had the article. I had remembered it was Jerzy Kosinski's *The Painted Bird*, but I now believe I had my birds mixed up). The journalist retyped the first hundred pages of the book, put his own name on it, and submitted it to all the major publishers.

None of the publishers recognized it, and none of them thought the book deserved publication. When his article appeared, there was a great outcry from the publishers. They said it was unfair to send a manuscript—any manuscript—in over the transom and expect it to be noticed. Books were supposed to be submitted by agents. The journalist followed their description of how to get an agent to sell a book. He sent his retyped manuscript to a number of well-known agents and waited for their replies. None of them recognized the book, and none of them felt they could undertake to sell it.

After a couple of early slip-ups I learned that no good can come of telling anyone you're a writer, so I kept it to myself.

The journalist had set out to prove that for a person like me, getting something in print was impossible. Instead, he told me exactly how to do it. Like him, I wrote to the Authors' Guild and asked for their alphabetical list of reputable agents. I began to go through the alphabet, sending out letters of inquiry, attaching to each a one-page synopsis of my book.

An agent whose name began with B wrote back a couple of weeks later and asked "Who are you?" I sent a letter telling him. He wrote again and said, "Send me the manuscript. I'll read it." So I did. Next he wrote, "I like it. I'll try to sell it." He took it to the editor Suzanne Kirk at Scribner's, she liked it, and Scribner's published it. The Mystery Writers of America gave the book an Edgar.

I don't think that any account of first publication would be complete without attaching a couple of bits of advice. One is that the most important thing a writer does is try to become a better writer. We improve by writing, not by publication. At its worst, the process of publication is a distraction from the real business of sitting down alone in front of an empty piece of paper and making up a story.

Even though there are now four or five times as many books published each year as there were when I started, it's still just as difficult to get anything in print.

Whether things are going well or badly, it's useful for a writer to remember that the most powerful force in human life is luck. The second most powerful force is persistence.

If a book is a failure, a true writer will do exactly what he would have done if it had been a huge success: he'll sit down and begin to write another.

People Who Need People

BRIAN FREEMAN

Brian Freeman writes psychological suspense, including the novels *Immoral* and *Stripped*. His books have been published in forty-six countries and sixteen languages. Check out his site at www.bfreemanbooks.com.

I f you're like most writers, you dream of publishing books because you love the writing process itself. It's solitary. It's all in your head. No strangers allowed. Right now, I'm sitting alone in my home office, and the fall leaves are drifting from the trees outside my window, and early Minnesota snow flurries are whipping against the glass in fuzzy dots. Perfect, hmm? That's how you want to spend your days.

The trouble is, if you want to make a business out of writing books, you have to face a hard truth. You need people. You can't do it alone. I may be sitting by myself in my office right now, but I've already sent e-mails to editors and readers all over the world this morning. Later today, I've got two book signings, and I have to sign stock at a third store. For a job that takes place mostly in my head, I have more contact with people now than ever before. For an introvert, that means dragging myself kicking and screaming into an extroverted world day after day. It means exposing myself to rejection or (worse) lack of interest.

I'd rather be home writing. But that's part of the price we pay. So before you decide that writing books is the life for you, think hard and make sure that you want everything that comes along with it. This is a business, not a hobby. It means putting yourself on the line and selling yourself, not just scribbling words on paper. It means putting your fate in the hands of others. Decide first if it's really the life for you.

Okay, that didn't last long, did it? You know you want it. Sure, it means crazy travel schedules and higher taxes and smiling until your face aches, but how cool is it to have people reading your book? Seeing it in the stores? Occasionally getting a check with actual money? (Much less than you dream, but hey, money is money.) True, I had no idea what the reality would be like, but I would have signed up for it in a heartbeat, and I haven't looked back since the dream came true.

So how do you get here? How do you take the first step? It's easy to subscribe to the fiction that if you write it, they will come. Ha. If you write it, you have to sell it. And you need other people to do that.

Getting published is as much a psychological challenge as a business challenge. It means checking your ego at the door, which for writers is often the biggest stumbling block. If you want to write books as a business, then you are writing for other people, and you have to accept the validity of their thoughts and opinions. You can ignore the rest of the world if you are writing just for yourself—but no one will pay you to do that.

You need to know if your writing is any good, and the only way to find out is to have other people read it. Harsh, isn't it? Other people will decide whether you know how to write. Deal with it. That doesn't mean that you should declare yourself a failure if one person rejects you. Don't worry, plenty of people will reject you along the way. But you do need objective criticism, not from friends, not from family, but from people who will pull no punches about the quality of your work.

My advice—get those critiques before you start sending to agents and publishers. Don't even think about posting something to New York until you've gone through a rigorous editing process driven by one or more honest opinions from people who recognize good writing. Talk to other writers. Talk to booksellers. Ask local book clubs to look at your work. Yes, it means putting your ego in someone else's hands and risking that they will squeeze it until your sweat and blood drip out. But that's what you have to do. You have to take that risk. It will be the hardest thing you ever do.

If you want to write books as a business, then you are writing for other people, and you have to accept the validity of their thoughts and opinions. You can ignore the rest of the world if you are writing just for yourself — but no one will pay you to do that.

When you're ready to test the waters in the industry, you need people again. Most agents receive hundreds of queries every week, and few queries receive more than a glance (usually from a lowly staffer, not the agent personally). If you want to get attention, you need to find ways to get around the crowd pushing at the door, and find someone who will escort you through to the back. Cultivate relationships with people who know people. Find people who have connections. You never know who they will be. Tell them what you do, and ask for their help. Yes, that's right — ask for their help. Another huge challenge for the solitary writer.

For me, my break came when I discovered that a lawyer I had worked with had an acquaintance who was a well-known literary agent in London. I asked for his help. He got her to read my manuscript — not a staffer, not an intern, but the agent herself. Six weeks later, I had two book deals in the U.S. and U.K. After twenty years of trying and failing, it happened that fast. But that was also the longest month of my life, because once my agent took the book out to the publishers, I had no control whatsoever. It was all in other people's hands. That was the first step in beginning to share responsibility for my career with editors, salespeople, PR reps, booksellers, and readers all over the world.

Yes, I love the writing days, alone in my office. The snow has tapered off now. The dry leaves are scraping together. But I wouldn't be here without a lot of help from a lot of people. Your book may be your child, but you know what they say — it takes a village. The sooner you swallow hard and get out there and talk to people, the faster you'll see results.

Writing Lies for Fun and Glory, But Very Little Money (So Far)

CARL BROOKINS

Carl Brookins is the author of *The Case of the Greedy Lawyers*, *Old Silver*, *A Superior Mystery,* and *Inner Passages*. Learn more about Carl and his books at his Web site, www.minnesotacrimewave.org/carlbrookins.

....

Not so very long ago I was swearing out loud at yet another mystery novel in which the author had metaphorically dropped the ball. My wife, a retired, successful publisher, tired of hearing my complaints, suggested I try my hand at writing a mystery and see if I could do it better.

Seizing the moment as it were, I took some courses in writing a mystery from the Loft in Minneapolis. There I discovered some of what I didn't know about writing crime fiction. Persevering, I came then to the understanding that I did have some stories to tell, but first I had to write the book. Okay, that was the original idea, wasn't it? Ah, but then I began to talk with authors, with writers already far down the winding road ahead of me.

After writing your novel, they told me, you must secure an agent. Otherwise you will find yourself at the mercy of charlatans who will rob you blind. Sure, says I, how hard can that be, assuming I write a good novel? You'll be surprised, says they. It can take a year or more of writing queries, waiting for answers, sending off your manuscript and waiting some more. And then? I asked.

And then, came the reply, your agent will try to sell your book. If she, or he, is successful, which could take a year or more, you'll then hear the publisher's acquiring editor tell you that it will be approximately another eighteen months until the book is actually released to the eagerly awaiting public. I thought about that and upon adding up the time, discovered that I could be dead or at least seriously in my dotage before my first novel made it to the bookstore shelves. There must be another way. And it turns out there is.

All of this assumes you have written a dandy novel. If your publisher doesn't edit your book, you better get it edited yourself. And not by your wife or cousin or…. Hire a competent editor, one who will really help you make your book better.

I bypassed the agent route, but not because I don't think agents are important. They are a vital link in the procession to publication. But they are not the only path.

I sold my first novel directly to a small independent publisher who promised to release the book less than a year after I signed the contract. Whee. And so it happened. I sold my second, third, and fourth mysteries the same way. You can do it too.

But there are potholes and pitfalls to watch for. Different ones. I have the advantage of living with a woman who knows about book contracts. I have the advantage of years of dealing with all kinds of folks in business and academic circumstances and I know how to do research. Do not let your eagerness to be published get in the way of common sense. Know with whom you are working. There are phonies in every field, here too, charlatans eager to take your money. They will wring you out if you aren't careful. Recommendations by those who have already carved a furrow are terribly important.

Now let's suppose you've gone ahead anyway. You have in your hands a copy of your first novel. The next surprise is something called distribution and promotion. What, you thought the publisher does that? Hah. No such luck, buddy. *You* do a lot of that. Most of it. Read your contract. If you want your book to sell, you are going to become a salesperson. If you want to interest the publisher in a second book, you definitely need the first one to sell well. So you get out there and sell it. It isn't that hard, but it does take time. And planning. And research.

Your publisher may sign a distribution contract with a wholesaler. That's cool, but it has little to do with you. You also have to be prepared to carry books with you when you visit bookstores. The best way to get a bookstore owner to purchase copies of your new novel is through personal contact and by putting a copy in the bookseller's hands.

Some things I've learned about promotion, another term for selling books, are these: Research is good. It's vital. Ask questions. Tap the knowledge of more experienced authors. They are wonderful sources of ideas, help, and inspiration. Attend workshops, go to fan conferences, listen and ask questions. In the mystery field, authors tend to be supportive and helpful. So do publishers representatives and also agents.

Here's my story about the lonely road of book touring and promotion. Some time ago a group of authors were talking about the rigors of individual touring. Fellow authors Ellen Hart, Kent Krueger, Deborah Woodworth, and I formed a promotional group we call The Minnesota Crime Wave. Cute, right? The idea was to tour together, sharing expenses, the workload, and by extension, the rewards. So how's it going?

Five years later, after four national tours, we have a web site, a thrice-yearly newsletter, a legal partnership, and more requests for appearances than we can schedule and still have time to write our books. We have made friends all across the country and book sales show steady increases. The trick is to balance all these promotional and marketing efforts with the time needed to write the next book, and the one after that.

The upshot of all this effort is that in spite of numerous rejections, it is possible, even in this tough age—you'll be told numerous times—to become a legitimate published author. Be disciplined, persevere, write those stories, edit, edit, revise, and edit some more. I'm doing it. You can too. Oh, and did I mention research?

The Poster Child
for Persistence

HILARI BELL

Hilari Bell enjoys board and fantasy gaming, but her favorite activity is the decadent version of camping she practices with her mother. They have a pop-up trailer with a fridge, a sink, a stove, and (if electrical hookups are available) a space heater, heating pads, and a toaster. Camping days are spent in reading, hiking, and reading some more. Hilari says, "Camping is the only time I can get enough reading. Well, I take that back—when it comes to reading, there's no such thing as enough." Visit her at www.sfwa.org/members/bell.

W riting friends call me the poster child for persistence — the first novel I published was the fifth I'd written, and when it sold I was working on novel thirteen. What finally made the difference? Harry Potter. I slid into publication on Harry Potter's big, beautiful coattails. When I first started writing you couldn't sell a fantasy novel for children or teens to save your life. An editor once told me, "First you have to sell three or four realistic novels, about real kids, preferably humorous. If they do well then maybe, *maybe* someone will look at your fantasy." Then Harry Potter hit, and every editor in the country started pulling fantasy out of their slush piles.

But even after Harry Potter turned the market around publication didn't happen overnight. My agent had been trying to sell both my YA and adult novels for four years before she found herself at a writers conference, sitting next to an editor who said she was looking for YA

SF with a strong female protagonist. "Have I got a story for you," my agent said. "It's already under consideration at a couple of houses," she lied. (It had already been rejected by everyone she'd sent it to.) "But I didn't promise them exclusive consideration, so I could probably let you take a look at it." A good agent is a wonderful thing.

To make a long story short, the editor bought it. It did pretty well so she bought another, and then another, and I now have seven books published, two more coming out this year, and six more under contract after that—persistence really can pay off.

The one piece of advice I'd give an unpublished writer is to attend writers conferences. You may already be going to science fiction conventions, but they're not the same, and for a serious writer SF cons aren't nearly as valuable. I met my first agent, who couldn't sell my books, my second agent who did sell my books, and the editor who published my adult SF novel all at writers conferences. And do you remember where my agent made that first sale? Mind, you have to do some research to find a good conference, and even a good conference isn't a magic key. But a lot of people make connections at writers conferences, and if you make enough connections, sooner or later, one of them might pay off.

Never Give Up

JEREMIAH HEALY

Jeremiah Healy is the author of the John Cuddy private investigator novels and, as "Terry Devane," of the Mairead O'Clare legal thrillers. He is also a lecturer on the DVD *Getting Your Novel Published*. He can be reached at www.jeremiahhealy.com.

As a kid growing up, I'd always written short stories, but as an adult, I was never able to get any published. Then, in 1983, I found I would receive tenure as a professor at New England School of Law in Boston (the dream of every Irish-American: inside work, no heavy lifting, lifetime employment). I said to myself: "You've always wanted to write a novel; you're reading and enjoying private-eye fiction; and, therefore, maybe you can write what you enjoy reading, but even if not, you'll probably enjoy trying." So I spent that summer off from teaching penning (literally: no computer yet) a manuscript entitled *Blunt Darts*.

Despite the fact that as a trial attorney I had represented authors against their publishers in New York City, and that as a professor I'd written scholarly articles on the rights of freelancers, I did *not* have the good sense to begin with a literary agent. Instead, I started sending the entire manuscript cold (as was still possible then) directly to editors (also still possible then). Using *Writer's Market*, I made an alphabetical list of publishers who indicated an interest in "crime novels." Twenty-eight publishers rejected *Blunt Darts* before the twenty-ninth, Walker

& Company (via editor Ruth Cavin, still working today though at St. Martin's Press and the patron saint of *many* a first-time author) accepted it. Now, since I was working through that list alphabetically, appreciate that I had only Yale University Press and Zebra left.

Well, thankfully Ruth's belief in me paid off for Walker. After publication, *Blunt Darts* received a major award nomination and was placed by *The New York Times* on its holiday list as one of the seven best mysteries of that year, and the paperback rights went for *five* times the hardcover advance at a spirited reprint auction (also possible back then).

Aspiring writers today *must* get a good literary agent. Attitudinally, though, I'd be inspired by Winston Churchill. When asked by a reporter after the Second World War for the three "secrets" to defeating the forces of Adolf Hitler, the great British prime minister replied, "This is the lesson: never give in, never give in, never, never, never, never ..."

Pretty good guideline for an aspiring novelist, too.

On Agents

KEN KUHLKEN

Ken Kuhlken's stories have appeared in *Esquire* and numerous other magazines, been honorably mentioned in *Best American Short Stories*, and earned a National Endowment for the Arts Fellowship. With Alan Russell, in the novella *No Cats, No Chocolate*, Ken has chronicled the madness of book promotion tours. His novels are *Midheaven* and the Hickey family mysteries *The Loud Adios* (St. Martin's/PWA Press Best First PI Novel, 1989), *The Venus Deal*, *The Angel Gang*, and *The Do-Re-Mi*. Visit him at www.kenkuhlken.net.

W hen I was in high school, I heard about an agent named Swifty Lazar who could sell something plagiarized off a soap label for a fortune. I wanted him to be my agent.

But I settled for G., an associate with William Morris. He either promised to make me a star, or I misunderstood. A year later, he gave up.

Next, K. read a story of mine and contacted me. He was with a good agency. I said sure, but when I finished my novel *Midheaven*, he declined to send it out. So I gave it to B., a Viking Press editor who stopped at the University of Iowa where I was studying. After a year, M., another Viking editor, found *Midheaven* in a tall pile left behind when B. ran off to Georgia to grow peaches. M. wanted the book. K. wanted to handle the contract. I said sure. But when I finished my next novel, *Yanqui*, and K. declined to send it out, I moved on.

A friend suggested I query P., his agent. P. was successful and smart. He liked my work, but then he bought out a large agency and had to cut back so he turned me over to an associate, L. She sent *Yanqui* to R. at Simon & Schuster. He wanted it, but when three weeks passed and he still hadn't gotten approval from the editorial board, L. withdrew the submission. Remembering that Viking bought *Midheaven* after a year, I objected.

Then I swore off agents, and might've sworn off writing novels, except I was addicted.

Tom Hickey, the protagonist of my novel *The Loud Adios*, was an M.P. during WWII. After my friends Dennis and Gayle mentioned the St. Martin's Press/Private Eye Writers of America Best First PI Novel contest, I discovered that Tom Hickey had been a private investigator before he got drafted. I sent *The Loud Adios* to that contest and won.

Dennis suggested I let A., his agent, handle the contract. I said sure. A. took her cut for that and the next two books with St. Martin's. But she sold nothing, so I moved on, to S. who represented several of my favorite writers. I told him I wanted a contract that would assure my next book got a paperback reprint, so I could build a larger following. Two books later, either he or I or both of us gave up. I moved on.

My next agent was a friend of my friend Alan. D. usually represented nonfiction, but he wanted to tackle the mystery and thriller market. He tried, and I might be with him still, except I told him I was returning to the Hickey family, the series I started with St. Martin's. He advised me not to, because mysteries don't pay. He wanted me to write thrillers.

I sent *The Do-Re-Mi* to Poisoned Pen Press, which doesn't insist on agented submissions. They offered a hardback and paperback deal, and agreed to reprint my three St. Martin's Hickey family novels in paper.

So far, of my five published novels, I've sold five. Agents have sold none. But my theme isn't don't go with an agent. My theme is, if you don't have an agent, don't mope, and if you have one, don't feel certain you can afford to quit your day job.

My take on agents is, if you can work with one who gives evidence of the ability to sell in your genre, and you find her agreeable and not so absorbed by successful clients that representing you comes second—if such a treasure comes along, take her on.

Otherwise, remember that agents don't run the only game in town.

Romeo and Juliet
With Needle Marks

MARK ARSENAULT

Mark Arsenault has been a newspaper delivery boy, a newspaper truck driver, a Sunday paper section inserter, a paste-up artist, and, since 1989, a reporter. He cut his teeth in the news business at *The Gardner News*, in Massachusetts, as a reporter and columnist, before moving to the Marlboro Enterprise in the 1990s. After a years as a reporter in Marlboro and ten months as the night city editor, Mark persuaded *The Sun*, of Lowell, Mass., to hire him as a reporter in 1994. It was during his time in Lowell that Mark discovered the setting and the character inspirations for *Spiked*, his first mystery novel. He is also the author of *Speak Ill of the Living*, and *Grave Writer*. For more about Mark and his highly entertaining books see his site at www.markarsenault.net.

I was so ticked off, I had to write fiction.

This was early in my career as a newspaper reporter, when I wrote for a mid-sized P.M. daily in Lowell, Massachussetts, a mill town of red brick and cobblestone on the Merrimack River, the birthplace of actress Bette Davis, writer Jack Kerouac, and the pilot who dropped the bomb on Nagasaki.

On a routine assignment to cover a dead body found under a bridge, I stumbled onto a community of homeless heroin addicts. They huddled together, cooked over campfires, and shot up their arms, invisibly, right underneath our feet. They lived—and some had died—on a ledge beneath that railroad bridge. That bridge carried one of the city's busiest downtown arteries over freight tracks.

My guide into this world was a heroin addict named Julia, the most honest person I had ever met. She had nothing to lose, and so no reason to spin. The dead man had been her common-law husband. They had been together a decade, including two years under the bridge. What I had found was a love story about two people with nothing in life but each other. They had tried many times to clean up, but heroin is a jealous master, and Julia's lover died of an overdose.

Ten years later, I still feel a tickle in my gut when I think about their story. This was Romeo and Juliet with needle marks.

I pitched a feature narrative to my editor. We can use this story, I said, to bring our readers into this underground world.

Eh. He wasn't interested. Told me to drop it.

I suspect he wanted to spare the city fathers the embarrassment of explaining a heroin den literally beneath their feet.

I felt my face flush as I argued to the edge of insubordination. The editor got angry.

Go write about some *respectable* people, he told me.

At the time I was two missed paychecks from homeless. So I couldn't quit in protest.

Julia wanted to see her story in the paper ... I think she looked at my writing as a validation of her lost love; to see it all in print would prove that true love existed, even under a bridge.

I hinted that I was having trouble getting the story in the newspaper.

"If you can't write it for the paper," she replied, near the end of our last conversation, ten years ago, "can you write it for me?"

I decided to tell Julia's story in fiction—in a mystery that blended my world of journalism and her world under the bridge.

Having never been a serious reader of mysteries, I bought ten or fifteen novels and read them for education.

Then I wrote. The first ten thousand or so words read like a long Sunday feature story. Terrible. Eventually, I shucked the controlled, skeptical newspaper voice, and, for the first time in my career as a writer, consciously took sides. The project that began as my way to tell a story without getting fired grew into a desperate struggle of man-against-paper. Could I even do this? Write a whole book?

There is nothing lonelier than a blank page, especially if you have no editor or publisher waiting for you to fill it. I kept writing—not because I thought it would be published, nor did I have anything to prove to my former editor. I wrote only because I hate to quit.

Five years later, I returned to Lowell to sign my first novel, *Spiked*, at a downtown bookstore, about a mile from that railroad bridge. Julia never showed up. She may not even know the book is dedicated to her. I can barely remember what she looks like, but I have imagined she turned her life around, found new love, got married, moved to a cozy house in the'burbs. I haven't tried to find her. I don't want bad news.

Everything I Knew
Was Wrong

MICHAEL SIVERLING

Michael Siverling is the author of *The Sterling Inheritance*, winner of the St. Martin's Press Best First Private Eye Story Award. A sequel story, *The Sorcerer's Circle*, was published in December 2006. More information on the Midnight Investigations series may be found at the Web site, www.midnight-investigations.com.

This is the story of how my novel *Clarke's Law* won the 2002 St. Martin's Best Private Eye story award, and never got published.

I learned after I set out on the journey of becoming a published writer that these days it's not enough just to be a writer; you have to understand the business of writing. So along with practicing the craft of storytelling, I studied the market, trying to discern trends of what kind of story is selling currently, the best way to approach a literary agent, and all the myriad things I thought a person needed to know to be able to see their words get into print. I even based my choice of genre (mysteries) on the fact that I was a working criminal investigator, thinking that my background might at least give my work the aspect of credibility. As it turned out, none of my efforts did me any good at all.

In early 2002 I was at a particularly low point in my quest. I had made the decision to separate myself from the agent I had worked so hard to find and found myself in the position of starting over completely from scratch. I had just finished writing my latest novel, *Clarke's Law*, the story of Jason Wilder, a young man who had turned his back on the family business, which just happened to be private investigations, because he wanted to be a musician. The backstory was that Jason returned to the business upon the death of his father and so starts to work for his mother, Victoria Wilder, the owner and chief investigator of the Midnight Investigations Agency.

As luck would have it, some mutual friends had introduced me to Robin Burcell, a fellow criminal investigator and the author of the Kate Gillespie mystery series. It was over lunch that Robin reminded me that St. Martin's Press underwrites two mystery novel contests a year, one for traditional mysteries and the other for private investigator novels. As it happened, my most recently completed book was a PI story. And so, being agentless and with nothing to lose, I submitted my story. I read the contest rules carefully, saw how St. Martin's didn't request the writer submit any biographical information (so much for my background as an investigator), and shipped my manuscript off.

These days it's not enough just to be a writer; you have to understand the business of writing.

Months went by, and then came the e-mail from Ruth Cavin, editor at St. Martin's, telling me that she liked my story, but there was another that was under close consideration, and she wanted to know if I would be willing "to make some changes" to my novel.

Was she kidding? Let's see now, make some changes versus not getting published. Quicker than it took to write this sentence, I e-mailed Ruth back and happily agreed to do whatever she felt was necessary to help the story.

The next thing I knew, I got an enormous e-mail outlining everything that Ruth thought was wrong with my novel. Starting with the plot. "Surely you can think of something more plausible," she wrote. In fact, the only thing Ruth did like was the character of Victoria Wilder, the head of the detective agency, referred to alternately as either "Mom" or "Her Majesty." By the time I finished reading and absorbing Ruth's massive missive, I was left with the inescapable fact that I was going to have to write a completely new novel.

I was invited to attend Bouchercon, the annual international mystery writer's convention that was held in Austin, Texas, that year, where I was presented as the winner of the St. Martin's PI Novel Award. It was all pretty overwhelming, and people probably thought I was trying to be funny when they would ask what my soon-to-be-published story was about, and I told them I didn't know. During the convention I had breakfast with Ruth Cavin and pitched the new plot I was going to use, all about a mysterious homicide that occurs near an old theater. I didn't bother to tell Ruth that this was the plot to my novel *The Return of the Cat Felons*, which St. Martin's had previously rejected. Although to be fair, every other publisher my agent approached had rejected it as well, despite the fact I had used the word "Cat" in the title (my research had shown that mysteries with the word Cat in the title outsell others two-to-one). By the end of breakfast, I'd promised Ruth a brand new novel by the first of the year.

And as soon as I got back from Texas, I jumped into my task of melding the characters from one novel into the plot of the other. I set myself a hard deadline, and I was proud when I was able to complete the new novel and send it in on time. Then came the e-mail from Ruth that said this story didn't work either.

I still remember the sinking feeling I had as I read the lengthy letter stating everything that was wrong with the new story. I was now convinced that I was going to go down in St. Martin's history as the only guy to win the PI Novel Award and never actually get a book published. By now I felt all I could do was either quit and return the advance money or write a third novel. I carefully studied Ruth's letter, and I went to back to work. I'd give Ruth updates as I went and couldn't resist the impulse to ask her in the midst of one letter, "Are you sure we want to keep the Mom character?" Which prompted Ruth to inquire as to my state of mental health.

As the saying goes, the third time was the charm. I will never forget the day when I received the e-mail from Ruth that read: "Well, looks like you gone and done it." I was told there was still a lot more work to do, and that the next step would come when I received the copyedited manuscript for my review. I was told not to worry about it, as I would have two weeks to review the copyedited manuscript before I had to send it back.

So imagine my joy when on January 24, 2004, I received the copyedited manuscript with a note that read: "Please return this with your corrections by January 24." As for the manuscript itself, there were so many red pencil marks on it that it looked like someone had been gored by an ox over the pages. I made a frantic phone call to New York and informed St. Martin's that I just received the manuscript, and I was told I could have five days to review and return it to them. So I took some emergency time off work and got to it, constantly under the fear that in the rush to complete my part of the editing on time I was going to miss some small but crucial aspect that would completely undermine the entire story.

Then came the day I got my advance reading copy (ARC), only to find a glaring error right on the blurb on the back. One of the many elements that I changed in Jason Wilder's backstory was the fact that I no longer had him being a musician. But the ARC proclaimed: "Private Investigator Jason Wilder has the toughest boss in River City. His own mother. And given the choice, he'd rather just play guitar." So I made another frantic call to New York, but all Ruth said was, "Ah, don't worry about it. Those things just go to reviewers, and no one's going to pay any attention to the back of the book." Later, my heart went out to that frustrated reviewer who wrote: "The blurb on the back mentioned the main character is a musician. I read that book cover to cover and I didn't find any musical references at all!"

But finally, in July 2004, two years and three complete novels later, *The Sterling Inheritance*, formerly titled *Clarke's Law*, reached the bookshelves.

As I write this, my sequel, *The Sorcerer's Circle*, is coming out from St. Martin's in December 2006. And just so you know, when I submitted that manuscript, I got back a three-page e-mail outlining everything that was wrong with it and why it was completely unpublishable.

Someday, I hope to break out of this pattern.

The Best Query Letter Ever

DUANE LINDSAY

The query letter is designed solely to get agents or editors to request sample chapters—proof that you can write. The wisdom on query letters states that the penguin letter, black on white and one just like the other, is the professional way to go. A query letter is made up of four parts: the opening, the hook/synopsis, your biography, and a closing.

The Opening

A short introduction suggesting why you are writing to this particular agent. The introduction tells the agent you know a bit about her and can contain personal information. Since you have to research the agent to find out how she wishes to be queried, add a personal note to remind her that you did your homework:

> I read in *Writer's Digest* magazine that you are seeking new authors. I would like to introduce my novel *The Grifter's Daughter*, winner of the 2006 Colorado Gold Writer's Contest.

OR

> I just read [name of book the agent represents] and loved it. I believe you'd be a perfect agent for my novel…

OR

I met you at Thrillerfest last week and you requested my submission package for *American Jihad* ...

The Hook/Synopsis

This is one or two sentence mini-proposal for your book. The hook is a short, enticing description of your book. For purposes of a query letter the hook and synopsis are one and the same.

> Can Dixie Lefeauf, daughter of a legendary con man, manage her misfit crew, build a new home, *and* bring down a crooked evangelist in storm-ravaged New Orleans—even with the unwanted help of her father?

OR

> After losing his parents in the collapse of the twin towers on 9/11, Arab-American Aden Saud takes the war to the terrorists, where killing the right man can save thousands, but killing the wrong one would haunt him forever.

The Bio

This is where you bring in anything to support your cause. Why should they be interested in you? How does your experience relate to your book? Anything that might pique their interest will move you from the huge send-it-back pile to the small request-sample-chapter group.

> I recently won the prestigious Model Train Engineer award for the best track layout in Central America [and my book is a mystery dealing with model train enthusiasts]. It was a winner in the XYZ contest.

Entering a contest (and winning or placing) is a great way to beef up your biography. It tells the agent that you're actively working on getting known, that your writing is good, and that you have good story ideas. The caveat here is if the contest isn't particularly well known you should add some details the agent might find impressive, e.g., "My manuscript placed first out of five hundred entries or fifth in a national competition drawing ten thousand entries."

Ideally your bio will have something to do with the book or marketing, but anything that will evoke a "Really?" response is a good thing to include.

> I recently visited close to three hundred bookstores to research
> how best to sell my book.

OR

> My article on home shopping was recently printed in the August
> issue of [*magazine title*].

The Closing

Tell the agent that your book is complete and give the genre and the length. Let her know that sample chapters and a synopsis are available. Thank her for her time.

Format

The entire letter should be business standard—single spaced, Times New Roman or Courier, twelve-point, one-inch margins, black ink on white, high-quality paper (no Xeroxes or cheap printers).

Enclosures

Always include a self-addressed, stamped envelope (SASE) for them to reject you. This is a standard procedure, costs little, and gives them that warm fuzzy feeling you're a professional.

We recommend including three to five pages of your manuscript as well. Some agents are only interested in the writing anyway and never read the query until they've seen if you can write. This saves a step. If they're not interested in you, you've saved (them and you) a step. But if the writing is impressive, they might give you a second glance.

Header and Footer

This advice doesn't come from the other how-to books. It is exclusively our own way to differentiate our penguin letter from all the rest.

Use any awards as a header and footer since they're both eye-catching and fill up space that would otherwise merely be a margin. For example, in 2006 I won the Colorado Gold Writers Contest for *The Grifter's Daughter*. The same year I was a finalist in the St. Martin's Best First Private Eye contest. Those two facts became my header and footer for the query letter. They were the first and last things seen and impossible to miss.

Unlike a sentence in the body of the letter (which might not get read if your opening isn't compelling enough to make the agent spend time with your letter), the header/footer is definitely going to be seen.

In Search of ...
a Publisher

P.D. CACEK

When not being flippant about her career, P.D. "Trish" Cacek maintains the dream. A multi-award-winning author, she's written over two hundred short stories, five novels, and even taught a few writing classes. Her most recent appearances have been in *Night Visions 12* and *Masques V*, as well as in two new collections: *Eros Interruptus* (2006) and *Sympathy For The Dead* (October 2007). Currently living in a haunted house in Fort Washington, Pennsylvania, Trish is working on a new novel, *Visitation Rites* ... about a haunted house. Check out her Web site at www.pdcacek.com.

There was never any question of my being a writer.

By age five (even though I barely understood what the whole "ABC" thing was about), I had filled ten *Big Chief* notebooks with stories. Of course they weren't more than *scribbles*, but I could pick any one of them and "read" (recite) the "story" written there. At that point my parents thought it was cute ... they were, however, less enthusiastic when I decided my major in college was to be English/Creative Writing Option. They thought I'd either starve to death or end up behind a counter somewhere asking people if they wanted to add fries to their menu selection.

Such little faith in their child's ability, don't you think? Well, I certainly thought that and decided to prove them wrong. I did this, simply enough, by sending out short stories to establish myself and build up some credentials. (I still feel this way—it is a *very* exceptional "first-time author" who can bypass this step.) I was nineteen … then twenty … then twenty-one …

Hmm.

Could it be that my stories were just "too unique," as one editor wrote in his rejection letter? (This, by the way, ranks alongside things like "Sorry, I have to wash my hair tonight" and "But we can still be friends, right?") Well, of *course* it could. By this time I had my degree in creative writing (with honors) so I *knew* I could write. Silly, silly editors … it was sad, really. So, what did I do—I broke my own rule and decided to write a *novel*. It all made perfect sense, especially for a genre horror writer like myself.

This was the eighties, you understand—and the horror glut was on. How could I possibly fail to achieve the recognition (and greatness) destined to be mine?

Very easily, as it turned out.

My first novel, *The Wind Caller*, was brilliant. Absolutely brilliant, I tell you … so I had no idea *why* none of the (@*#^!%$) publishers I sent it to could see that. It was the industry; had to be. I'd read some novels at this time that were *bad* … so it had to be that my *good* novel was, again, just "too unique." But I'd show them; I wouldn't let a little thing like "their" obvious lack of insight stop me. Oh no! I'd continue to write and send out, and when I was a big name they'd be sorry!

(Yes, we *all* go through this at some point.)

So I continued to write (two more novels and probably fifty more short stories) and it really wasn't because I wanted to "show them," whoever "them" was at the time—it was because I couldn't think of anything I loved to do more than write. Okay, I'm also a little stubborn … but all writers need to be. There are too many people in this world who will tell you to quit. In the end, it's up to you.

For me the "end" came when I was thirty-nine.

After receiving the last batch of rejection letters, I looked up at the cracked ceiling plaster of my office/den/guest bedroom and told God that if I wasn't published by age forty, that was it! I was finished! No more writing! Period.

I got my first acceptance letter when I was thirty-nine-and-three-quarters years old.

Who says God doesn't have a sense of humor?

Odd though it may seem, during the decades of not being published, a strange thing happened ... I learned my craft. Nothing comes quickly: It takes time, and each rejection is just a stone to kick aside. If you stop too long to stare at that stone, you might forget the path you're on ... so just take it in stride.

The three things I can offer are: Don't give up. Don't lose the dream. Believe.

Oh, and about *The Wind Caller*...

About three years ago I decided to "take another look at it, maybe clean up a couple things and try sending it out again." I knew it wouldn't take much work, since it was *perfect*. Oh. My. God! The first thing I wanted to do was send letters of apology to every publisher who'd ever seen it; the second thing I wanted to do was burn it and then sow the ground with salt. It was that bad! Really ... horrible. What I did was sit down and rewrite it from beginning to end. Leisure Books published it in 2004.

Like I said, don't give in.

Who Done It?

ROBIN HATHAWAY

On Robin Hathaway's fiftieth birthday, her husband told her, "It's now or never." And so she began. She wrote three mystery novels in three years featuring Dr. Andrew Fenimore, an old-fashioned cardiologist who still made house calls. Robin's amateur sleuth was patterned after her husband, who just happened to also be a cardiologist. *The Doctor Digs a Grave* won the St. Martin's/Malice Domestic contest in 1997 and an Agatha Award in 1998. It was followed by *The Doctor Makes a Dollhouse Call*, *The Doctor and the Dead Man's Chest*, and *The Doctor Dines in Prague*. Her fifth novel in this series, *The Doctor Rocks the Boat*, appeared in 2006. Robin's second series features a young female doctor, Jo Banks, who provides medical care to motel guests via a motorcycle in south Jersey. *Scarecrow* and *Satan's Pony* will be followed by *Sleight of Hand* in 2007. Her Web site is www.robinhathaway.com.

....

O ver the years I often uttered the plaintive refrain, "Someday I want to write a novel."

I had majored in English in college, taken every creative writing class offered, written many short stories—and even started a novel. But they all lay in the bottom of my desk drawer. When my husband and children pointed this out to me, I would say, "I know, but I don't have time now." And I didn't. My husband and I were running a printing business, Barnhouse Press. One printing press was in the barn, the other in the house. (The kitchen, to be exact.) I was raising two daughters, nine cats, and three ducks. And I was helping my husband part time in his office. (He was also a cardiologist.)

On my fiftieth birthday, my husband casually remarked, "If you're ever going to write that novel, you'd better get started. Time marches on."

I scowled at him. On top of everything else, I was now looking after my elderly parents who were both ailing. I had no plans to follow up on my husband's suggestion. But he had planted the seed, and a few days later I found myself in the local stationery store. I bought a pack of yellow legal pads and some ballpoint pens. I began to scribble at the kitchen table every morning. If my husband or children came in, I would hastily hide what I was working on.

"When can we read it?" they would ask.

I would merely smile and say, "When it's done." I was having a wonderful time. I had no idea I would enjoy writing so much. Until one day my husband jumped in and spoiled it all.

"Don't you think it's time you sent it out?" he said.

I was shocked. If such an idea had occurred to me, it was to happen years from now, at some foggy future time. Reluctantly, I agreed. But before I sent it out into the big world, I let my family read it. My magnum opus was a mystery with a cardiologist sleuth named Dr. Andrew Fenimore, who bore an uncanny resemblance to my husband. It was entitled *The Doctor Digs a Grave*. My husband was the most ruthless critic. A perfectionist by nature (a good thing for a doctor to be), he meticulously corrected my grammar, punctuation, spelling, and even my prose. His favorite comment, which he frequently penciled in the margin, was "Bumpy!" This meant that my sentence was either too long, awkwardly constructed, or had a dangling participle. I had a conniption fit whenever I saw that word.

Then began the rejection years. By this time I had joined two mystery writers' organizations: Mystery Writers of America (MWA) and Sisters in Crime (SinC), and I had learned how to prepare a manuscript for submission.

Double space, provide one-inch margins on all sides, put your name and address in the upper right-hand corner of every page, and—most important of all—include an SASE (self-addressed, stamped envelope) ... if you want it returned, that is.

And returned it was, over and over and over again. Sometimes I would revise it; other times I would just send it right back out again. When I began this depressing process (in the 1980s) writers could still send manuscripts directly to the publisher ("over the transom," it was called), and they could count on someone reading it, even if it were a youngster just out of college. But gradually, in the 1990s, this custom disappeared, and writers were required to have an agent to submit their work if they wanted it to be read. So I began sending out queries to agents, enclosing my first chapter and a synopsis of my novel. Like clockwork, more rejections arrived. Most were mimeographed slips, but a few were signed by a human hand, and once I actually got a bona fide letter. "This has promise, but is not for us," it read.

By now, I was in my sixties, and I was becoming deeply discouraged. In fact, one night I told my husband I was ready to give up. Julie, my oldest daughter, was working and living in New York by then, and Anne, my younger daughter, was away at college. We had sold the printing business, the cats had used up their nine lives, and the ducks, well, we won't go into that. But for the first time since I had married I had plenty of time on my hands. My husband said, "Why don't you write something else?"

Right away, I felt better and proceeded to write not one, but two sequels to the first doctor book: *The Doctor Makes a Dollhouse Call* and *The Doctor and the Dead Man's Chest*. I continued to attend meetings of MWA and SinC sporadically, but I stopped sending my manuscripts out. One day, a member of Sisters in Crime told me about a contest: The St. Martin's Press/Malice Domestic Contest for "Best First Traditional Mystery." (The title was almost a book in itself.) The woman gave me an application and said, "Why don't you try it?"

The application sat on my desk for weeks. One day, when Julie was home on a visit, she saw it there and noticed the deadline was coming up. She prodded me to fill it out. "What have you got to lose?" she said.

"Okay," I said, "But this is it. This is the last thing I'm going to do."

Months went by. Nothing was heard from St. Martin's. I forgot all about it. I continued to work on my mystery series, but with waning enthusiasm.

At this point I reached for a chair and said the immortal word: "Oh."

One day, about nine months later, my phone rang. I picked it up and a pleasant woman's voice said "Is this Robin Hathaway?" Since that is my pen name, and I hadn't been using it very much lately, I had to think a minute. But I finally said, "Yes."

"Well, I've called to tell you, you've won."

Won what, I wondered, completely at sea. The lottery?

In answer to my silent question, she said, "You've won the Malice Domestic Contest. And St. Martin's wants to publish your book."

At this point I reached for a chair and said the immortal word: "Oh."

This brilliant reaction was followed by a violent migraine headache that lasted three days.

In 1997, at sixty-five, my novel, *The Doctor Digs a Grave*, was published by St. Martin's Press. And in 1998 the book went on to win an Agatha Award—named for Agatha Christie. Since then I've published four more Doctor Fenimore mysteries and started a new series featuring a young female doctor, Jo Banks.

Recently I had my picture taken on a Harley for the cover flap of *Satan's Pony*, a mystery I wrote about a biker gang. But my most satisfying achievement was a review in *Publishers Weekly* that said, "Hathaway's nimble prose makes quick, enjoyable reading." When I showed it triumphantly to my husband, he merely grunted and said, "You can thank me for that!"

A Snowball's Chance

SANDRA BALZO

While waiting for her debut mystery, *Uncommon Grounds*, to be published, Sandra Balzo wrote short stories. The first, "The Grass is Always Greener," appeared in *Ellery Queen's Mystery Magazine* and won both the Robert L. Fish Award and the Macavity Award from Mystery Readers International for Best Short Story of 2003. Her second story, "Viscery" (also *EQMM*), won the Derringer Award and was nominated for a Macavity. *Uncommon Grounds* was nominated for an Anthony and a Macavity Award, and will be followed this year by *The Milkman Always Rings Twice* (Severn House) and *Dial Auto-Grind for Murder* in 2008. She can be reached at www.SandraBalzo.com.

....

W hen I was downsized from my corporate public relations job after twenty-four years, I did what every PR person with a few months of severance under his or her belt does. I decided to write a book. I'd spent my career writing, but now I wanted to see my words—not in a newspaper, magazine, or press release, but in a book. A novel.

As you might suspect, the writing well outlasted the severance, but when I finally finished *Uncommon Grounds*, I packaged it up carefully and mailed it to the first agent on my list. When that box left my hand, I was certain those 65,000 words formed the best traditional mystery written since Agatha Christie had hung up her pen.

By the time the manuscript landed—irretrievably—in the mailbox, I was certain it was the *worst* thing ever written. I couldn't understand why I was sending it to someone who would actually read it. *And* tell me what they thought.

Now, in a movie, it would turn out that I was right the first time. *Uncommon Grounds* was brilliant. Agents and editors fought over me.

This wasn't a movie. *Uncommon Grounds* didn't sell for six long years.

Luckily, during that time I had the help and encouragement of my writing group and the mystery community—perhaps the most supportive group of writers and readers you'll ever find.

You know what they told me?

Simple: Never give up. Never *ever* give up. I heard story after story of authors being rejected ten, twenty, thirty, a hundred times. And they told me to keep writing.

So I did. I wrote another book, and then I rewrote *Uncommon Grounds* and sent it off again. When nothing still seemed to be happening, a friend suggested I try my hand at a short story.

That sounded like a good idea. A short story was, at least, short. I wrote that story and dropped it in the mail to *Ellery Queen's Mystery Magazine* without giving it a thought. By this time I was used to rejection, or so I told myself.

The truth? Rejection still hurt. Rejection never *stops* hurting.

But *EQMM* bought my story.

Not only that, but after it was published, that same story—"The Grass is Always Greener"—won the Best First Short Story award from Mystery Writers of America. It was also nominated for two more awards and won one of them. Then *EQMM* bought my second story, and that won awards, too.

One day not too long after that, I got an e-mail. I was being offered a book contract for *Uncommon Grounds*. I still hadn't found an agent, but I'd found a publisher. When it came out, *Uncommon Grounds* garnered great reviews, and my publisher went back to press three times.

So, I ask myself, what happened? What was I doing differently than I had been doing for the last six years?

The answer? Nothing. Nothing different, at least. I was just trying to keep my head up. I was working hard. And I was doing my best.

Early in my PR career, I had a boss who wanted me to spend more time on office politics and self-promotion. Exasperated one day, she asked if I thought it was enough to work hard and do my best.

My answer, then, was *yes*. Yes, I did think that was enough. And I still do.

You see, I figure I spent those six years working hard and doing my best to push a snowball uphill. That snowball was my writing. My words. And, to be honest, I'd begun to think I had that same snowball's chance in hell of seeing them published.

But eventually, I'd reached the top of the hill and that snowball started to roll down the other side, picking up speed as it went. The short stories, the book, the awards. All the hard work was paying off. Things were finally rolling for me.

Now, I'm no fool. I know there will be more hills, and more snow-balls to push up those hills—that's what life is all about. That's what writing is all about.

Our words are our building blocks. With them, we can build bridges or we can build walls. We can build a book, or a resume, or an e-mail. An angry letter to the editor, or a poem to someone we love.

But whatever we choose to do with our words, they should give us joy. And we should never *ever* give up on them.

Fear? We Don't Need No Stinking Fear!

SHANE GERICKE

"Shane Gericke is the real deal, and this is an A-grade thriller," Lee Child enthuses. "One of those scary rides through criminality that can melt away a fifteen-hour flight," John J. Nance agrees. The bestselling superstars are applauding *Cut to the Bone*, the new crime thriller from Shane Gericke, who hit the national charts in 2006 with his debut *Blown Away*. Gericke previously spent twenty-five years as a journalist, most prominently as a senior financial editor at the *Chicago Sun-Times*, and still writes for national magazines. He's a founding author of International Thriller Writers and lives in the Chicago area. Visit him at www.shanegericke.com.

S cared? Do it anyway.

I became a best-selling author because of those four little words. You can too.

Pitching your work to publishers is the writer equivalent of a blade in the gut. The secret fear, of course, is that they're judging not your words and ideas, but you.

You're right. They are. They're handing you a wad of dough and tying their good name to yours. So they're gonna study you like a bug on a board. Which generates a fear of failure that pounds body and soul like hail.

Don't let it worry you. Fear simply means the stakes are high enough to reward your winning personality and incredible work. It's a good thing, not bad. So whatever makes you afraid, just take a deep breath, smile, and do it anyway. You'll be glad you did.

The first time I faced that was 1982, when I applied to one of the nation's largest newspapers. Here I was, four years out of journalism school, asking the *Chicago Sun-Times* to hire me as an editor. They indulged me for some reason, and I arrived for the interview.

"We're launching a major expansion," the managing editor growled, all eyebrows and sternness. "News, business, sports, everything. We're going to take down the *Chicago Tribune* to become number one. To do that, I need a good man on the business desk. One who eats and drinks *The Wall Street Journal*. Lives and breathes stock tables. Spends every waking moment thinking of fresh ways for our business section to compete, fight, and win."

The secret fear, of course, is that they're judging not your words and ideas, but you.

The eyebrows crushed together.

"Are you that man, Shane? Do you have what it takes to make us number one?"

Gulp.

Tell the truth, I'd never read a stock table, let alone inhaled it. At heart, I was a cops-and-robbers guy — I lived for fires, crashes, and axe murderers. True, I was the "business editor" at the small suburban daily at which I worked, but that mostly meant I rewrote the business press releases into something resembling news. To win this job in this biggest of leagues, I'd have to convince the man with the steel-wool brows that I was the real deal. Even though he'd surely laugh me back to the suburbs when he smelled the fear on my coffee breath .... .

"Yes, sir, I am," I said, with every bit of mustard a twentysomething can squeeze. "I love business. I eat stocks for breakfast. I'll do whatever it takes to get the job done."

The managing editor stared.

Then, he winked.

"Welcome aboard," he said.

And a long, happy match was made.

But a decade-and-a-half later, after writing the umpteenth version of "Bank Buys Bank," "Dow Wow," and "Thousand Workers Whacked," it was time to scratch an itch that started with discovering the Hardy Boys in grade school: writing thriller novels. I wanted "Gericke" in the pantheon of authors I admired most—Spillane, Parker, Sandford, Lynds—and I wasn't going to do it breathing stock tables.

Which brings me to the second act of "Scared? Do it anyway."

I left the newspaper to write full time. Finished my first manuscript in a year flat. Sent it out. It didn't sell. Wrote another. Didn't sell. Wrote another. Didn't sell.

The fourth one seemed the charm. It was a gripping tale of derring-do and attracted a premier literary agent. Who called the editor of a top New York publisher and pitched it to the gills.

She didn't want it either.

It *is* a terrific story, the editor said, with solid, likeable characters. I loved the first half of the book. But the second half sucks. It's really too bad, but I'll have to take a pass.

Cue anvil on Wile E. Coyote.

I was scared. Some "author" I'd turned out to be. I'd made a big mistake trading a solid paycheck for ether, and I seriously toyed with ending this foolishness and getting a "real" job. Leave book-writing to people who knew what they were doing.

Then I considered the editor's response. If I read one way, it was, Sorry, Charlie.

But if I turned it upside-down and squinted enough, I saw a road-map to *yes*. All it involved was six more months at the keyboard, a head-to-toe rewrite, and no guarantee I'd be any further ahead then when I started.

"Can we re-pitch this?" I asked my agent after explaining what I had in mind.

"Only one bite at the apple, I'm afraid," he said.

"What if I volunteer to redo the entire book along the lines of what she loved in the first half? On pure spec, with no expectation she'll say yes. No contract or even promise of one. If we did all that and ask nice enough, do you think she'd give me one more shot?"

"Let's find out," he said.

The result was a two-book deal led off by *Blown Away,* my May 2006 debut that became a national bestseller with translations in Turkish, Chinese, and Slovak. The sequel, *Cut to the Bone,* came out June 2007 and has garnered praise from the best-sellingest authors on the planet.

So was I scared?

Shitless.

I did it anyway. It worked out fine.

My final example comes an author who defines success — P.J. Parrish.

P.J.'s actually the pen name for sisters Kristy and Kelly Montee, who pooled their life-long loves of writing by teaming up in 1995 to create the Louis Kincaid novels. And did so fabulously — their books are snapped up worldwide.

Kelly's "do it anyway" tale is about blurbs, those book-cover quotes that promise thrills, chills, and nonstop roller coaster rides. It's the author's job to collect these eye-bites, which means asking some seriously famous authors to (a) take time from their jammed schedules to (b) read your manuscript cover to cover and (c) write a catchy blurb that (d) helps make *you* a bestseller.

And, do it for free.

"It's a sucky feeling to ask for blurbs," Kelly writes on DorothyL, an Internet resource for mystery writers and fans. "You have to be brave and try to pretend it's not groveling, it's just part of the business of selling books."

That sound you hear is a million authors nodding.

"My sister and I were sitting at the Bouchercon signing table," she continues. "Next to an author that, of course, had a much longer line than ours. That alone is humbling enough, but this was also an author who I had read and very much admired. But, like I said, you gotta be brave.

"So, after his book line went down, I nudged Kris and whispered, 'Why don't we ask him for a blurb?' After a few minutes of embarrassing awestruck fumbling and more whispering, she finally leans over and asks.

"He sighs but graciously tries to cover it because he is a prince of man on top of being a good writer, and he starts to give us his publicist's or agent's card. Then suddenly he changes his mind and offers his home address for us to send him the book after Bouchercon.

"It was probably one of the best and most effective blurbs we have received."

Afraid?

Doesn't matter. Do it anyway.

I promise you won't be sorry.

Writing in the Cracks
of the Day Job

ZOË SHARP

Zoë Sharp started writing the Charlie Fox crime thriller series, featuring her ex-Special Forces-turned-bodyguard heroine, after receiving death threats in the course of her work as a freelance photojournalist. Charlie Fox has been described as the "must-read heroine of mystery" by Ken Bruen and "today's best action heroine" by Lee Child. *First Drop*, published in the U.S. in 2005, was short-listed for a Barry Award. Sharp blogs every week about the writer's life on her site, www.ZoeSharp.com, where you can read extracts of her work, download them as MP3 files, or watch the video trailer for her latest book.

Writing is a job. It fits into a lot of other categories, too—compulsion, therapy, joy, art, and occasional nightmare. But, at the end of the day, it's a job. And—unless you're very lucky—it's not your only occupation.

I still have a full-time day job working as a photojournalist, something I've done on a freelance basis since I sold my first magazine article back in 1988.

In the early years, this background was enormously useful to me as a fiction writer. It taught me to turn in good clean copy, on time, on topic, and to length. It not only introduced me to the astounding idea that someone wanted to read my words, but it also enabled me to make a living putting them on paper. Too good a living to want to give it up. Particularly since I now provide all the photography for my husband's nonfiction writing, so if I gave up my day job, he'd also have to give up his.

So, I've always had to find the time to write fiction as well as maintain a demanding day job, and it *can* be done. In fact, my day job feeds my writing in all kinds of ways. Quite apart from the fact you meet fascinating people in professions that might just come in very handy for research, it gives you a structure.

Like many people, if I have all day to write something, then writing it has a habit of taking me all day. I'd love to work like mad, have it done by ten o'clock, and take the rest of the day off, but it doesn't happen that way. So knowing I *haven't* got all day to write something—in fact, I might only be able to squeeze an hour or so here and there—makes me buckle down and get on with it. If you're not a night owl, setting your alarm an hour earlier in the mornings and getting up to write with a cup of coffee before you start your normal day achieves a surprising number of words over a few weeks or months. I used to write that way and found my alarm calls getting earlier and earlier because I couldn't wait to get back on with the book.

Like many people, if I have all day to write something, then writing it has a habit of taking me all day.

The day job means that we're traveling a lot of the time, usually by car. I discovered while I was writing book five in my Charlie Fox series, *Road Kill*, that I could work successfully with my laptop on my knee in the car. And, no, not while I'm driving—I'm usually the navigator on these trips. Twisty back roads do produce mild carsickness, but a relatively stable slog down the motorway now enables me to get the majority of my day's target achieved.

Ah, yes, that's another thing. A daily target. I know some writers who would throw up their hands in horror at the idea of aiming to produce a set number of words every day, but it works for me. It focuses my mind on the job at hand. I may sit down tired and restless, but I try hard to get the words done, and, more often than not, I get into the swing of the scene I'm writing and get on with it. It's too easy, when you're tackling a 100,000-word novel, to think, "What the heck—one day's not going to make any difference." And, before you know it, a month's gone past and you've written nothing. Inspiration is one thing, but perspiration gives it shape and form. You want words on paper; sometimes you've just got to sweat them out.

I initially tried setting a certain number of words per day. But what do you do if you have a couple of duff days? Add the extra on to the day after? Then the target becomes so big you're disheartened before you begin.

Once I'm into a book, I decide on a reasonably sensible number of words I'd like to write each month then break it down into a daily target. If I have a good day and exceed my target, the number of words a day I need for the rest of the month comes down slightly, too. If I have a bad day, I just divide what's left among the remaining days.

Writing a book is a huge task. I feel you need lots of little victories to sustain you along the way. Just ten thousand words a month—which even on a short month works out to just 333 words a day, or just over a page—will see a novel completed inside a year.

Writing continuously has the advantage that you don't lose the thread of the story. To further help with this, I do a summary at the end of each chapter. This is different from an outline, because it's a blow-by-blow account of the book as it's written.

In the summary, I list all the main points of what happened in each chapter and highlight any threads I need to remember to pick up or refer to later. I also include information like what day it is—starting from the first chapter at Day One, so I keep an eye on the passing of time—and any injuries any of the characters have picked up along the way. In the current book, *Third Strike*, my main protagonist, a bodyguard, managed to get herself hit by a moving vehicle while saving the life of her latest principal. Obviously, she sustained a few knocks and scrapes along the way. It would be very easy to forget this two chapters further on and have her leaping about with no aftereffects.

Of course, these are just a few tricks to keep you going. To begin with, you've got to have the ideas, the vision, and the ability to expand them into a full-blown story, and the will to write it all down. I'm just reassuring you that you can still do all this, in a reasonable time span, without giving up the nine-to-five.

Holding Back
the Years

A.J. HARTLEY

A.J. Hartley is the best-selling author of the archaeologically inflected thrillers *The Mask of Atreus* and *On the Fifth Day* (Penguin/Berkley). As Disintinguished Professor of Shakespeare at the University of North Carolina at Charlotte, Dr. Hartley is also the author of numerous articles and books on English Renaissance drama, and the editor of the performance journal *Shakespeare Bulletin*. In an attempt to fuse his two strangely divergent identities, he is currently working on a thriller about a lost Shakespeare play. His web site is www.ajhartley.net.

I honestly don't know if people will find this story inspiring or depressing, something that will pump up the struggling writer or prompt her to dump her PC in the nearest ravine. I'm not sure what I make of it either. But it's true, and the ending is happy. So there's that … .

I wrote my first novel when I was nineteen. It was bad, the kind of mystery they call "cozy" these days, but with added pretensions to high literary values. I had never taken a creative writing class and knew nothing of plot, character, or pace except for what I had gleaned osmotically from my random reading habits. It took me about a year to finish it, and the moment it was done I set about mailing it out to whatever big, famous publishers seemed most likely to back a dump truck full of money up to my parents' front door. It was, I figured, no more than I deserved.

No one bought it. No one so much as nibbled. I'd be astonished to learn that anyone read more than a few pages of the thing before mailing out the obligatory polite rejection.

Over the years I accumulated quite a stack of polite rejections. I got them after I painstakingly rewrote the original sally into Agatha Christie territory, and I got a whole stack more when I penned my next effort, a kind of fantasy adventure with a comic touch. Having learned a little more about the business of publishing courtesy of *Writer's Market*, I was now being rejected mainly by agents. Publishers, I had discovered, rarely accepted unrepresented manuscripts, so I dutifully sought an agent while working on (wait for it) a sequel to the novel I couldn't sell. Genius.

I tried everything: mass mailings to agents, selective submissions with sample chapters, query letters, the occasional phone call follow-up, and—just for devilment—periodic mailings of entire unsolicited, unrepresented manuscripts to major publishing houses. This went on for a while. Years, in fact. And each time I would receive:

1. Nothing at all.
2. Polite form rejections.
3. Less polite, sometimes even mean-spirited, scribblings on the corner of own query letter ... .

Once in a blue moon I'd get something more promising—a note to keep at it, a request for more—but none of it ever panned out, and with each rejection I would rant at my girlfriend about those idiot agents and publishers who didn't know a good thing when they saw it. One time, after my mystery set in a Catholic seminary in England was rejected for the hundredth time, I was particularly struck by the agent's observation that I clearly knew nothing about either England or Catholicism. I wasn't certain how to take this, since I lived the first twenty years of my life in England and spent two of them in a Catholic seminary. Was my writing that bad? Or—as I came to suspect—was the author of the rejection (his signature conveniently scrawled into illegibility) merely assuming I didn't know my stuff because it didn't square with his preconceptions? In the end, of course, it didn't really matter because—as his confident condescension revealed — he was the person in power, while I was the lowly supplicant. It was one of those laugh-or-cry moments, when all you can feel is a maddening sense of impotence and injustice, however righteous your indignation.

And of course that indignation loses its full-throated quality as you enter your second decade of failure. It gets undermined by that nasty, poisonous little voice that mutters at you while you're trying to get to sleep, the one that always says the same thing: "They're right. You should quit. Stop wasting your time. You can't do it." Because by now girlfriend had become fiancée had become wife, and I had moved from undergraduate to M.A. to Ph.D. with nothing to show for it in terms of my fiction. I should say that my girlfriend/fiancée/wife never once suggested I should give it up. It was, she once observed, part of who I was.

And there lay the rub. Writing had something of a pathological hold on me. It was a sickness, an addiction, and I couldn't stop. As I finished each book, or each movie script (I was achieving similarly impressive failures as a screenwriter), I would sit back for a few months, let it start the rounds, suffer my occasional sojourns in the Slough of Despond as it accumulated the inevitable rejections, and then I'd start again: a new project, maybe a different genre this time. Perhaps if I made the protagonist a woman ... .

And so it went. We moved houses, got jobs, traded in cars and computers for newer models, went through the life stuff that you never quite see coming, and through it all I kept writing. I felt good about book number six and sent it out to a few carefully targeted agents. Two requested the complete manuscript. Both offered me representation. I chose, and then stood by the phone for three months waiting for details of my first sale. The book circulated, had a couple of near misses, and then died quietly. Book number seven revisited my mystery roots and met the same fate. I was still standing by the phone, but now I was waiting for my hard-won agent to fire me. She was, after all, making nothing off an author she couldn't sell.

When my wife got pregnant and our domestic landscape started to shift, I began to take that nasty little voice in the back of my mind seriously. I didn't have time to write anymore. I couldn't afford it. It felt a little like cutting off a diseased limb, a sacrifice made for the health of what was left.

Knowing how an infant would monopolize our lives, we took a last summer holiday to Greece, and while visiting Schliemann's excavations at Mycenae, an idea started to shape itself in my head, a mystery with its origins in both the Trojan War and in more recent, darker history. But when would I write it, and how would I justify spending so much time sitting in the familiar glow of my computer?

My son was born three months premature and that, as you might imagine, changed everything. My wife and I spent six weeks sitting beside his hospital incubator, and if that doesn't change your perspective on the world, nothing will. Oddly, the forced inactivity and something else—something like a need for normalcy—drove me back to the computer, and I finally hammered out my Greek thriller, *The Mask of Atreus*.

My agent liked it, and in February 2005 she started sending it out. For a couple of weeks we heard nothing, and then the obligatory rejections started coming in. Among them were plenty of near-misses but I was used to them. As far as I was concerned, an enthusiastic rejection wasn't good enough anymore. Not after twenty-two years of writing. Not nearly good enough.

One day in April I had just returned to my office after a meeting when my phone rang. It was my agent, and she sounded different. I could hear it immediately. It wasn't just that she had good news. She had strange news.

We had been offered thirty thousand dollars for *The Mask of Atreus* by a publisher *in Greece*.

A week or so later we got an offer from Brazil. Then Penguin-Berkley in the U.S. Within two months we'd done deals in a dozen languages with advances close to five times what was then my annual salary. When the book went to press in the States, the print run was over 200,000 and the book made the *USA Today* best-seller list for the first three weeks it was out. One week it reached number six on the Barnes and Noble

Mass Market list, behind a Janet Evanovitch and four Dan Browns. Not bad for a first-time author.

The fact that I wasn't a first-time author except in terms of publication, that this was actually my eighth complete novel, never bothered me. All those years, the rejections, the furious pronouncements of how I would never write another word, all fell away and became — as they are here — prequel, a kind of teleology of success. It's a trick of perspective, of course, but a useful one, if only because suddenly all that I used to think was failure now looks merely like apprenticeship.

I am not vain or stupid enough to believe that talent will win out, that good writers will always succeed, that the industry will sniff out the sheep from the goats, that publishing is a meritocracy. That's all nonsense. I'm not even sure that the book that succeeded was clearly superior — rather than merely more timely in market terms — to those that didn't. But I do know that persistence counts for a lot in publishing, that determination and labor are often as good as luck, and that talent is easier to recognize when it is safely gilded by success. Right now I'm where I always wanted to be, and though I suspect I've learned a lot along the way, I think the real reason that I finally got here is because I never stopped.

Your Goal Is Not to Be Published

CHARLES BENOIT

Charles Benoit is the author of the Around-The-World adventure mysteries *Relative Danger* and *Out of Order*. His latest, *Noble Lies*, is published by Poisoned Pen Press. Visit his Web site at www.CharlesBenoit.com.

Your goal is not to be published.

As a writer, I'm sure you recognize the above sentence as an example of what we in the biz call "an attention-grabbing opening that pulls the reader in." You also recognized, no doubt, that it is an ambiguous sentence, the kind that we writers would want to clarify in the revision process.

As it's written, a casual reader might assume that I am suggesting that your ultimate aim is to fail in your attempt to see your books in print. While this is not the advice I'm offering, it does seem to be the advice many writers choose to follow.

Some writers appear to do whatever they can to keep their books from being published, starting with not writing them. We all know dozens of people who tell us how someday they'd like to get a book published—usually a biography—because they have a unique story to tell, a story that they then proceed to tell us whether we want to hear it or not. And while the stories are often (but not always) different, they all end with the line, "Now I've just got to find the time to write it." Sadly—or fortunately, depending on the story—these would-be authors spend their writing time telling people they can't find time to write and are, therefore, assured of reaching their goal of never being published.

Your real goal is to write a book that people would pay good money to read … You can't achieve this goal if your reason for writing is to just see your name on a bookshop shelf.

Other writers do indeed write books, and some even finish them, but they don't let this fact keep them from their goal of not being published. These writers either allow no one to read their manuscripts — ever — or, if they do allow them to be read, refuse to listen to any advice, no matter how small. These manuscripts are divinely inspired, unalterable, and perfect in their present form, to be safeguarded from the impure thoughts of writing groups, teachers, agents, and editors, and are, perhaps, better off not being published after all since the reading public would fail to grasp their brilliance anyway.

But you are not one of these writers, so I must clarify my clever opening sentence.

Your goal is not *merely* to be published.

I know, I know, an *adverb*, but it works. To be merely published is simple. There are dozens of big-name publishers, oodles of independents, small houses, university and workshop presses, print-on-demand sites, vanity imprint companies, and Kinko's. If your goal is to hold in your hand a bound copy of your book, if this is why you write, it will happen. That's why *merely* being published is not your goal.

Your real goal is to write a book that people would pay good money to read. We're not talking friends and family members (who will try to get a free book off you anyway), we're talking strangers — strangers with limited budgets and unlimited options as to how to spend their money, handing it over for the chance to read *your* words. Not just once but *every time* you publish a book. You can't achieve this goal if your reason for writing is to just see your name on a bookshop shelf. Your words will betray you, and your readers—for the short time that you have them—will see through you. And if you're doing it just for the money, that'll show too. You have to be writing because you have a story that must be told and you are the only one who can tell it.

All that said, let me tell you that it is mind-blowingly cool to see your books on the shelves, to sign your name on the title page, to answer fan mail, to spot someone reading your latest in the airport, to be stopped on the street by someone who recognized your face from the author photo on the dust jacket. And it is most definitely cool cashing checks of any size from your publisher. But don't make those things your goals.

You are a writer.

You *will* be published.

Just make sure you'll be read.

Being Orphaned

CHRISTINE GOFF

Christine Goff is the author of the Birdwatcher Mysteries: *A Rant of Ravens*, *Death of a Songbird*, *A Nest in the Ashes*, *Death Takes a Gander*, and her latest, *Death Shoots a Birdie*. Christine can identify more than two hundred Colorado bird species. Her books are intriguing and captivating, and hard to put down. She can be contacted through her Web site at www.christinegoff.com.

As a writer I decided that I would do the one last thing I could think of to move my work from unpublishable to publishable quality. I signed up for a ten-day intensive writers' retreat. It was expensive, in Kentucky at the end of May, and featured a well-known agent and teacher giving instruction. She was amazing, and I was encouraged enough to return the following year with my revisions in hand. Another agent who was attending asked if he could represent my work. Of course, I said yes and felt redeemed. Then came the long wait for my new agent to sell my work. I waited, and waited, and waited, and then ... my agent, Peter, called me asked me if I had ever considered writing a birdwatcher's mystery.

"A what?" I said.

"A birdwatcher's mystery," he replied. "I have an editor who wants one."

Well, Peter had been at my home in Evergreen, knew I watched birds because of the long list of birds spotted that was pasted next to my window, so I gave it a try—and dismally failed in my first attempt. Then, after consultation with my agent and the editor, I set the book in Colorado (a place I know), filled it with an eclectic mix of birders (biologists, retirees, forest service personnel, young people, old people—in other words, real bird-watchers), and came up with a plot centered around the illegal trading of peregrine falcons to the Middle East. I sent my agent a four-page synopsis, two paragraphs on the next two books I envisioned in the series, and thirty pages of manuscript, and I waited. And I waited. And I waited.

Finally, the editor called. He liked the pages, hated the proposal. Well, he didn't hate it, he just wanted something different. He wanted a love interest. He wanted more detail. He wanted cozier.

He called on a Friday afternoon, so I asked, "When do you want the changes?"

"If you could fax them to me on Sunday, that would be great."

Stunned, I ordered carryout pizza for the children and worked, and worked, and worked, then faxed and waited, and waited, and waited.

Finally, my agent called. It was one of those days. The kids were scream-ing at each other over the TV in the living room. The groceries were melting on the counter. The neighbor's dog was barking at my dog through the screen door, and I couldn't send him home because he only speaks Hebrew, and I don't. And my four-year-old answers the phone.

"Mommy, it's Caesar."

"Who?"

"It's Peter," said my agent in his thick British accent. "Is this a bad time?"

"No."

His tone spoke volumes. I knew the news was bad.

"Give it to me straight," I said. "I can take it."

"Berkley Prime Crime wants to offer you a three-book contract."

After the celebration I got to work on the book—and then one week after signing the contract, I was orphaned.

My editor left Berkley for St. Martin's Press, and I had no editor in the house.

Luckily there were three editors who saw the potential in the series and offered to take it on. My editor, Cindy Hwang, "won," and I now have five books published and more on the way.

Life Is Not a
Four-Letter Word

ANN PARKER

Ann Parker is a science writer by day and author of the critically acclaimed Silver Rush historical mystery series by night. Her debut, *Silver Lies*, won the Willa Literary Award as well as the Colorado Gold Award and was a finalist for Western Writers of America's Spur Award and the Bruce Alexander Historical Mystery Award. Publishers Weekly's starred review of *Iron Ties*, the second in the series, notes "Parker's outstanding second Silver Rush mystery finds her heroine, Inez Stannert, corset-deep in the intrigues of Leadville, Colorado … Plenty of convincing action bodes well for a long and successful series." Visit Ann at www.annparker.net.

As I write this, I know I'm late. Late in getting a story out. Late fixing dinner. Late responding to emails. Christmas is also roaring down upon me like a freight train, and if Santa Claus doesn't hoof it over to the local big-box toy store or the Internet equivalent pretty darn soon, there's gonna be hell to pay on the morning of the twenty-fifth.

And … tomorrow I'm driving six or so middle-graders to a school trip to the Tech Museum, trading in one of my precious vacation days from work to spend hours on the clogged San Francisco Bay Area freeways, white-knuckle driving, with said middle-schoolers in the back seats talking and whispering about who-knows-what (on one hand, I don't wanna know, but on the other hand, I'll be listening, you betcha).

So what does this have to do with writing?

In a word: everything.

This is life. And writing comes from it and is a part of it. The trick is finding a way to weasel in the mechanics of writing into everything else without going crazy.

So, this is for all you multi-tasking supermachines who have some combination of day jobs, spouses, elderly parents, babies, teenagers, children over the age of majority, pets ... Well, you get the idea. And you know who you are. You are the ones with the mental to-do lists that could easily fill many double-spaced manuscript pages. The "who, me sleep?" folks.

I'm here to claim my place among you and to stand up and say, yeah, it can be done. You can write. You can get published. You can do it and still live life. And still get some sleep as well.

It helps to set realistic goals. Okay, so you've got a day job that keeps you running forty-plus hours a week and it pays the bills and keeps the youngest in diapers. Is it realistic to toss said job out the window in pursuit of the "ideal" writer's life?

I'd say... No. Be realistic. How do the bills get paid?

But there's always a moment, somewhere, sometime (waiting at lights? In the evening when the babe's in bed?) to jot down a few words here and there. (I've managed 349 already here, this late evening, barreling along on a laptop sitting at the kitchen table full of dirty dishes.) Be flexible. Allow housekeeping to slide a bit. The dust bunnies won't bite, and you can always wash a needed cup by hand (or even better, give that job to the teenager who lurks in the corners of the house, perpetually plugged into the latest electronic gizmos). Train yourself to use those moments; don't assume that you need large, uncluttered blocks of time to write.

If those little moments don't appear, there's always pen(cil) and paper. I've scribbled notes on the back of grocery receipts, school notes, work papers, whatever's handy, for later reference.

And don't underestimate the power of the unconscious to solve your writing problem. Many's the time I've faded off to sleep ("faded" probably being the wrong word; it's more like falling off a cliff into the dark void when the day's been hectic), obsessing over some corner I've written myself into, only to find a way out has miraculously evolved by the time the alarm clock rings in the morning.

Another suggestion: celebrate every step of the way. And I do mean every step. So you've always wanted to write and you got that first chapter drafted? Hey! Do something special for yourself, whether it's buying a mocha with extra whipped cream or taking a quick turn around the block with the stroller. Finished your first draft? Once you've written "The End," it's definitely time for a treat. Maybe champagne. Maybe a new pair of shoes (for you, not the kid). Look at each step as getting you closer to your ultimate goal of being published. That means that every rejection you get from a publisher or agent is another step. Like Lamaze during childbirth, you greet that breath and then say goodbye. Each rejection, each "not for us" or "liked it, didn't love it," is bringing you closer to the "I loved it" and the "we want to publish it." But if you don't persist through every single "no," you'll never get to the final answer: "yes."

A word, too, about writing and the "downside" of life: the big life events that hit you, slam you into the wall until you can hardly breathe. Whether it's illness or death in the family, or other emotional/physical crises, some people write through them, finding solace in the written word. Others need to curl into a ball for some indeterminate amount of time and set the writing aside. There's no right or wrong way to deal with these times, and it certainly does no good to beat yourself up if you're one of those who can't write through it. In the end, living fully will help make you a better writer.

Everywhere you look, there's some little gift that you can take with you and use. The conversation of middle-schoolers in the back seat of the car yields insights into adolescent culture and interactions. The snarky comment of a co-worker can find its way into some bit of dialogue. That two-day-old half-filled cup of coffee that you just found behind a stack of reports at work … Hmmmm. That's what two-day-old coffee dregs look like? I can use that!

Well, there's more I could say, but now it's really late. I hope this provides some encouragement to those of you who are juggling so much already and trying to write as well. Life, in all its chaos, its joy, its pain, is the raw material of stories—even if those stories are set in another time or even on another planet. If I were to get "Zen" on all this, I suppose I could say life doesn't get in the way of writing; it is the way of writing. So look around and realize: In your busy, full, and hectic life, you've been given a gift better than any that Santa could leave under a tree.

Open it and use it.

Fish Where the
Fish Are Biting

RAY WHITE

Imagine you are an unknown, unpublished writer with no industry or agent contacts but you have a manuscript you want to get published. Not hard to imagine that, is it? Because that's where most of us are at the beginning of our writing careers—clueless and beautifully naïve about our chances of getting into print. So, what's the first step? After you've written and edited that manuscript and had your critque group tear it apart, of course.

Easy.

As an unknown, unpublished writer, whose favorite uncle probably isn't an editor at Random House, you must make contacts in the publishing industry. The best way to do this is to attend writers conferences. Why? There are lots of good, valid reasons I'll delve into later for going to conferences, but the most important one is that agents and editors go to conferences in order, at least in part, to look for new submissions, new voices—you. I call this the "fish where the fish are biting" approach, and if you believe, as I do, that you create your own destiny, you will be there talking to those agents and editors, getting to know them, and learning if they are the right people for your submissions.

Most conferences offer one-on-one sessions with agents and editors. But those meetings are only one of several opportunities you will have to talk to them at the conference. A word to the wise here: even in a private meeting you will only have five or ten minutes to deliver your sales pitch, so you need to have your presentation down pat. It must be organized and professional. You should have a short, catchy title and above all be able to answer the question "What's your book about?" in twenty words or less. This isn't as hard as it sounds. (We learned by selling our book at garage sales and the Colorado State Fair.) Hard, after all, is learning to write a gripping synopsis, and we cover that too.

While meeting with agents and editors, remember that only part of the process is introducing yourself. Equally important is learning about them—their personal tastes and interests. Giving agents and editors some time to talk will help separate you from the dozens of other writers who pitch and never stop talking. If you build a rapport that will touch them as a person, and not just as an agent or editor, it will help your cause. Also, while talking to them after a session or at the bar that night, you might discover that they don't represent historical romance or thrillers or whatever manuscript you've just spent years pouring yourself into. This isn't a loss for you. It's an opportunity to ask them if they know anyone who's looking for your type of work. These conversations are very much win-win. You've saved yourself the cost of sending off a manuscript that will be rejected and you earn points for doing your homework well enough to not waste their time.

And you might just discover that they are the right person for your manuscript, in which case you will be able to send them a submission with the all—important *"Requested Material"* on the package—more on that later.

There are other reasons to go to a writers conference—meeting other writers, choosing from a full slate of very informative panels on every aspect of the writing profession, attending question-and-answer sessions with industry insiders … all of these could make a conference well worth your time and money.

Plus there are often contests to enter. Winning a contest can give your biography quite a boost. For example, Denver features the prestigious Colorado Gold Writer's Contest every year. There is a first-place winner in each of four categories (romance, mainstream, science fiction, and mystery), and the entries are judged by the attending agents and editors.

It's usually a given that if you win your category, the agent who voted for you will want to read your manuscript. For example, Duane Lindsay entered his novel *The Grifter's Daughter* in 2006 and won the mystery category. The agent, with whom he hadn't been able to get an appointment, presented the award and immediately asked him to send the entire manuscript to her attention marked "requested material."

Giving agents and editors some time to talk will help separate you from the dozens of other writers who pitch and never stop talking.

The words *"Requested Material"* on the package mean that it bypasses the slush pile and goes directly to the agent. If you include a cover letter reminding the agent who you are, chances are good that she'll read it.

Now, we all know writing is a lonely occupation, and that's another good reason to go to conferences. They are full of writers just like you, people with whom you can share your war stories or get advice from, people who will constantly remind you that you are not alone — and, who knows, you just might meet your future agent and or publisher there.

Everyone says you must be ready to answer when opportunity knocks. Well, let me tell you, opportunity doesn't go around knocking on doors. That's your job. Every query letter you send out, every conference you attend, every contest you enter is you knocking on a door.

Knock on enough of them and one will open.

A Guy Can Dream, Can't He?

DARRELL JAMES

Darrell James is a fiction writer living in Pasadena, California, with his wife/ manager, Diana. His stories have appeared in numerous mystery magazines, including *Futures Mysterious Anthology Magazine*, *The Armchair Aesthete*, and in the book anthology *Landmarked For Murder*. He is the 2004 winner, as well as the 2003 finalist, in the prestigious Fire to Fly Competition. His solo anthology, *Body Count: A Killer Collection*, was released in February 2006. Find Darrell at www.authordarrelljames.com.

I had a dream that I would become a famous crime writer. In this dream, I would follow in the footsteps of the greats — Mickey Spillane, Raymond Chandler, Elmore Leonard. I pictured television commercials and billboards proclaiming the long-awaited arrival of my latest bestseller. I would arrive in New York's LaGuardia Airport to a crowd of jostling fans. A driver would sweep me past and into the back of a limo where I would be couriered to the posh offices of my Manhattan publisher. There I would be plied with wine and cheese as we discussed the marketing strategy for the launch. And there were women in my dream. Lots of them. Throngs of pretty young fans, pushing and shoving as I left the building. Baring their breasts for me to autograph and sending me lacy little panties in the mail. Money would arrive in shipping containers. It was the mid-nineties, and I had made a decision to write.

I began my career with a novel titled *The Walking Man*, laboring under the *Field of Dreams* Theory that "if I write it, they will come." There were false starts and more scrapped revisions than saved. But two years later I typed *The End* on my manuscript, and my wife and I celebrated with a bottle of champagne. (Okay, actually two bottles followed by a round of great sex.)

But time was wasting. Outside my front door would be the agents and publishers lined around the block and armed to the teeth, ready to fight for their chance to represent my work. Fans were gathering beneath the tree in our yard and on the neighbors' lawns, awaiting the long-awaited emergence of the great author.

Right!

Outside my door, there were no lines of agents. No publishers. There were no fans. And the friends I had, weary of hearing of my aspirations, had all seemingly drifted off to seek other stars to wish upon.

What followed, those next years, was what I like to refer to as "The Trail of Tears." Rejection letters placed end to end would have stretched from the publishing houses of New York to the front stoop of my townhouse in Southern California. A second novel was later completed. Two screenplays made their rounds through Hollywood. More than a dozen short stories were colonizing paper mites in a cardboard box beside my desk.

Call me a fool, but I still had images of receiving my umpteen-thousandth Edgar to the applause of millions. I still dreamed of success, holding on to nothing more than a quote by the great motivator and one-time mentor, Paul J. Meyer. It says: "Whatever you vividly imagine, ardently desire, sincerely believe, and enthusiastically act upon must inevitably come to pass." It began to happen for me in 2003.

That February a letter came in the mail that said I had been chosen as a third-place finalist in the Fire To Fly Competition for my short story "The Bridge" and that, as part of the reward, my story would be published in the winter issue of *Futures Mysterious Anthology Magazine*. Un-f#*&ing-believable!

But wait, there's more.

After a month of sex-and-champagne celebrating, *Futures* wrote to say that they were also interested in publishing "Lydia," a second story that they liked but that had not made it into the finals. *Who are these people?*

I've come to think of 2003 as "The Summer of Manna." In June that year, I received a note from another magazine publisher saying that they would like to publish my submission. Thirty days later a well-known noir magazine accepted yet another. By now I'm reeling. Toward the end of summer I got word that a screenplay of mine had been accepted as a semifinalist in the prestigious Slam Dance Screen Competition. And by late in the year my stories were appearing seemingly everywhere. *Yes*'s were falling from heaven.

In 2004 I won the Fire To Fly Competition again with a story called "Running in Place." And later that year I was accepted into my first book anthology. On its heels came the publication of my first solo anthology, *Body Count: A Killer Collection*.

I've come a long way since those years on the Trail of Tears. These days I write with a certain confidence that my novels and short stories will find their place in the world. Agents and publishers respond favorably to my queries. And I've signed hundreds of books for fans who tell me they like my work and can't wait for more.

As of this writing, the shipping container of cash hasn't arrived, and I've yet to get the limo ride from the airport. But it's coming, I know it. And somewhere out there, at perhaps this very moment, an attractive young woman is stuffing her undies into an envelope with my name on it.

Rubbish, you say? Well, hey … a guy can dream, can't he?

How I Started

MARIAN KEYES

Author of more than eight novels full of quirky, off-beat humor, with a touch of heartbreak, Marian Keyes has established herself as a must-read in her native Ireland, in England, and in America. Visit her site at www.mariankeyes.com and become familiar with her delightful stories, including her latest novel, *Anybody Out There?*

My story—like nearly everything else about me—is a bit odd. I didn't begin writing until I was thirty; I'm the only writer I've ever met who doesn't have seven unfinished novels gathering dust in her underwear drawer.

I had no idea that writing was something I wanted to do—I've never done a creative writing course, and the message I got growing up in Ireland was that while it might be perfectly fine to *read* books, it was other kinds of people who wrote them. (Impressive types with a big mahogany desk and stables and spectacles that they'd whip off from time to time and say, "I'm glad you asked me that question, George.") A lot of oral storytelling went on at home and it was fine, oh perfectly fine, to be doing that *in your spare time*, but the whole focus was upon education and getting a good job with a health plan and a pension and possibly, if you did really well, a company car.

So I left school, and I was eighteen, and I was clueless, and I got into college to study law, and I might as well have been studying carrots or hammers for all the interest I had in the law—anything would have done just to stave off real life for another three years. Eventually I got my degree and everyone else in my class went off to become barristers, and I went off to London and became a waitress—and I thought I was the cool one.

Eventually I got a job in the accounts office in the restaurant (possibly because I was such a bad waitress), and after the restaurant went to the wall (nothing to do with my waitressing skills, honest) I got a job in the accounts office of an architectural college. I worked there for 187 years, or at least that's what it felt like. It was a very small office, and there were three or four of us, and we used to put a lot of energy into how much we hated our jobs, and how late we could arrive, and how early we could leave, and how little we could do, and how much we could complain.

The poor students used to hate coming down to the accounts office: When it was my turn to do the petty cash, you'd swear it was my own money I was giving out—I was so mean to them. And sometimes I'd pretend that the combination lock on the safe was broken, and that they'd have to come back later. Or other times I'd pretend that I hadn't been to the bank yet and—yes, they'd have to come back later. Obviously I was very unfulfilled in my work, but I'd no idea that I could do something else and still had no idea that I wanted to write.

Parallel to this, something that had always been there began to develop further in my late twenties—a very close relationship with alcohol. This had been fine in my early twenties, when everyone around me partied hard, but then they all started getting married, and having babies, and getting promoted, and buying couches and curtains and stuff, and I wasn't moving on in any way. And then people began using the word alcoholic around me, and I was quite annoyed. Just because I didn't have a couch .... .

So I was coming up to my thirtieth birthday, and life was shutting down—I tried not to see anyone, because all I wanted to do was drink, and all they wanted to do was stop me from drinking, and that isn't exactly a recipe for fun. I knew I was very unhappy, and I kept thinking about suicide, and every night when I went to bed, I'd pray that I wouldn't wake up, which is no way to live.

Despair, however, is a great thing (mind you, that's not how it felt at the time); my life felt so hopeless that something had to give. And something did. One afternoon, just after my thirtieth birthday, I read a short story in a magazine which had won a prize, and something about it—it was fun—made me think, "I'd like to do something like that." There and then I wrote my first short story, which I was really quite pleased with, all things considered. This was a watershed, because I had never before done anything that I had felt was worthwhile, that I was proud of in any way.

Over the next four months, I wrote four more short stories, which were all a reflection of my state of mind at the time—one was about a woman who had died and was walking around in her own life without knowing she was dead. Another was about a credit card who falls in love with his owner. (Even at my bleakest, I was able to be funny.) I had a sort of inkling that my stories could save me.

But they didn't. In January 1994 the wheels came off, and I attempted suicide and ended up in rehab. I was monumentally lucky because while I was in there, I got an overview of my life and saw the shambles it was, and I saw that alcohol had been implicated in every terrible thing that had ever happened to me and that if I could stop drinking, then everything might work out.

After six weeks, I re-emerged and it was like being born again. I hadn't a clue how to do anything—how do you have confrontation, how do you celebrate, how do you deal with your feelings without alcohol? However, because I was feeling so hopeful and positive, I decided to send my short stories off to a publisher. I also sent off a letter saying I'd started a novel—but I hadn't, and had no intention of doing so. I'd decided that a novel would take far too long to write. Easily nine months, even *a year*. A short story, by contrast, could be knocked out in an afternoon if you were quick about it, and then you could show it off and everyone would say how great you were.

However, the publishers wrote back, and although they claimed to like my short stories, what they were really interested in was my (imaginary) novel. It was the biggest "Oh my God" moment of my life. I berated myself for my lie, asking myself how I always ended up in such tricky situations. I thought the best thing would be simply to ignore it and hope I never met the people from the publishers, but then—another watershed moment, obviously the year for them—I decided to give it a go.

I had nothing planned; I had no characters, I had no plot. However—although I had never noticed up until that point—I wasn't entirely without material. My life had been packed full of pain and disasters (an absolute must if you're planning to write): alcoholism, depression, disastrous relationships with men, a rigid Catholic upbringing, frizzy hair, freckles, being a Virgo, being the eldest child, always feeling like an outsider … the list was a long one. And I must say, while none of it had been particularly pleasant to live through, it came in fairly handy once I had embarked on my book (it wasn't remotely autobiographical, but used quite a few of my emotions).

Terror—in this way very similar to despair—is a great thing. Because I was so afraid that I'd be unmasked as a liar I didn't have time to agonize about what I should write. I just launched into it, writing from the heart, writing in my authentic voice because I didn't have time to manufacture any other. The recording in my head which told me on a second-to-second basis how useless I was at everything was still there, but I was too panicked to listen to it. "Not now!" I kept yelling at it. "I'm trying to *write*!"

In a week I wrote four chapters (about 12,000 words) and it sort of, in a rough way, seemed to hang together.

At the time I didn't know how I'd managed that, but in retrospect it's clear that because I'd always read so much, I had a blueprint in my head of the narrative arc of a book. (Even if at the time I didn't know about words like "narrative" and "arc.")

I sent the chapters to the publishers, and they offered me a contract for three novels.

Now, hold on a minute! Before you start burning effigies of me, can I tell you that I know my story is very unusual and I know that most aspiring authors have to go the rejection slip route. Don't be disheartened by my ridiculous good fortune. The thing is that I always regarded myself as one of the unluckiest people on earth, and if something that wonderful can happen to someone like me, it can happen to anyone.

My Scabby Ego

JESS LOUREY

Jess Lourey spent her formative years in Paynesville, Minnesota, a small town not unlike Battle Lake, the setting for her Murder by Month Mysteries. She currently lives in Alexandria, Minnesota, where she teaches Creative Writing and Sociology full time at the local college. When not writing, raising her wonderful kids, getting rejected, or teaching, you can find her gardening and navigating the niceties and meanities of small-town life. She is a member of Mystery Writers of America, Sisters in Crime, The Loft, and Lake Superior Writers. Her Web site is www.jesslourey.com.

.....

Four hundred and twenty-three rejections. One novel. Not very good odds, but I'm working with them. It started when I was five. I wrote this poem for my grandfather:

> Grandpas are full of love
> Grandpas are full of tickles
> But grandpas are especially full of pickles.

People loved it. Aunts hugged me, cousins were jealous, uncles asked me to immortalize them next. My poetry skills have not evolved since that day, but the enchantment with words and their power to make people see the world through my eyes has grown inside of me like a watermelon seed.

I finished my first novel when I was twenty-six. It featured three women traveling across the United States, three women suspiciously like myself and the two best friends I had taken a road trip with a couple years earlier. Like most first novels, it was embarrassingly self-involved, full of overwritten description and twenty-pound dialogue tags: "'Why doesn't my alcoholic father accept me for who I am?' Hannah asked pityingly, rubbing the burning, salty tears from her chocolate brown eyes."

Amazingly, no publisher would take a look at the first three chapters. (The fact that I was submitting directly to publishers shows just how green I was.) I tried some light revising, working under the new-author misconception that my work was great and the world just wasn't ready for it yet. When the adding of more adjectives didn't net me a three-book deal, I took a sabbatical from writing the Great American Novel and got a real job.

But, like most writers, I couldn't stop thinking of book ideas, writing down sparks of description or snatches of conversation that I overheard and would love to write about, feeling lazy and envious when I read a fantastic novel. When the nagging sense of ignoring something important got too strong, I started writing *May Day*, the first in my Murder by Month series.

It turned out mystery writing was an excellent fit for me. I enjoy structure, adventure, humor, justice. My first draft was complete, I thought, at 45,000 words. Confident that I had found my niche, I sent out fifty query letters and received fifty rejections. I researched the field, poring over the Mystery Writers of America and Sisters in Crime web sites, reading all that Predators and Editors had to offer me, camping out in Jeff Herman's fantastic reference book as well as the *Literary Marketplace* and Association of Authors' Representatives database. Out of all those resources, two points stuck with me: no one would read a book shorter than 50,000 words, and if you're writing a mystery, publishers only want series.

I hired a freelance editor and pumped it up to 52,000. Next, I wrote *June Bug*. Then, and only then, did I begin my systematic plan of attack to wear down the publishing Behemoth. I sent out 200 query letters. When the rejections started trickling in, I sent out 150 more. Not an agent or small press was spared. If they represented books, they heard about *May Day* and *June Bug*.

If you're keeping score, that's three books written, zero books published. Why did I put so much effort into this? Because when I write, I feel like I'm in the right place at the right time. How did I know *May Day* and *June Bug* didn't suck on five different levels like my first novel? Because I had done the research, including reading nearly forty books in the mystery genre, I had studied what made them great, and I had sought out and adhered to feedback from a reliable and well-recommended editor.

Finally, a bite. I found an agent. We never met—she lived out west on a commune, where she edited technical manuals and studied the healing power of crystals. After six months and a handful of offers from publish-on-demand companies, we parted ways amicably. I found another agent shortly after that, and after a year of rejections from New York publishing houses, she found my books a home with Midnight Ink, an innovative new imprint of a respected Minnesota publishing house.

Because when I write, I feel like I'm in the right place at the right time.

May Day came out March 2006, has received critical acclaim, and is available anywhere you can buy books. *June Bug* came out in March 2007; *Knee High by July* will come out in September 2007 and *August Moon* in March 2008. I'm also developing a series which I hope to shop to larger publishing houses and working on a mainstream fiction novel outside of the mystery genre.

So, as of today, I'm at 423 rejections and one novel. Most people would have given up a while ago, and there is a word for those type of people: sensible. The rest of us? We're called writers.

The Fiery Road to Publication

JONATHAN SANTLOFER

Jonathan Santlofer is a highly respected artist whose many awards include two National Endowment for the Arts painting grants. His artwork has been written about and reviewed in the *New York Times*, *Art In America*, *Artforum*, *Arts*, and *Interview*, and is included in numerous public and corporate collections. He serves on the board of Yaddo, one of the oldest arts communities in the country. He is the best-selling author of *The Death Artist*, *Color Blind*, *The Killing Art*, and *Anatomy of Fear*, an illustrated suspense novel, all published by William Morrow/Harper Collins. Visit his web site at www.jonathansantlofer.com.

H ad there been no fire I might never have written my first novel. I had been an artist, a painter, since graduating from Pratt Institute with a Masters of Fine Arts degree, first setting up a studio in Hoboken, New Jersey, and later in downtown Manhattan; and with that particular mix of hard work and good luck I had, by the eighties, actually done it: become a success in New York's contemporary art world. I was not exactly king of the art world hill, but exhibiting on a regular basis, recognized as a serious artist, and making enough money from part-time teaching and selling my artwork to support myself.

In 1989 I had a show in Chicago. Five years of work, half of it previously sold and gathered from collectors, the other half new; nothing left on my studio walls but outlines, "ghosts," of where the paintings had been made. The show opened on a Friday and burned to the ground on Saturday.

I will not bore you with the details of my personal anguish except to say I dropped out of the art world and moved to Rome where I made drawings from Renaissance masters, and … started writing a novel. *Why?* Because I needed something creative to replace what I'd lost. It's as simple as that.

My novel, written in the first person, was about a mid-career artist who'd lost it all. I worked on it for a year before I realized I could not bear the protagonist's voice (mine) and so decided to kill myself on the page. It was a relief to be rid of that whiner and it showed me what I really wanted to write: crime fiction.

When I started again I created an entirely new character, Kate McKinnon, an ex-policewoman with a blue-collar background who had retired from the force early, married a rich New York lawyer, and had become an art historian. A woman who had it all, who thought her crime-fighting days were in the past. Of course she was wrong.

What I wanted was to write a terrifying and funny thriller about a serial killer in the New York art world, a world I knew intimately (the art world part, not the killer part). I chose to write in the third-person — safer, I thought, as I was writing about a woman, and it gave me access to every character's point of view.

It took me five years to complete a decent first draft, working almost exclusively at night (during the day I was teaching and trying to find my way back to meaningful artwork). I told very few people what I was doing, just my family and a few close friends. I did not want people to know if I failed, though for some reason I believed I could do it — finish the book and sell it. That part is unexplainable. Blind faith? Perhaps.

I got up the nerve to show the draft to one of my friends, who proclaimed it "enjoyable," and to my sister, a poet, who said, "Jonny, this is *not* shit!" Two votes of confidence, sort of. I showed the next draft to a friend, who liked it enough to put me in touch with a literary agent, who also liked it, but felt something was missing — though she could not tell me what.

I rewrote again (another year passed), and I gave it a title, *The Death Artist*. After that rewrite I gave it to a writer with whom I'd become friends at the arts colony, Yaddo, where I was painting by day and writing at night. She liked it so much she gave it to her agent, who called after three days to say she was halfway through it and liking it very much. We met a week later. She was extremely enthusiastic but thought there was a structural problem in the plot that needed to be addressed. I wasn't sure; she was. What she suggested would cause a ripple effect and require a major rewrite. I pondered the changes for a day, decided her idea had merit, and figured I had nothing to lose but sleep. For the next three weeks — day and night — I rewrote the book. It transformed a good mystery into a thrilling page-turner.

She took me on and sold the book in less than a week. *The Death Artist* has been translated into French, Spanish, Italian, German, Japanese, Dutch, Turkish, Greek, Czech, Russian, and several other languages. It is still out in paperback, and still selling.

I wrote a second book, *Color Blind*, then a third, *The Killing Art*, both Kate McKinnon mysteries, a character I grew to love. For me, each book is not only a challenge, but an opportunity to do something new, to learn, to get better at my craft. For the latest, *Anatomy of Fear*, I created a new character, Nate Rodriguez, a police forensic artist, who draws right on the page. This made it possible for me to combine my two loves, writing and art, since I am the one who makes Nate's drawings — and there are over one hundred of them in the book.

In many ways it feels as if I have figured it out: How to create something uniquely my own — a new kind of illustrated novel — and that my life has come full circle by putting my artwork in the book, pictures and prose coexisting.

I would not suggest a literal fire, but sometimes you need something that completely throws your life off its trajectory to do something else. After losing five years of artwork I am simply not afraid of losing, of changing, of starting again. As for the blind faith ... well, you've just got to have it in yourself because no one else will.

Follow the Yellow Brick Road

KATHY BRANDT

Kathy Brandt is the author of the series featuring scuba diver and underwater crime scene investigator Hannah Sampson. Clive Cussler calls Kathy a "terrific writer"; of her most recent book, *Under Pressure*, he says that "the scene with the sharks inside the aircraft is enough to cause nightmares." Her articles have appeared in dozens of national magazines, and she is at work on her fifth book, a standalone mystery titled *Out of Sight*. Visit her site at www.ksbrandt.com.

I started *Swimming with the Dead*, the first book I had ever written, on a snowy February day in Colorado when the Caribbean setting seemed a better place to be. For a year, I got lost in that tropical paradise with my character, Hannah Sampson. Then, suddenly, I came to the end—the book was finished. Now what? I could tell you I got that mystery published when the first editor I met, hungry to make her mark with a fresh new talent, insisted I sign with her house for mega bucks. I could tell you that story. After all, I write fiction. But in truth, my road to publication was a one-step-at-a-time, follow-the-yellow-brick-road approach that ultimately paid off.

I made appointments to meet editors and agents at conferences to pitch my manuscripts. I sent queries to agents because I'd decided an agent was the best path to a big New York publisher. I sent dozens of letters over the course of six months. By the time I sent that last letter, I was sure I'd become the most skilled query letter-writer in the history of query letters. I kept sending them, made sure I had six or seven out at a time, always making it clear I was submitting simultaneously. I knew it could take years if I sent only one letter at a time and then waited the months it would take for a reply. The day a rejection hit my mailbox, I was putting a stamp on another envelope. It kept hope alive.

My rejections ran the gamut. Some returned my own query letter with a "not interested" or "didn't fall in love with it," scrawled across the top. Others enclosed pieces of paper so tiny I thought the SASE had come back empty until I spied a narrow strip of paper in the bottom. Agents apologized for sending form letters. "We get so many submissions," they explained. Some sent personal responses. "I loved the story, but the character's voice is too biting," one told me. While another said he "loved the voice, but found the plot wanting." I never considered spending months rewriting my character's voice or replotting the entire manuscript. Instead, I sent out more letters. I don't envy these agents or begrudge them their form letters and terse responses. I know what they say is true — hundreds of submissions each month. Hundreds, I think and cringe.

When I look back on the process, I see that I was lucky and that it went perfectly. After six months of letter writing and manuscript mailing, I signed with my agent. Less than two months later I was signing a three-book contract with one of those big New York publishers.

Little, But Mighty

LAURA BRADFORD

Laura Bradford is the author of the Jenkins & Burns mystery series. *Jury of One*, an Agatha nominee for Best First Novel of 2005, was issued in mass-market paperback for Harlequin's Worldwide Mystery Book Club. *Forecast of Evil*, the second book in the series, was released in 2006 and is also scheduled to be a Worldwide Mystery title. To learn more, visit her site, www.laurabradford.com.

I t's there every time I open my cell phone and scroll through my stored numbers, holding court alongside family and friends, the kids' doctor, and school.

It's a number I'll never dial, yet I saved anyway—a treasured memory of a call I never imagined would come so early in my career.

But come it did ... complete with a voice on the other end announcing my Agatha nomination for Best First Novel of 2005.

My novel. My *small press* novel.

The decision to pursue a small press was as much an act of ignorance as it was anything else. I hadn't researched the business enough to know the differences between a small press and a large publisher other than the obvious geographical ones. The little guys tend to be scattered throughout the country, the big guys centered in New York.

What I *did* know was simple. The small presses would look at my manuscript without agent representation. The large houses wouldn't.

And for a stay-at-home mom of two young children, that time-saving piece of information was all I needed to know.

I popped my labor of love into a manila mailing envelope and shipped it off, rubbing the contents on the top of my kids' heads for good luck.

Weeks turned to months, my thoughts returning to that envelope again and again. I wondered if it had been read, if it was being considered, if they loved it, if they hated it. Until, eventually, I stuffed it in the back of my thoughts for the sole purpose of maintaining my sanity.

It was there, in its tucked-away state, when word finally came — Hilliard and Harris Publishing Co. of Frederick, Maryland wanted to publish my first mystery novel, *Jury of One.*

The next year was a blur of copyrights, dedications, acknowledgments, proof corrections, and lip-nibbling. I was on my way to being a published author. The only thing I'd ever wanted to be.

But, as the big day loomed, the second-guessing started. I was beginning to learn about things like distribution and name recognition, booking signings, and visiting bookstores. And the more I learned, the more glaring the differences between small presses and large publishers became.

Had I made a mistake? Was my beloved book doomed for failure before it ever saw the light of day? Time would soon tell.

And tell it did.

Less than three months after its official launch, mass-market paperback rights for *Jury of One* were purchased by Harlequin's Worldwide Mystery, my book chosen as one of their direct-to-consumer book club selections. Suddenly my small press book was finding its way into the eager hands of avid mystery readers.

It was an exciting time. I checked the Harlequin site monthly, waiting for word of my launch month — eager to see my name, and *Jury of One's* new cover art, below this powerhouse's banner.

My name. *My* book. My *small press* book.

And it was then, while my thoughts were occupied, that an unknown number showed up on my cell phone one evening. Truth be told, I debated ignoring it, figured it was a wrong number.

Fortunately, it wasn't.

That call was *the* call. My now-stored-in-my-cell-phone-for-the-rest-of-my-life *Agatha Call*.

Suddenly, the belief I'd had in my novel was now shared by others. By *readers* who recognized a fun story regardless of the size of the publisher. By *readers* who liked my story enough to write my name on a ballot for Best First Novel.

Jury of One didn't win the Agatha, but that's just fine with me. For now.

Because if all goes well, that number will appear on my screen again one day. Only this time, I'll know who's calling.

A Sixth-Grade Education

MICHAEL A. BLACK

Michael A. Black holds an MFA degree from Columbia College. A police officer in the Chicago area for the past twenty-eight years, he's had short stories published in anthologies and in both *Ellery Queen's Mystery Magazine* and *Alfred Hitchcock's Mystery Magazine*. His novels include *A Killing Frost, Windy City Knights*, and *A Final Judgment*, all featuring private investigator Ron Shade, as well as stand-alone thrillers *The Heist* and *Freeze Me, Tender*. The first book in his Doc Atlas series, *Melody of Vengeance*, was released in January 2007. Forthcoming are *Dead Ringer*, a collaborative novel with Julie Hyzy, and his new police procedural, *Random Victim*.

I wrote my first mystery story when I was in sixth grade. Up until that time, the only things we were allowed to write were themes such as "How I Spent My Summer Vacation" or "What I Want To Be When I Grow Up." My teacher, Miss Rehack (her name has been changed to protect the guilty), finally relented after my continued badgering and agreed to let me write something more creative. The only two stipulations she insisted on were that I have it ready by Monday and that I would read it aloud in front of the class that same afternoon. All other restrictions on language and such were implicit at my school. Besides, even if I'd known any "bad words," I probably wouldn't have been able to use them in the right context.

I went home Friday afternoon with a smile on my face, thinking, wow, I'm really going to get to write a short story.

Joy soon turned to gloom when I sat down at the kitchen table to begin. What was I going to write about? Private detective shows and Westerns proliferated the tube in those days, and I quickly settled on a tough private dick named Mike. (It wasn't that I was self-aggrandizing at this young age, but remembered a TV show called *Mickey Spillane's Mike Hammer* that my dad liked watching.) So after deciding on my protagonist, I figured I needed an equally formidable villain.

What could be more suitable than a good guy gone bad? I quickly came up with a crooked copper named "Lt. Johnson." (I used the abbreviation because I didn't know how to spell Lieutenant.) Looking back on this, after having spent most of my life in police work, I guess there's a certain irony here. But on to the story.

I don't really remember much else about the plot, other than our hero shot the crooked cop with one of those scuba spearguns. (Obviously this was yet another item borrowed from one of the TV shows at the time, since I didn't know how to swim back in sixth grade.) I do remember taking about a half a notebook page describing Lt. Johnson's unfortunate death spasms, though. Proud as hell of my accomplishment, which I finished late Sunday afternoon at the expense of my other homework, I readied myself for the accolades I was sure I'd receive the next day when I read it to the class.

I waited with a relish of anticipation, which was uncharacteristic because I was an incredibly shy child and usually hated our oral readings. But this time I would be reading something that I had written. My own creative work ... "May I have the envelope, please?"

The morning's lessons passed quickly, and so did lunch. Ducking the bullies who usually tried to beat me up and steal my lunch money, I reported back to school early and sat through a long-winded recitation as Patricia Peloquinn read her poem to the class. After heaping praise on Pat's iambic pentameter, Miss Rehack turned to me and asked, "Michael, are you ready to share your story with us?"

I should probably parenthetically note that Miss Rehack was an awesome being who looked to be seven feet tall to us. She wore thick glasses and often had hair that was an odd shade of blue. This was

public school, so she was no ruler-toting nun, but she was extraordi-
narily strict and could scare the bejesus outta us with only a stern look.

"Yes, ma'am," I said as I stood and hurried to the front of the class,
clutching my sheaf of notebook papers.

I positioned myself at center stage and began reading. I knew the
story so well that I even had a variety of voices ready. (I was really
a ham in those days, once I got warmed up.) Throwing everything I
had into the performance, I raced through the adventure, even using
a Jonathan Winters-like sound effect for the launching of the spear
from the gun.

But I guess I was born to be a writer, because I didn't listen to her and kept writing stories anyway.

When I finished, a hushed silence settled over the room. I beamed as
I looked around, seeing my classmates sitting all prim and proper, their
hands folded on their desks. Miss Rehack tilted her head slightly down-
ward, glared at me over the thick frame of her glasses, and snapped her
fingers. I walked over to hand her my story, upon which she scribbled
in big red letters: *D—Poor work*.

"Michael," she said, "don't you *ever* try anything like that again."

She told me to sit down, and Ernie Eggleston, one of the tough kids
who usually took my lunch money, tossed the tip of a pencil eraser at
me and hit me in the head. The rest of the day seemed like an eternity
as, one after another, my classmates turned to look at me and snicker.

After the bell rang and we collected our coats and headed home, one
of my friends came up and asked, "What'd she give you?"

"A 'D,'" I said.

He shrugged. "Well, I didn't think it was that bad."

Little did I know, I was getting my earliest lesson on the pitfalls of
writing. I managed to attract someone's attention with a pitch, got my

first deadline, wrote my heart out on a story, and got my first rejection slip. Only this was more like a slap.

After all these years, Miss Rehack's words still ring clearly in my memory. But I guess I was born to be a writer, because I didn't listen to her and kept writing stories anyway. So to all of you unpublished writers out there reading this, take heart. Perseverance will win out. Keep your strength.

Miss Rehack left the teaching field a couple years after this incident. If I didn't know better, I'd swear she became either an editor or a literary agent.

Confessions of a Late Bloomer

KRISTINE SMITH

Kristine Smith's first novel featuring science fiction heroine Jani Kilian, *Code of Conduct*, was released in 1999 and shortlisted for the Philip K. Dick Award. The other books in the series are *Rules of Conflict*, *Law of Survival*, and *Contact Immanent*. Her next book, also featuring Kilian, is scheduled for release in late 2007. In 2001, she was awarded the John W. Campbell Award for Best New Writer. Her site is www.kristine-smith.com.

I tend to keep my mouth shut when writer friends discuss the age at which they first started writing. So many of them seemed to have started in grade school, completing first novels before they graduated college or, in some cases, high school. Yes, these might have been very bad first novels, but they were still complete stories with beginnings, middles, and ends. They were *books*.

I sink lower and lower in my chair when I hear of the first short works sold by age twenty-five. The novels written and sold by age twenty-five or thirty. I wonder if there's something wrong with me. What took me so long?

Confession time. I did not begin writing seriously—by seriously, I mean for publication—until my early thirties.

This wasn't for lack of encouragement. Since grade school, I had always been told that I could write, and that I wrote well. My essays earned As. I could always string sentences together. But save for the odd school assignment, I had never attempted to invent a tale. I had no trunk stories. No unbearably bad novels written in wirebound notebooks and illustrated by hand. I never once considered writing as a career, or even a sideline. I read voraciously, but I never imagined my name on a title page.

I felt the first vague rumblings in college. I started writing the story of a young woman rebelling against a repressive regime, and had completed about two handwritten pages when my roommate asked me what I was doing.

"Writing a book."

"Oh. How many pages have you written?"

"Two."

She laughed in a lightly mocking sort of way, and I ... stopped. I didn't have the wit to reply that every book ever written started on page one. I just stopped. Looking back, I realize that I just wasn't ready yet.

Finally, in my early thirties, as so many of my friends returned to school for their MBAs, I decided to give a writing course a try and call it my MBA. My instructor, who wrote science fiction and fantasy, saw something worth building on and encouraged me. I started attended writers conferences and science fiction and fantasy conventions. I met writers and absorbed their advice on everything from contracts to choosing agents to how to behave at parties.

And I wrote. Evenings. Weekends. Blew up in frustration countless times. Quit forever, only to restart a few months later. Finished one draft, over eight hundred pages in ten-point Times New Roman, a mess of tangled plots and stalled characters, and immediately began the rewrites. Produced another mess, then started on the next draft until, six years later, I had finally strung enough sentences together to tell the tale. I talked to writer friends and, with their help, found an agent. I sold *Code of Conduct* in a three-book deal a month before my fortieth birthday.

What wise words follow? You're ready when you're ready. You learn as you have to. If you want it badly enough, you make the time. Talent helps, but you need to finish the book. Am I really telling you anything you haven't heard a hundred times before?

You just need to be at the point where you're ready to listen.

Two Books in
One Week

KAREN ROSE SMITH

Best-selling and award-winning author Karen Rose Smith has seen sixty novels
published since 1992. Writing for Harlequin and Silhouette, *The Bracelet* (2007),
spotlights the story of a Vietnam veteran whose war experience impacted family
relationships throughout his thirty-three year marriage. Her series for Silhouette
Special Edition will begin in 2008. Visit her Web site at www.karenrosesmith.com.

After six years of writing and the completion of thirteen manuscripts, I sold two books in one week! Unbelievable? It was for
me. The dream of being published began for me in 1984. After
a vacation, I began having back pain. At that time, the treatment was
bedrest. I had to stop swimming and biking as well as aerobic dancing.
I felt lost. As an English major and teacher, I turned to writing, at first
penning short stories. But as they stretched longer and longer and there
was no market for them, I decided to try a book.

I'd read romances since I was a teenager and loved them. It was the
natural genre for me, especially since I was fascinated by relationships.
Little did I suspect they would become my career. My sights were set
on that first sale. Yet after I completed an entire manuscript, I knew
writing was an integral part of me and I'd probably never stop. The
thought of quitting after one never occurred to me. After five, I queried
agents. I'd finished seven manuscripts when an agent took me on. But

I didn't sell until I'd completed *thirteen* manuscripts and was working on number fourteen.

I'll never forget the day I received the call. I always had a few manuscripts circulating, but I'd become accustomed to my agent forwarding rejection letters through the mail. That spring, my husband and I had decided to buy a new house. It was time to move on with our lives, even if I didn't sell a book. That evening we were going to talk to an insurance agent about life insurance. I received the call from my agent about five o'clock that I'd sold to Meteor/Kismet. At first I was in shock. After reality set in, I recall driving to the agent's office unable to wipe the smile from my face the entire time. I didn't want to talk about insurance. I wanted to discuss my blossoming career! Because now I had one.

Since we were moving, we had posted the sale of household items in our community paper. I was showing a couple the merits of our microwave a week later when my agent phoned. I asked her if I could return her call later. She said something to the effect of, "I think you want to talk to me now. Silhouette just offered you a contract for *Wish on the Moon*." That couple examining the microwave probably didn't know what to think when I whooped with delight and suddenly cared little about selling the microwave.

Do I wish I had sold after I'd written my first manuscript ... or seventh? No. Those years of writing and submitting taught me self-discipline. They taught me how productive I could be. When I had to set deadlines with contracts, I knew exactly what I could manage. I'd also honed my craft so I was ready for those sales ... ready with more ideas ... ready to be a published writer who stays published and appreciates every minute of it, every project offered to me, every idea that takes hold and becomes a book.

Timing might be everything, but I believe hard work, perseverance, and persistence pay off, too. Reaching for dreams becomes a habit when you've had experience to make your arms strong. I'm still reaching for dreams and don't intend to ever stop.

The Bob Richards Story

JERRY B. JENKINS

Jerry B. Jenkins is the author of more than 150 books including the number-one best-selling Left Behind series with Tim LaHaye. Their latest collaboration is *John's Story*, the first of The Jesus Chronicles. Jenkins is the founder of the Christian Writers Guild, www.ChristianWritersGuild.com, an organization that serves tomorrow's professional Christian writers, as well as Jenkins Entertainment, a filmmaking company in Los Angeles. The following story is taken from his nonfiction work, *Writing for the Soul*.

D uring my junior year in high school, the buzz around school was that we were going to have a famous assembly speaker: Bob Richards. An Olympic pole vault champion, Richards had had his picture on Wheaties boxes and was now a motivational speaker. I also happened to know he was active with the Fellowship of Christian Athletes.

My journalism teacher, Mr. Carey, told me that I, as sports editor of the Forest View High School *Viewer*, would get the privilege of attending a press conference with Richards and the sports editors of other high school papers in our district. I prepared a long list of questions.

Richards was inspiring at the assembly and back in those days was allowed to speak, if obliquely, about his faith. I made a note to ask him to expand on that at the press conference. But somehow a whole lot more people than the sports editors had been invited, and I found myself in a big room with three hundred other kids. I crossed out question after question, knowing that if I was lucky I would get to ask just one. I narrowed it to the faith issue. I stood and waited my turn, and finally Richards called on me. I asked him to say more about his personal faith, and he grinned broadly, apparently realizing that, since I had brought it up, he had the freedom to say what he wanted. And he had a lot to say.

I wrote that story, and Mr. Carey submitted it to *The Chicago Tribune*. They published it under the headline "High School Scribe Scores." Soon it was picked up and reprinted in a Christian youth magazine, *Campus Life* (now called *Ignite Your Faith*), and suddenly I felt like a real writer.

It was a thrill to see my name in the school paper, let alone a major daily and then a national magazine. I began stringing for local papers before I was old enough to drive, and I've never looked back. By age nineteen, I became the full-time sports editor of the paper I had been stringing for, and I figured I still had sixteen years to reach my goal of the same job at the *Tribune*. But God had other ideas, as He often does.

A Killer Nonfiction Proposal

RAY WHITE & DUANE LINDSAY

We read six books that explained how to write the perfect nonfiction book proposal. We wrote our proposal and sent it to an agent who immediately explained that we didn't have the slightest idea how to write a proposal.

The good news, though, is that we learned pretty quickly, and that you won't have to learn the hard way.

Basic Rule: Unlike a fiction novel, a nonfiction work need not be completed before sending it out. Even if you have written a complete nonfiction manuscript, you should submit a book proposal first—not the manuscript. Here's why:

Agents and editors aren't just busy; they are swamped, receiving literally hundreds of submissions a month. They simply don't have *time* to read complete manuscripts.

Publishing is a business. More than half of a book proposal is a business plan that explains how and why your book will make money. If an agent likes your idea, he needs it in a form that he can present to other people. Agents present your material to editors, and editors submit your idea to an editorial board. They make the final decision, and they don't have enough time to read your whole book.

A nonfiction book proposal is a snapshot of the book as you think it should be. As a result you should be as clear in your own mind as if the book were sitting in front of you. Your proposal will show exactly what your book is to anyone who reads it.

The book proposal is your first and best shot at convincing somebody to pay you for your work. It should intrigue them (what a great idea!), then answer any questions they may have: Will it sell? To whom? How does it compare to other books like it (precedents/competition)? Can you write it? What does it look like? What is the size? How many pages? The proposal will have the following sections.

Title Page

This should be the name of the book, the subtitle or tag line, if any, as well as the author's name and contact information.

Table of Contents

This is for the proposal, not your book. It should look like this:

The Overview

An overview is a one- to three-page mini-version of your proposal, similar to the inside flap of a novel. What is your book about? Why is it exciting?

Start off with a one or two sentence attention-grabber. This is called the *hook*. Look at any best-selling paperback for an example of how to write three or four sentences that will snag a reader's attention.

Include a paragraph or two on each of the following: the main benefits and features of your book, who its audience will be, and why they'll buy your book instead of another one that is already published. Add a paragraph that explains why you're especially qualified to be the author of this text.

The Audience

"There are three types of untruths," said Mark Twain. "Lies, *damn* lies and statistics."

Yet the publishing industry, who knows the statistics better than you, wants you to tell them the number of people likely to buy your book. To whom will it appeal? How many of those people are there, and how many of them read your type of book?

We went to writers conferences, searched the Internet, called people, read a lot of books, and settled on a number we believed would find our book entertaining or useful enough to want it. We could have just as easily settled on any other number to make our point but we went with the following:

> This year an estimated seven hundred thousand book proposals will be submitted to publishers, up from half a million five years ago. This increase in submissions goes hand in hand with ever-increasing use of personal computers and an explosion of new magazines for writers and new publishing venues such as e-publishing and e-zines. These writer's magazines and e-zines total more than one million annual subscribers. Every one of these proposals represents a writer who will want to buy *How I Got Published*.

The point is to make the best case possible for how many people will want to read your book. Is it about fly-fishing? Fine, how many subscribers does *Fly Fisherman* have? How about the Federation of Fly Fishers? Get online and check them out. Is your book computer related? There's a huge market for those books. How big? Not a clue. That's what you have to find out.

The Competition

Here's another place you have to research. Are there any books similar to yours? Of course there are. The absolutely worst thing you could say about your book is, "There is nothing at all like this book," because (1) that's not true, and (2) the publisher wants to know what kind of audience your book might have, and if there isn't any, who would buy it?

Let's face it, there *has* to be something out there like your book. In our case we knew there were a lot of how-to-get-published books. The problem was to shorten the list so that it didn't look like the market was totally glutted. Eventually we settled on four books we had been studying and listed those, along with comments about why they were good—you only say good things about the competition—and why ours was going to be better.

This is an area that takes another huge amount of thought. Why is your book, which is similar to other books that sold a lot of copies, *different enough* from those others that people will buy yours?

Like the statistics, it is a question that has to be answered. Here is one way. What are five or six of the best-selling books that compete with yours? Narrow them down to no more than three for the proposal, which is enough to make your point. Show them in this format:

> *Putting Your Passion Into Print* by Arielle Eckstut and David Henry Sterry (Workman, 2005). A very good book with an unusual gimmick—offering a contest that would lead to an agent deal. Good for them!

How does your book differ from each of those books? Specifically, what does your book do better than they do? Explain how your book covers the ground more thoroughly or has better graphics or more celebrity endorsements or comes at the issue from another, more revealing direction. In our case this book was less about informing you how to get published than it was about inspiring you to keep trying until you do. The difference? All those great success stories by authors who did it.

About the Author

Why are you exactly the right person to write this book? Do you have any special qualifications? Are you well known; do you have any famous friends?

Write a brief biography of yourself, pointing out your many accomplishments. Have you been published before, even in local papers? Have you won awards, been anywhere appropriate to the book?

Are you an ex-playmate or a public speaker with a large audience? Are you well known in several circles for your witty style and iconic wit?

This is the place to pitch not just your great idea for a book but yourself as the writer of that book. Duane played that gig with the Rock Bottom Remainders which gave us an "in" with some famous authors, and I simply had chutzpah enough to ask.

Format

What will your book look like when it's published? For the most part your publisher will determine that. But since you are doing a proposal they will need your best guesstimate as to book length. How many words will it be? Publishers use 250 words per page as a count to estimate how many pages the book will be. Will there be any drawings or photographs, index or glossary or appendices?

These answers help the publisher determine how much your book will cost to produce. Is this a six-hundred-page opus with charts and graphs, color plates, and expensive paper? Is it a coffee table book filled with beautiful photographs taken by award-winning photographers? Or is it a trade paperback on inexpensive stock that will sell like gangbusters—at a lower price?

How, you ask, can you know this? Well, it's your book; how do *you* see it? When you were researching the competition, were you impressed by the expensive paper, hard cover, and graphics? Or did you buy the book because it jumped out at you with a colorful cover, a cool or clever title, and bargain price?

Promotion Strategies

Let's say a publisher buys your book. Yay! Now what? The publisher usually won't do much to promote your book—that's up to you. So you need to come up with a marketing plan that takes full advantage of the critical six-week post-release window. They will do what they can to promote it, but it is very much up to you to sell them on the idea that *you* will help them sell your book.

Are you willing and able to go on tour? What kind of tour? Will you do book signings all over the country, or stay local and do a few conventions? Will you do radio interviews or television walk-ons?

One writer we know does mailings to book clubs and offers to read his book to any group that will have him. It takes up a lot of time but sells a lot of books, too.

Do you have an idea for marketing your book online? A great Web site or a history of successful self-publishing will help convince the publisher that you understand the business.

It's been pointed out that an author is 40 percent a writer and 60 percent a salesman.

Show the publisher how you plan on getting your book in front of a reader. Will you hire a publicist? Odds are the publisher won't, especially on a first book. Can you afford one?

When I was talking to Clive Cussler at the inaugural International Thrillerfest Conference in June 2006, he told me his initial success was due to being good at marketing rather than being a good writer. The better your marketing plan, the better your chances of convincing a publisher to take a chance with you.

Outline

Since our book was filled with stories from authors, we first just listed the writers' names, thinking the draw of big names would help sell our concept. This looked incredibly boring, so we changed our outline to a table of contents format, exactly like the one you read in the front of the book. We added snappy or humorous or inspiring titles next to the authors' names to get your attention. We made it look the way what we'd want to see it if we were browsing in the bookstore.

Sample Chapters

The agent or editor wants to know—can you write? It's not enough to have a dynamite idea if you come across as an airhead. So even though you don't need to do the entire book, you have to create two or three chapters with interesting titles, clever openings, and strong writing. This is your chance to shine, so make the most of it.

That's it, really. Once you've done all this work, all that's left is to put together a query and *send it out.*

Chiefs Did the Trick: Interview With Stuart Woods

Stuart Woods is the author two nonfiction books and 34 novels including *White Cargo, Grass Roots,* and *The Run*. His novel *Chiefs* won the Edgar Allen Poe award from Mystery Writers of America, and *Palindrome* earned another nomination. *Imperfect Strangers* won France's Prix de Literature Policiere. Still, Stuart is best known for his Stone Barrington novels. His latest book, *Fresh Disasters,* pits Stone against the New York mafia. Visit Stuart's site at www.stuartwoods.com.

....

Stuart, how did you first get published?

I sold the rights to *Blue Water, Green Skipper* to Stanford Maritime, in London, and they sold the American rights to Norton. My first agent submitted *Chiefs* to three publishers with 100 pages and an outline, and all of them declined. Michael Korda at Simon & Schuster, in particular, cordially despised it, so I sold the book to Norton for $7,500. In hindsight, it was a mistake to sell the uncompleted book, because I would have gotten a great deal more for it finished. I would not advise any other budding author to make this mistake.

Did your publisher do anything to promote the book? Did it make the New York Times *best-seller list?*

Norton had almost stopped publishing fiction at that time, and they did absolutely nothing to promote it. Their attitude was, "If it starts to sell, maybe we'll take out an ad." Whatever the hardback did was by word of mouth, but I changed agents, to Morton Janklow, and he got a very good paperback deal with Bantam. When the miniseries came out the paperback got a second wind, and we probably sold 600,000 in all.

Wait a second, how did you manage to simply "change agents to Morton Janklow," and for that matter how did you find your first agent?

I'll answer the second part of that question first. The designer of my yacht, Ron Holland, had a contract with Stanford and introduced me to his editor. I had no agent.

Since I'd already sold *Blue Water, Green Skipper* I didn't have any problem finding my first agent. I asked my editor at Norton to recommend one. He recommended three, and I chose one of them.

After completing *Chiefs* I felt that my agent was not sufficiently enthusiastic about the book and that his goals for its various sales were too modest. Pat Conroy recommended me to his agent, Julian Bach, and a friend at *Saturday Review*, Susan Heath, read the manuscript and recommended me to Morton Janklow. I met with them both, they both wanted to represent me, and I chose Mort. That was twenty-five years ago, and I have never regretted that decision.

Your books are regulars on the New York Times *best-seller list. Did* Chiefs *get you there first?*

Chiefs certainly made my reputation, and it did crack the list in paperback, as a result of sales spurred by the TV mini-series, but I didn't make the *Times* bestseller list, in hardback, until my 15th novel.

What advice do you have for beginning authors regarding getting published and promoting their books?

Write something. So many "writers" fail to do this. Buy a copy of *Writer's Market*. Getting published is easy; writing something worth publishing is hard.

Things I Wished I Knew

LOUISE PENNY

Louise Penny is the author of the Armand Gamache mystery series. Her first book, *Still Life*, was named one of the top ten mysteries of 2006 in the U.S. and won the Creasy New Blood Dagger in the U.K. for best first crime novel in Britain, as well as the Arthur Ellis award in Canada. A former journalist, she lives with her husband in a small village south of Montreal. Her site is www.louisepenny.com.

Like most writers I was turned down more often than I care to remember, or cared to admit to my agent. Now, when it's too late for her to dump me, I might as well admit it. A few things would have helped had I known them earlier. This is a small attempt to make your life a little easier, if you're an unpublished author.

First—finish the book. Most people who start books never finish them. Don't be one of those. Do it, for God's sake. You have nothing to fear—it won't kill you. It won't even bite you. This is your dream; this is your chance. You sure don't want to be lying on your deathbed regretting you didn't finish the book.

Read a lot.

Read books on writing and getting published. I read *Writing Mysteries*, edited by Sue Grafton and published by Writer's Digest. I also read *Bestseller* by Celia Brayfield and a bunch of other books including *The Complete Idiot's Guide to Getting Published*.

If this is your first time writing a book, why would you assume you know what you're doing?

Why put that sort of pressure and expectation on yourself? You might very well have an innate appreciation of character and structure and pacing. Some people do, and don't need these books. Frankly, I'm not totally sure how much good they did me. But I know for sure they did no harm. And it was comforting to "listen" to other writers and know they struggled with the same things. I felt much less alone and inept.

I suffered from writer's block for many years. Terror had taken hold. I was afraid that, once tested, I'd prove my worst fear true — I was a terrible writer. What cured me was a sudden realization I was taking myself way too seriously. And that I was trying to write the best book ever published in the history of the world. And if I didn't, I was a failure.

If you've actually finished your first book — well, you're amazing! You're already so far ahead of the pack they can barely see your dust!

I decided instead to just have fun with it. To write what I loved to read. And to people the book with characters I'd want as friends. Clearly we all choose our own characters — but make sure you're going to want to spend lots of time with them. They don't have to be attractive, kind, thoughtful. But they do need to be compelling. Look at Scarlett O'Hara. A petty, jealous, willful, vindictive character, almost without redeeming traits, whose tragedy is her failure to change. But she's riveting.

Be true to yourself.

Write what you want even if friends and relatives think you're nuts. And be very careful who you show the first draft to. Once finished I'd strongly suggest you make a list of readers, friends, acquaintances, friends of friends, who'll read your work and critique it. This is a crucial stage. But remember, your "baby" is fragile as is your ego at this stage. Mine certainly was. I'd invested so much of myself, a too-harsh criticism or cruel critique (always said with a knowing smile) could have made me toss the whole thing away. I wish I could sit here and tell you I was strong and determined and centered and courageous about the first draft of *Still Life*, but I wasn't. And you're probably not absolutely sure your first book is any good either.

Here's the trick. You need to get it into the hands of other people. You need to be open to criticism and guidance and suggestions. But you need to choose those people wisely. Some people are simply petty. Some people see it as their God-given purpose to find fault. This process isn't about finding fault. Frankly, anyone can do that. It's facile. No book is perfect. It's about making the book even stronger. You need supportive, encouraging, thoughtful readers. People who'll offer critiques in a kind and constructive way and who understand the difference between truth and opinion.

A novel should be more than 60,000 words in length. Publishers and agents judge length not by the number of pages, but by the number of words. Your computer will have a word count option. In Microsoft Word it's under the Tools heading. You might aim for 60,000–90,000 words for a first book. There are always exceptions—some very successful debuts are mammoth, but you're simply making it more difficult to find a publisher. Still, more than anything, you need to be true to yourself. If it needs to be 150,000 words, then go for it. But my first draft was 168,000 words. I cut it in half, and it made the book much stronger. Once my ego and pride were set aside I was able to "kill my young."

Persevere. Believe in yourself.

If you've actually finished your first book—well, you're amazing! You're already so far ahead of the pack they can barely see your dust! Most people never even start that first book. Of the few that do, most never finish. If you've actually finished, well done! Frankly, as far as I'm concerned, the pact you made with yourself, probably as a child, is complete. You wrote the book. You did it. And, if it's never published you should have no regrets. I'm serious. You've accomplished something most people only dream of.

Still, chances are, you want to get it out there, and why not? Here's how I did it, and my suggestions—remembering that every writer has his or her own story and no one of us is "right"; it's just our opinion and experience.

Make sure your manuscript is as good as you can get it. Edit, edit, edit. Print out a copy for yourself. When you think you've finished, set it aside for a few weeks then sit down and read the hard copy. For the sake of convenience I print it out single-spaced, double-sided and get it bound. Much easier to hold, and it feels like a real book! Thrilling.

When it's time to send it out, print double-spaced, in twelve-point, on white paper, single-sided.

Do not bind the manuscript.

Print your name and a key word from the title on the top of each page, in a corner (e.g., Penny/Still). There's an automatic function for that on your computer as well. You don't have to do it manually.

Number the pages from the first page to the last. Don't start the numbering fresh with each chapter.

Don't worry that the manuscript will appear to be huge. Always scares me when I see it at first. Looks like a dog house.

Aim high. Might as well be turned down by the best. Buy those huge thumpin' bricks of guides to agents and publishers in your country—read them carefully. There will be essays on writing query letters, and each listing will tell you what the agent/publisher specializes in. Don't waste your time or theirs by sending them a mystery when they only deal with nonfiction.

Send multiple queries. It takes a long time for them to get back.

Go to conventions and network.

Enter contests.

Okay, here it is. This is how I got a leading London literary agent and three book deals with Hodder/Headline in the U.K. and St. Martin's Minotaur in the U.S. Ready?

I entered a contest.

I was surfing the Web and came across the Crime Writers Association in Great Britain and noticed their Debut Dagger contest.

If you're an unpublished crime novelist, I beg you—go to this site: www.thecwa.co.uk/daggers/debut/. Go to their "welcome" section and from there read down to the "debut dagger" part. Click on that.

There were eight hundred entries worldwide in my year (2004). They shortlisted fourteen, and I was one. I knew then my life had changed. As a reward for being shortlisted we were all invited to the awards lunch in London. My husband Michael and I went. I came in second—and networked like mad. I cannot overstate the importance that award has had on my career. I met my agent Teresa a couple of nights later, actually at a private party—but she knew my name and my submission. All good London agents who deal with mysteries read all the shortlisted CWA submissions.

Now—I did something else that was crucial to my success. Before the awards I did my homework and found out who were considered the top agents in London. When Teresa introduced herself at the party I was able to look her in the eyes and truthfully tell her I'd heard of her and she was considered a top agent. I think that made an impression. If nothing else it showed a degree of work and commitment on my part. In my experience you get out what you put in. The harder you work, the more research you do, the more knowledge you have, the better your chances of success. Which isn't to say some people don't walk in totally unprepared and have great success. And why not? I have no problem with that at all. Any way that works is fine with me. But for myself, the more prepared I am, the calmer I am, the better my brain works. Again, it's giving myself every chance of success, instead of handicapping myself through either fear or laziness.

There are other awards out there. The Crime Writers of Canada has just created the Arthur Ellis Award for Best Unpublished Mystery and another important and exciting one for writers of traditional mysteries (like *Still Life*) is given out by St. Martin's Press and Malice Domestic, which is a fan-run convention in Washington. Very prestigious, very knowledgeable and sophisticated people. The great thing about this prize is that St. Martin's agrees to publish your book if you win. You'll find information on it at www.minotaurbooks.com. You have to kind of root around in the site to find it, but it's there.

There — my brain is empty.

If any of you have other suggestions for unpublished writers, please go to the "contact me" page on my Web site and send them to me. We need to support each other. Isabelle Allende once said that the end doesn't justify the means, the end is decided by the means. If we're petty and greedy and shallow and put our need to win ahead of our humanity, then nothing good will come of our careers.

Others have helped me, and I'd consider it a real privilege to help you.

Critiquing and the Green-Eyed Monster

L.L. BARTLETT

L.L. (Lorraine) Bartlett is the author of *Murder on the Mind*, a Jeff Resnick paranormal mystery. Her bookseller mystery series will debut in 2008. Learn more about Lorraine and her books at her site, www.llbartlett.com.

I f it weren't for several of my critique partners I can guarantee that I would not now be a published author of novel-length fiction. I've received wonderful, thoughtful comments from people (almost all women) who wanted me to succeed and have cheered me on. (And I hope you know who you are!)

That said, I'm sure most every author who has joined a critique group has had at least one bad experience. I've had more than my fair share, and most often the "problem" was the same, and most definitely mine: I was determined to see my work published, whereas some of my critique partners were more in love with the idea of writing than actually sitting down at the keyboard and creating.

To get published, I felt I had to keep working at it, despite reams of rejections. When something wasn't working, I would try something else. During my tenure with one group (for two, or was it three years?), I finished two suspense novels. Yet my first published pieces were to the confession magazine market. It became a contest amongst the members: which one (of five) of us would get published first. I don't remember who actually "won," but I do remember that only one other person got published: she sold one confession; I sold six. Talk about jealousy! Needless to say my days with that group were numbered.

For several months I was without a group and felt aimless. I thought I'd found gold when a local romance-writer acquaintance introduced me to her new critique group, which was an offshoot of a writing class and focused on mysteries. Although I didn't have their shared history, and the critiques were hard, sometimes very hard, to take, I hoped my writing would improve because of that input. (Meanwhile, my acquaintance dropped out after a couple of months.)

It soon became apparent that not a lot of writing was happening within the group, because meeting after meeting I'd be the only one bringing in any work. Of the two to three hours we'd convene (at neutral ground in a local restaurant), most of the time would be spent socializing, with the critique happening only after the meal was over and the plates cleared.

During the three years I was a member I brought in to be critiqued three novels (one of which went on to be a finalist in the Malice Domestic/St. Martin's Best First Traditional Mystery contest) and three short stories (one of which was accepted by an anthology and another sold to a magazine). At times some of my critique partners were anything but positive. Often scathing remarks would be noted on my manuscript pages. Behind my back, complaints were made: "she writes too much." To my face I was told, "This isn't the type of mystery I care to read. Please don't bring another."

After a while an "us-against-them" kind of mentality developed. Two of the other women were appalled at the mean-spirited comments I'd receive. It seemed to one of them that half the group wanted me to be writing a different kind of book, and their comments were aimed at steering me into their vision of what my work should be. More than once a very kind woman apologized to me on behalf of the group.

The breaking point came when three members of the group decided to self-publish an anthology, something the other three of us weren't interested in underwriting (or contributing to), and we were abruptly tossed from the group. I'm sure our former critique partners felt smug in ridding themselves of us—especially me—but we only felt relief. I'm happy to say the three of us have continued to meet and critique.

Under a year later I sold my first book in hardcover to a small press, with a subsequent mass-market paperback deal, and sold (on proposal) a cozy series to a major New York publisher. (Meanwhile the group's planned self-published anthology has never seen the light of day.)

I wish I could say that these experiences were the last of my brushes with jealousy surrounding my work. Unfortunately, I've lost touch with several friends since I announced my sale—people who'd been dabbling but hadn't finished anything. People who couldn't bear to hear about my successes because they hadn't achieved their own goals. (And again, it came down to my choice to keep writing, keep submitting, and their choice not to.)

Bottom line: Despite a lot of negativity I learned to take the comments I deemed of value and ignore the rest, and not to let others' petty jealousy stop me from attaining my goal of publication. I have no regrets.

Despite Lazy Agents, Crooked and Dead Publishers, Perseverance Paid Off

MARILYN MEREDITH

Marilyn Meredith is the author of the award-winning Deputy Tempe Crabtree mystery series; the latest is *Calling the Dead*. She's also written *Wishing Makes It So*, a psychological thriller which was awarded Best Thriller for 2006 by the American Author Association and Best Horror by USA Book News. She is a member of Sisters in Crime, Mystery Writers of America, EPIC, and Public Safety Writers of America. She was an instructor for Writer's Digest School for ten years and served as an instructor at the Maui Writer's Retreat and many other writer's conferences. Visit her at www.fictionforyou.com.

The difference between a nonpublished and published author is the published one didn't give up. I'm proof of that statement. Back when I began, the publishing process was in the days of typewriters and carbon copies. My first book I sent out nearly thirty times before it was accepted by a publisher. Every fifth rejection, I rewrote the book. Finally, I received a slim envelope with a contract rather than the box with the manuscript inside. There is another lesson here—be sure the book is as good as possible before sending it out.

The editor who accepted that book left the house, and the one who took her place wasn't impressed with my next book. I did find another publisher and the book came out—but before I received any royalties, the man and his son who owned the company were jailed for fraud.

Fortunately, before it was all over, I was sent all the books that had been printed and the proof sheets.

I sent my first Christian horror novel to a small independent publisher who asked me to make the book camera-ready. This meant I had to learn how to use a new computer program. To do this, I enlisted the aid of a friend who owned a computer store. He taught me what I had to do and let me come to the store every day before he opened for business. Not only did that mean I was in the store every weekday from six to nine in the morning, but also, it was hard work. Once I was done, I called the publisher. His wife answered with the news that her husband had died and she didn't want to continue with the business. (Several years later, I found an electronic publisher, Treble Heart Books, who was brave enough to publish two of my Christian novels.)

Everyone says to find an agent first. That may be good advice, but for me, having an agent didn't help. Over the years I've had five agents. One, who had a great reputation, took on my Deputy Tempe Crabtree series. Every year I'd send her the next novel and she'd send me encouraging words. Finally, after four years, I asked for a list of my rejections. She sent me three rejection letters. I decided I could do better on my own.

My first mystery was published by a Canadian company. A book-signing was arranged, and the store ordered fifty books. In the meantime, that publisher also went out of business. Those fifty books were the only ones printed. I met a small, independent publisher who was willing to republish the book. Fortunately, she also was interested in publishing my mystery series. We had a great relationship for four books. Sadly, she had a stroke and passed away.

Electronic publishing is another venue I've tried. I wrote a police procedural, found a publishing house, and sent in the manuscript. It was accepted, and when I received the contract I learned the house only published electronically. This was at the very beginning of the e-publishing industry. Since that time I've been published by four e-publishers, and most of them have now branched out into doing print books as well.

Once again, I began the search for a publisher for my series. I'd met the publisher of Mundania Press at Epicon (the conference for electronically published authors) and was impressed by his knowledge of the publishing industry. I submitted my next Deputy Tempe Crabtree novel, *Calling the Dead*, and it was accepted.

This is merely an overview. There were many more struggles, upsets, and disappointments. The point is, if I'd been discouraged by any of the many rejections, less-than-honest publishers, the death of publishers, and the other problems along the way, I could have given up.

Because of the many stories in my head that I'm compelled to put into writing, I never let any of the bad events stop me. If you are a true writer, you have to write, and nothing should stop you. Write the best you can, don't let anything discourage you, and you will be published.

When I Couldn't Get an Agent

MARTHA POWERS

Martha Powers has written thirteen novels and has a humor column online. Her latest book is *Death Angel*, published in 2006. She lives in Vero Beach, Florida, and spends way too much time on the golf course. Visit her at www.marthapowers.com.

When I couldn't get an agent for my book, I wrote to Michael Korda at Simon & Schuster. I had spent two years sending out query letters to agents. Although I wasn't a newbie, having published eight historical romances, I was changing genres. I had a suspense thriller that I felt was strong enough for a mainstream publisher. I made lists of agents who brokered deals similar to the kind of book I was writing. I thought with my track record I was a shoo-in.

Oh, and did I mention I was hoping for a million-dollar advance?

Disillusionment came quickly. I sent out query letters to the top five on my preferred agent list. Three informed me they weren't taking new clients and the other two never responded. It was then I began to have an inkling this might not go according to plan.

After I sent out the next five, I had several requests for the manuscript. Three agents wanted major changes to the manuscript. I would have made the changes if any of their ideas sounded reasonable or even close to my vision for the book.

It's not that I'm stubborn, although my husband would have a word to say about that. I knew the market I was writing for and I knew the kind of reader who would read the book. So I continued to send out query letters.

Eventually I reached the bottom of the agent list: Igor Hanschmucker, whose clients were mainly from little-known Baltic countries. I began to question the wisdom of continuing this plan. After all, I had sold my first five books without an agent.

I had originally decided to become an author so I could sleep late and go to cool parties. The biggest drawback was that I couldn't write. I was a history and geography major who didn't have a clue how to put a book together. Some people are natural writers. I'm a natural storyteller, but I didn't know how to translate the oral tradition to the written page. So I read everything I could get my hands on about the mechanics of writing. I joined a writing group, and they gave me invaluable tips on how to craft a story. Once I learned the technique, it was just a matter of telling my story and getting it published.

Only an idiot believes it's really that easy.

The first thing I learned was that you had to have a manuscript. You can talk about being a writer all you want, but unless you've got a completed manuscript, you're just kidding yourself. A compelling story idea won't be enough to interest a respectable publisher, except perhaps one involving a religious conspiracy, artwork, and Mary Magdelene.

So I wrote a manuscript.

I entered a contest run by the Romance Writers of America. A contest is an excellent vehicle for a beginning writer to get feedback on a manuscript. Usually the final judges are editors, and it's a chance to get your writing seen. In my case I won the contest, and one of the editors who judged the entries bought my book.

Contests and conferences are excellent ways for writers to not only attend workshops but to network with other writers. Through conferences run by both Romance Writers of America and Mystery Writers of America, a writer has the unique opportunity to meet editors face to face. Sometimes you can make a pitch or at least make a personal contact that ends up as a request to send the manuscript to the publishing house.

If you ask most authors, they will tell you that the reason they got published is that they refused to give up. I was at the bottom of my agent list and decided it was time to try a new plan.

I had seen Michael Korda interviewed on Charlie Rose's television show. In my eyes he was an unreachable icon, but in the interview he'd come across as very approachable. Since I had nothing to lose, I decided to write him a letter. Writers are told to make query letters one page long, and that's what I did. I gave him a one-line synopsis of the suspense thriller I was pitching, gave my publishing credentials, and finished with a sentence on my personal life: "I'm married to a confirmed bachelor and I have two teenagers, so I understand the mind of a psychopath."

Even Igor Hanschmucker would have taken me as his client with that kind of a query letter. That letter got me a trip to New York, a publishing contract, and, best of all, dinner with Michael Korda.

Are You Sure You Don't Want to Be a Lawyer?

MICHELLE GAGNON

Michelle Gagnon is the author of *The Tunnels,* first in a series of novels featuring F.B.I. Special Agent Kelly Jones, whose specialty is tracking serial killers. Gagnon's novel just came out in June of 2007, so her advice is fresh and worth heeding. See her site at www.MichelleGagnon.com.

When I was in high school my local newspaper, the *Providence Journal Bulletin*, held a holiday short story contest. On a whim I entered something I'd written involving a six-year-old boy, Spiderman, and Santa. To my shock and amazement it won publication in the features section the week before Christmas, and a hundred-dollar gift certificate to the local Hallmark store. That short story kept me in thank you notes for years afterwards.

I entered college convinced that the writing life was for me, but I was persuaded by my parents to sign up for a more diverse major on the off chance that I didn't turn out to be the next James Joyce. As my mother said, "Writing is hard, very few people make a living at it. You have to have something to fall back on." This was always quickly followed by, "Are you sure you don't want to be a lawyer? You're so good at arguing."

When the time came to take the LSATs I balked, choosing instead to pursue the far more stable and lucrative profession of modern dance. I studied with a company in New York and managed to pay the rent by also bartending, walking dogs, and performing in a Russian supper club dressed as an extra from Michael Jackson's "Thriller" video. Heady times, I assure you.

When I moved to San Francisco, I reconnected with a college friend who helped me get a gig writing articles for websites. I became a freelancer, specializing in interviews and articles on health, fitness, and travel. One magazine paid me to spend the day with politician and author Arianna Huffington; another had me talking to a young girl incarcerated for killing her lover's husband. It was interesting stuff, the pay was decent, and I enjoyed the work. But part of me was itching to write fiction again. I started slowly, compiling a series of short stories that featured the same main character (a character who was remarkably similar to me: same age, same basic life experience). After a year I managed to string the stories together and handed the finished product off to my friends, all of whom gave it glowing reviews. They were convinced I had a bestseller on my hands. Basking in their approval, I promptly submitted the first thirty pages to ten agents that I'd found in a guidebook. Wouldn't be long before my phone was ringing off the hook, I surmised. I debated how I'd narrow the field and jotted down the questions I'd grill them with. That was on September 10th, 2001.

The next day's events threw the world into turmoil. The ten agents I'd queried were all in New York, and their response time was understandably delayed. The few agents who eventually answered claimed that they had found my book humorous, but didn't feel like laughing just yet. Many other packages were returned unopened, victims of the anthrax scare that followed.

And so I waited. Six months later I tried again, sending it out to some of the original agents who had never responded, along with some new ones. Weeks turned into months, and the rejection letters started filtering in. Some were quite kind, others mere form letters. The absolute worst was one agent whose office had a checklist for why they were rejecting the manuscript. It was either: a) the quality of the material does not meet our high standards; b) we are currently not accepting new clients; or c) we feel strongly that you are a talentless waste of space. Although I might be paraphrasing with regard to C, since that was the one letter I refused to save in my files. In my case they'd checked all of the above, which struck me as far more labor-intensive than printing out a form letter.

Unabashed, I queried ten more agents. Then ten more. By the thirtieth rejection letter, I was starting to lose faith. By the fortieth, I was completely disheartened. The last ten letters I sent out with the kind of sad resignation reserved for the condemned.

Don't send out anything until it's sat in a drawer for at least a month. Then take it out and read it through again.

And so two years after I started, I gave up. I filed the last rejection letter and sat down at my keyboard again. I had in mind a coming of age story set on a college campus. But the novel kept petering out at the fifty-page mark. I tried telling it from different characters' perspectives, altering the setting, and changing the timeline, all to no avail. And then one night, ten pages into the story, I suddenly killed off my main character. I sat there, shocked; that had never been my intention, but I looked at the screen, debated for a moment, and decided to let the story take me where it would. Three months later I had the rough draft of my first novel, *The Tunnels*.

This time I waited before showing it to anyone. I set it aside and started working on something else. When I dusted off the manuscript a month later and re-read it, I was alternately despairing and hopeful. There were some great passages, and the skeleton of a story, but it was still rough. Three drafts later, after incorporating comments not just from family and friends but from the moderator of my writing group, I queried ten agents. One of those responded immediately, asking to see the first thirty pages. A few days later, she emailed and asked if her agency could exclusively review the manuscript. I agreed, and waited.

Months passed; I became convinced this was going to be a repeat of my initial experience. But lo and behold, a week before Christmas 2005, I received the phone call extending an offer of representation. Better yet, my wonderful new agent managed to secure a deal with MIRA books for a series of thrillers starring the same main character.

Just the other day I took out that first manuscript and flipped through it. Now I can see why it was roundly rejected. There's a lot of good raw material there, and someday I might take another crack at it. But there isn't a doubt in my mind that the end product will be dramatically different.

So my best advice is this: don't send out anything until it's sat in a drawer for at least a month. Then take it out and read it through again. Give it to someone that really knows writing, preferably not a friend who will try to protect your feelings. Don't be afraid to go through five, ten, fifteen drafts, whatever it takes, before you send out those query letters. And of course, above and beyond anything else, persevere. I only know of one writer who had absolutely no trouble getting an agent. A college professor passed his manuscript along to a friend at a well-known New York agency, who immediately called him with an offer of representation. "Gee," my friend said when we compared notes. "I had no idea it was so tough. I must've just been lucky."

Don't worry. I'm planning to kill him off in my next novel.

Talk About Naive

RITA LAKIN

Rita Lakin lives in Marin County, California, happily writing and running around the country publicizing her Gladdy Gold comedy mysteries. The first novel, *Getting Old is Murder* (2005), is in its fourth printing; the second, *Getting Old is the Best Revenge* (2006), is in its second; *Getting Old is Criminal* was released May 2007. She is also a partner in a musical comedy, *Saturday Night at Grossinger's*, which continues to play at various theaters around the country. Her short story "The Woman Who Hated The Bronx" will appear in the fall issue of *Bronx Noir*. Her site is www.ritalakin.com.

In a fevered pitch of inspiration I wrote a novel. Late at night or in pieces of weekends when I could steal the time. Then I tucked it away in a drawer and forgot about it. At that time, twenty years ago, it wasn't the passion for me that it is today. I was way too busy with my day job. (Hard to imagine isn't it? But I had responsibilities. Three children to support. House payments, car payments, little league, PTA. *Ad nauseum.*)

Then I met some editor guy at a cocktail party, and when I happened to force the subject of my dust-covered novel into the conversation, he handed me his card and told me to send it right away. I assumed he would have said anything to get rid of this pest.

He bought it in the next mail and enclosed a contract. Well, that was easy, I thought. Being young and stupid and the novice I was, I signed the contract, had no idea what I signed, and promptly forgot about it. I was under deadlines in my *real* job.

I just assumed they knew what they were doing. I had no idea that I could argue about the cover, which I hated. I despised the title, but did I think to argue? No. I was also so inexperienced; I didn't realize I might have asked for a hardcover deal. I was given a mass-market paperback. I also didn't have a clue about getting out there and promoting said book. Or anything else for that matter.

But I finally started to get excited. I got to correct galleys. Me, with galleys, wow! It was finally dawning on me that I really was going to have a book published! I'd be rich and famous and have my photo on the cover and I could quit my job. I could say, I'm an author! The dream I had but never believed would happen.

Demon of the Night, a thrilling tale about the Adam and Eve legend, came out. I called up the local book-stores day after day to find it how it was selling. Double wow! The book was selling out. Then, a while later, I called again to see how the next batch was doing. Well, there was no next batch. Seems like the publishing house went under. There would be no new books. The editor disappeared. There was no one to call or write to. Too late. Now that I was finally ready to assume the mantle of a published novelist!

That was that. And I still keep finding copies of the book on eBay and Amazon.com, and I buy up the copies so I can look at what almost was.

Now it's years later. Older, definitely wiser. I am a full-time novelist with a hit comedy mystery series about a group of little old ladies living in Ft. Lauderdale who accidentally become private eyes. *Getting Old is Murder*. My title, my choice. My chosen cover art. But what I've learned this time around is that a novelist spends 40 percent of her time writing and 60 percent on the road all over the country promoting her work, paying her own expenses. I've learned how complicated the contracts are, how to ask for the covers I want, and how to fight for what changes are to be made in my manuscript. Luckily, I'm with a great company, Bantam, and have a great editor to work with.

But what I've learned this time around is that a novelist spends 40 percent of her time writing and 60 percent on the road all over the country promoting her work, paying her own expenses.

"Easy" went out the window. Nothing is easy anymore, and I realize what a quirk of fate that first sale was. The moral of the story, if there is one, is if you're any good, just keep trying. Either a fluke of fate will come along or, more likely, you'll just have to work hard like the rest of us. And, believe me, it's worth it.

F. Scott Fitzgerald
Had It Wrong

ROBERT S. LEVINSON

Robert S. Levinson is the best-selling mystery-thriller author of six novels, most recently *Where the Lies Begin* and *Ask a Dead Man*. Number seven, *In the Key of Death*, is scheduled for publication in March 2008. His short stories appear often in *Ellery Queen's Mystery Magazine* (he's been an *EQMM* Readers Award winner several years running), *Alfred Hitchcock's Mystery Magazine*, and in "year's best" mystery anthologies. Learn more at www.robertslevinson.com.

His *Gatsby* has proven great, but not so much the oft-quoted aphorism found in a series of notes for a novel F. Scott Fitzgerald never completed: There are no second acts in American lives.

In fact, with all due respect and reverence, Mr. F. —

Wrong.

In your case and current state, sir —

Dead wrong.

There can be an Act 2, even an Act 3 or Act 4, for anybody who wants it badly enough, sets a goal, and pursues it with unreserved dedication and commitment. For example —

Me.

I'd sailed through careers in journalism, public relations, and writing and producing for television, all professionally and financially rewarding, but the desire always nagging at the back of my noggin was to write a novel and get it published.

Just one, if possible; thank you very much.

There came a day I looked into the bathroom mirror, saw my father's face staring back, and recognized I had to pursue my dream now; now, not tomorrow, before another decade disappeared and it became a dream unrealized through neglect, lost inside the file labeled What Might Have Been.

There's a song lyric from the vintage Broadway and movie musical *Damn Yankees* that goes something like, *There's nothing to it but to do it*. Were it so easy.

For me to do it, I had to build in enough time for focus and application by leaving all my business pursuits, turning my life upside-down — becoming a day person instead of the night person I had been for almost forever — and chaining myself to the computer on daily basis, from six in the morning until exhaustion and brain drain set in.

I drew on my penchant for show business history and trivia in concocting a mystery built around the not-entirely-crazy notion that Elvis Presley and Marilyn Monroe may have had a torrid, enduring love affair.

Never having tackled fiction before, it became a learning experience, trial and error as I wrote, edited, reworked, rewrote, and rewired while inching my way from one page to the next, following my storytelling gut rather than any outline, facing frustration and fear, maybe every twenty or so pages, realizing I'd written myself into a corner or hadn't a clue where to turn or twist the story next.

These were the times when it might have been easier to quit under some pretext. The need to reload the bank account by climbing back into a suit and tackling something for TV or a PR assignment. On a temporary basis, of course. Knowing full well it would be as temporary as forever if I weren't careful. Maybe, take a few days away from the writing, or a week, or a month. A year. Two. However long it took to rejuvenate the creative juices. You know, any handy excuse to easy-out, but — my dream.

What about my dream, damn it?

Remember that Academy Award-winning Best Picture of a quarter-century ago, *Chariots of Fire*, about a bunch of Brits competing for a place on England's track team at the 1924 Olympics in Paris? One of them, Harold Abrahams, has lost enough times to convince himself he doesn't stand a chance of winning and tells a lady friend, "If I can't win, I won't run." Whereupon she feeds him a dose of reality, saying, "If you don't run, you can't win." Harold recognizes the truth in her argument, competes, makes the team, and goes on to win a gold medal in the hundred-meter dash.

These were the times when it might have been easier to quit under some pretext.

Unlike some fledgling authors who surrender to frustration and fear of failure after ten pages, twenty, fifty, a hundred, my dream was never in danger.

Unlike Harold, I was never inclined to quit, and after four months of concentrated writing I had a finished novel I titled *The Elvis and Marilyn Affair*.

Mission Accomplished, right?

Wrong.

Half the mission.

Now came the really hard part, finding an agent and publisher.

Suffer more than a few sleepless nights as days of waiting turned into months of uncertainty and dread, fed by polite rejections couched in the most civilized of terms that nevertheless inspired in me thoughts of commissioning murder for real, not only on the printed page.

Resiliency.

What a wonderful trait.

They knock you down and, as hard and depressing as it might be, you pick yourself up, brush yourself off, and start all over again.

And the day comes, maybe a year later, that you've found yourself an agent who is anxious to represent you. And the day comes, maybe eight or nine months later, that your agent calls with the news you have a publisher excited about your book. And the day comes, maybe after fifteen months, that you walk into bookstores, one and then another and then another, and you see *The Elvis and Marilyn Affair* stocked with other novels on the New Releases tables and shelves.

And wonder of wonders, after ten years and five more novels — *The James Dean Affair, The John Lennon Affair, Hot Paint, Ask a Dead Man, Where the Lies Begin* — the joy of fulfillment remains undiminished.

Meanwhile, you out there:

How's your dream, your own Act 2, coming along?

The Rule of Twelve

SUSAN OLEKSIW

Susan Oleksiw is the author of the Mellingham mystery series featuring Chief Joe Silva (the most recent entry in the series is *A Murderous Innocence*, 2006) and the Anita Ray series with Hindu-American photographer Anita Ray, set in India. She compiled *A Reader's Guide to the Classic British Mystery* (1988) and coedited *The Oxford Companion to Crime and Mystery Writing* (1999). With two other writers, Oleksiw cofounded Level Best Books, which publishes an annual anthology of crime fiction by New England writers. The most recent title is *Seasmoke* (2006).

I am not a superstitious person. I don't keep a rotten apple in my desk drawer, like the poet Friedrich Schiller, to inspire me to put words to paper, nor do I sharpen a certain number of pencils each morning like Ernest Hemingway, lining them up like a stockade fence falling to the earth before the perfectly crafted sentence. If I need to have my desk tidy and clear of clutter before I turn on my iBook and face the blinking cursor, that is simply a normal tic in the life of a writer. The tic for Don DeLillo is a manual typewriter, and for May Sarton it's eighteenth-century music. Malcolm Gladwell needs a busy, noisy place, reminiscent of his newspaper days, to create the right kind of environment for his work. Gladwell's setting is positively serene compared to Hart Crane's need for raucous parties and loud Latin music.

But the Rule of Twelve is not a superstition; it is based on empirical evidence.

I learned about the Rule of Twelve in the second writing group I attended, in the 1980s, while I was struggling to publish my first stories since college. A fellow writer, more published than I (her experience supplied the first piece of evidence), explained the rule: A story sent out to twelve journals, or sent out twelve times sequentially, will be published by one of them. Was I skeptical? Yes, but testing this was hardly as threatening as getting a new desk, which I did recently. Deciding that the Holy Grail for me was a desk with drawers rather than the six-foot-long trestle dining table I'd been using for years almost sent me into therapy. But, as I said, I'm not superstitious. Unlike George Sand, Charles Dickens, Vladimir Nabokov, and Winston Churchill, I don't believe the only way to write is standing up. Robert Louis Stevenson and Mark Twain lay down to write. I use a chair.

There are those who believe that before you can be published you have to write out the first million words at the end of your pen (or your fingers) before you get to the really good stuff, the stuff that will make your agent swoon and editors call you on Sunday evening begging for your manuscript. I considered my options: a million words versus twelve submissions. As a rational person, I chose to test the Rule of Twelve. I polished one particular story and sent it out to twelve journals. And then I waited.

The notion that writers are superstitious gains credibility at every author signing and talk. The first question is often, "How do you write?" People ask this question as though the answer held the key to a finished novel, a prize-winning story. The answer in fact might, but not for the person asking it. Bruce Chatwin buys a box of Moleskine notebooks at a certain stationery shop in Paris, numbers the pages, and writes his name and address on the inside. This is a superstition—they can be used just as well for a travel journal, without numbered pages, which is how I choose to use them.

After what seemed an unreasonable length of time, in the twelfth month of the year, the story was accepted. I don't know what happened to the other submissions—they seem to have disappeared into the mail. Unlike Jack London, I did not obsess about the mail—stamps, letters, modes of delivery, postal system workers. I accepted the editor's reply as empirical evidence. The Rule of Twelve works.

I think it is important to keep in mind that writers live in fantasy worlds and therefore it is all the more important to keep superstitions at bay. Umberto Eco explains this nicely when he points out that certain projects call for a pen, others call for a felt-tipped pen, and still others call for a computer. Alexandre Dumas *père* used different colored paper for different genres, an orderly, rational approach to his work. Sensible and practical, I cleared a shelf in my bookcase for all my future publications.

The next time I noticed the effect of the Rule of Twelve was in 1992. By now I had an agent and a mystery novel, which she sent out to more editors than I can remember. She sent the manuscript to Scribner's, where it sank into oblivion. Despite calls to the editor and repeated letters demanding the return of the manuscript if it wasn't going to be accepted, we heard nothing. But I am a rational person. Unlike Gail Godwin, who keeps talismans from the graves of writers she admires—a beechnut from Isak Dinesen's grave in Denmark and a piece of rock from D.H. Lawrence's in New Mexico—I cleared my desk and went to work on another novel. I don't need a window overlooking the water in Venice, like Henry James, waiting for a ship to bring into view a needed detail for the story. The sidewalk outside my window works just fine.

On a cold Sunday evening in February, the telephone rang. It was Susanne Kirk. She wanted my mystery novel. It was a full twelve months since my agent had sent it to her. My bookshelf was filling up with more empirical evidence.

By now you should be convinced that superstitions have no place in the writing life. Empirical evidence is the only way to go. The Rule of Twelve works. Use it.

Love It or Leave It

GRANT BLACKWOOD

Grant Blackwood is the author of the Briggs Tanner thrillers *An Echo of War*, *The Wall of Night*, and *The End of Enemies*. Fast paced, edge-of-your-seat suspense, highly believable, yet with a touch of humor and human concern—in other words, exactly my kind of book. Readers of Clive Cussler and Robert Ludlum will love Grant's work. Visit his Web site at www.grantblackwood.org to learn more.

J uly 2007 will mark my twentieth year of chasing my dream of writing fiction for a living. There's an old saying in this business: "It takes ten years to become an overnight success." Of course, "success" is a fuzzy term. It's different for everyone, but if we take the above saying at face value, I'm either a very slow learner, or this is a very tough business. The truth is, it's probably a little bit of both. There is an upside to my slow absorption rate, though: I've had two decades to internalize some lessons that would've made my journey far less frustrating.

In May 1987 I was discharged from active duty in the U.S. Navy. I remember walking off the ship and heading down the pier, seabag over my shoulder as my former shipmates waved goodbye from the forecastle railing. I remember thinking, "Okay, now what?" Two answers popped into my head: One, go back to college; two, maybe try my hand at writing.

I first became intrigued with the idea of writing at the age of eighteen while reading a copy of Clive Cussler's *The Mediterranean Caper*. I imagined millions of readers just like me, curled up in his or her favorite chair, "living" an adventure that had been woven from the whole cloth of a writer's imagination. This realization was like an intuitive punch in the stomach. To do this for a living would be — you'll forgive a cliché — a dream come true.

Two months after walking down that pier, I was living in St. Louis and easing my way back into civilian life as I waited for the fall semester to start. I woke up that July morning and my first thought was, "I should really give that writing thing a try." I must have caught myself on the right day. Instead of putting it off, I sat down and started writing. I never looked back. And to my own surprise, I found I loved writing.

So this is the first lesson: You've got to love it. You've got to love writing. For some, that may mean they enjoy the process of stringing words together, of working with the glorious complexities of the language. For others, it may mean they relish the process of weaving a story born only of imagination and dedication. For some, it may mean both of the above and more. Whatever the case, if you don't love it, you probably won't last long.

Make no mistake: This is a tough business. The statistics of success and failure can be disheartening, the odds stacked against you staggering. A struggling writer's best weapon is a deep, abiding love of writing. Love will see you through the heartbreak, the frustrations, and the mind-numbing, logic-shattering capriciousness that can be the publishing industry.

A love of writing will help you take the rejection and march on. A love of writing will spur you to decipher and digest the myriad techniques every writer must have in his or her arsenal. A love of writing will keep you motivated when it feels like you're getting nowhere.

Most importantly, the love of writing leads to dedication, and dedication in turn leads to perseverance. At events and signings I'm often asked what I consider the most important trait in a writer. My answer is always the same: perseverance. With few exceptions, the writers that succeed in this business are the writers who have refused to give up. Period.

Become a Devourer of Worlds

When I was eight or nine, my mom gave me a copy of Ian Fleming's *Dr. No*. I'd always been a big reader, but *Dr. No* was the first "adult" book I'd read, and it set the tone for the rest of my life. After my introduction to Bond, James Bond, I started reading every thriller I could get my hands on. I devoured the world of thrillers—the good, the bad, the in-between.

When it came time to decide what genre I was going to write, there was no question. Thrillers were a natural fit. I loved thrillers and, most importantly, I knew them by heart.

I frequently tell that story to struggling writers who are trying to decide which genre is right for them. What do you most love to read? Chances are, that's what you should be writing. Not only will you enjoy the process more, but you'll have a built-in compass.

So, lesson number two: Know your market. Know it backwards and forwards, top to bottom. And then trust that knowledge. Be flexible (there'll always be something to learn in this business), but if you know your market—really know your market—you'll know what works and what doesn't.

Don't think. Write.

Like most writers, I've collected my share of rejection letters. For the most part I've been able to either set them aside and keep going, or learn from them and grow. There was a time, however, when I did neither.

After about ten years of diligently practicing my craft, submitting manuscripts, and collecting polite and not-so-polite rejections alike, I hit the wall. Invariably, all the rejection letters were the same: praise of my work and my writing followed by the big "but" (or "however" or "that said"):

"However, we don't feel we're the right agency for you."

"That said, we don't feel confident we can sell your manuscript."

"But, there are flaws in the story that makes the book unsaleable."

I'd heard it all before and had so far been able to take it in stride. This time, *however*, was different. I had no idea how to write a better book. I had no idea how to go from a "great writer" with a "gripping story" to a saleable author with a saleable book.

I shut down. Stopped writing. Withdrew into a world of introspection and self-pity. I read how-to writing books, joined writers groups, enrolled in writing courses. I did it all—except for writing. After about three months of this, I woke up one morning and realized I was no longer a writer. I wasn't writing. I wasn't trying. It was a slap in the face.

I sat down and started writing again. I didn't know how I was going to become that saleable author, but I knew I wasn't going to get there by not writing.

It had taken me an embarrassingly long time to absorb the lesson: writers write. Whatever else you do to grow as a writer, make sure you're writing. Put words on paper and let the rest worry about itself. If you love writing, if you've learned to persevere, and if you know your market, then stop thinking. Sit down and write and trust that you'll get better.

It worked for me.

Join a Critique Group

RAY WHITE

All of us who write know it is an isolating profession, requiring long hours in front of a keyboard with minimal distractions. We write and write and finish a scene and begin another and we think what we've written is good. Okay, sometimes we think what we've written is great. But how do we know?

We get other people to read what we've written, and not just any other people. I, for one, have so many relatives who think I'm the next Hemingway I don't even bother to have them read for me anymore (except for pleasure). So we get other writers to read our stuff, people who know what we're trying to do and can help us get there, preferably people who will tear our precious words to shreds. We join a critique group with, hopefully, weekly meetings that allow us to socialize with peers.

Critique groups teach us not only how to write but also how to grow a thick skin. Notice I said a *critique group*, not a fan club. If your group consistently tells you how great your writing is, find a different group. You want one that will hurt your feelings by explaining (tactfully) how your characters are shallow, your dialogue forced, and your plot predictable and asking why, if your protagonist got shot in his left arm in chapter one, is his right arm bandaged in chapter three? You want a group that will force you to do better, because only then can you believe them when they say what you wrote was terrific.

Honest criticism, given with the intent to improve your writing, is the greatest gift one writer can give another. But for most of us criticizing someone else is hard. That's especially true when we join a new group and we don't know anyone well. I remember my first group, five other writers, strangers all, none published in novel form. We began with just one rule, and it's probably the only rule any critique group needs: You can say anything except that another person has no business writing.

Seems like we always tried hard, at least I know I did, to find at least one thing in everyone's writing we could praise. We each brought at least one chapter per week to exchange with all the other members, so we each had to review five chapters per week. That's a pretty good workload if you're conscientious, but the problem was three of the writers consistently produced good work that was difficult to find fault with, two were beginners who tried hard and did decent work, and one was a beginner who didn't know how to give or use criticism. She wrote great vivid settings but her dialogue was wooden and her characters boring. Her critiques consisted of, "Good work; couldn't find a thing wrong with it." And in the six months of meetings she never listened to the rest of us as we tried and tried to get her to write like she talked.

The other unwritten rule of critiquing: You can't just say "I don't like it" or even "I loved it." You have to put in enough thought to say why and to offer a suggestion for improvement.

A writer's group brings you out of your shell and improves your writing. They can help you polish query letters, and almost everyone uses them to help craft a synopsis. Also, you never can tell who the members of your group may know, or what ideas they may bring to your work. Being able to brainstorm with others is the single greatest reason to join a critique group. Everyone is pacing around the room bouncing ideas back and forth, joking and laughing and creating magic. Your critique group is an essential part of your network. If you and your group work hard, you will help each other get published.

When Writers Write
About Writing

CHRIS KNOPF

Chris Knopf is the author of the Sam Acquillo mysteries *The Last Refuge* and *Two Time*. A principal of Mintz & Hoke Communications Group, Chris lives and writes in Connecticut and Southampton, New York. His site is www.sameddie.com.

....

Somebody once said—I used to think it was Ernest Hemingway, but now I'm not sure—"Writers are people who write."

This was the sort of seemingly moronic minimalism that got the big guy in a lot of trouble. The political climate within the arts and academia in recent decades has been hostile to Hemingway's legacy, especially since he's rightly perceived to be a tad misogynistic. (That Ezra Pound was an out-and-out Nazi sympathizer and F. Scott Fitzgerald, T.S. Eliot, and James Joyce all had wives who were certifiably insane, with barely a whiff of censure from the critical legions, I guess is beside the point, though it does raise questions of intellectual honesty.) But I think no writer of the modern period was more able to summarize gigantic truths, especially when writing or talking about the writer's life.

Part of the problem with the quote above is it usually leaves out the next sentence, which was, paraphrased, "People who aren't writers are those who only talk about writing." This gets at the main reason why most people who have both the talent and aspiration to write betray their potential. They don't write enough.

There are a few reasons why they don't write enough, though the most common is fear that what they write won't be any good. Worse, it will incite derision, ridicule, or disinterest. So, they are inhibited from starting the actual act of composing thoughts on paper (these days, monitors). They console themselves by spending a lot of time and energy thinking about writing, under the rationale that they are simply formulating the big ideas in their heads, which will, once properly constructed, fall effortlessly though their fingers and onto the page. This is a fallacy, of course. For a couple reasons.

Writing is, in great part, a type of thinking. It takes inchoate feelings and inarticulate thoughts and expresses them in a transferable form. Words make thoughts and feelings concrete, but also, the very act of forming structure inspires thought. Sometimes, there really is no idea until the words start to form.

Ergo, the only way to know if you really have a thought worth communicating is to put it into words. You have to actually write it down.

The other reason is more practical. You have to practice the trade. You can no more become a good writer by thinking about writing than you can become John Coltrane by imagining yourself playing the sax. Professional writers are obsessed by things like sentence structure, word count, punctuation, literary voice, style consistency, and concentration, just like world-famous wood workers are obsessed with things like router bits, bench dogs, chip out and finishing oils. You can't write a book or make a Chippendale highboy thinking only about the grand vision. They're both products of millions of little visions manifest in little acts of craft.

And it really doesn't matter what form you're writing in. Your heart may be committed to poetry, but your brain gets almost the same benefit from writing billboards. To extend the music analogy, a familiarity with Bach gives a jazz musician a killer advantage. It's the practice that counts, and the knowledge and experience that comes from practicing within a variety of formats and protocols.

Hemingway also said that "Writing is rewriting." This is also a simple statement pregnant with complex meaning. Many failed writers who write too little do so because they think they're supposed to hone and perfectly render every little piece of description or exposition as it's written. Very bad approach. Much better to disgorge everything you can on to the page, to get yourself into a chatty monologue with your presumed reader, and just let it go wherever it's going to go.

The next day, it might be all for naught. The work might be unsalvageable. But probably, there is something there. Now, with an objectivity developed over time, you start to rewrite. You lop off big chunks of unworkable babble — often the first things you wrote down — and start to shape the words into something more elegantly and originally expressed ... or, just as important, something persuasively, clearly expressed.

None of this is possible if you aren't writing. You've got to pile up your own mother lode in order to refine the gems.

Hemingway, that wordy guy, also said that he strove to write something that "was true."

True, in the sense that it was as close to real as humanly possible. Honest to his mind, and not contrived. But also true in the sense of a picture hanging true on the wall. In the sense of your aim being true. Even, balanced, harmonious, artfully composed. He believed that both definitions of the word true were mutually generative. Honesty encourages symmetry and vice versa.

To quote the last line of *The Sun Also Rises*, "Isn't it pretty to think so."

If the Shoe Fits

KATE PEPPER

Kate Pepper is the pseudonym of author Katia Spiegelman, who teaches fiction writing at New School University and lives in Brooklyn, NY, with her husband and two children. She is the author of *Seven Minutes to Noon* (Signet, May 2005) as well as *Five Days in Summer*. For more information, visit www.katepepper.com.

"If I don't sell this novel, I'll open a shoe store."

That's what I told my husband, and I meant it. Shoes were easy and fun—I quested for them on an intuitive level only a shoe lover would understand—whereas my career as a novelist, another passion, had been a struggle. My first two novels, published by a small press, had lasted a few weeks in bookstores before vanishing into the backlist. I was a published author but still had to do office work to survive. Then my publisher died and I couldn't find a home for my newest novel. My career was a bust before it really began. A dozen years, a marriage and two kids later, I was eager to dig into work again. The question was, *Do what?*

Like many mothers who temporarily detour out of the workforce to care for their families, I found that going back to work meant making choices. I did not want to be in a full-time job that kept me away from my children, and I didn't want to write another novel that wouldn't sell.

Outside motherhood, there were four things I was good at: typing, teaching, novel writing, and knowing a good shoe when I saw one. Typing for a living was definitely a last resort, avoidable so long as my husband had work. I was already teaching fiction writing as an adjunct and had been since my first baby was ten months old; it was satisfying work, but paid poorly. Novel writing was what I felt fired-up to do. It's an esoteric skill, relegating you to long hours alone, inventing characters and worlds that you manipulate to your liking; you might say it's on par with insanity. You churn out hundreds upon hundreds of pages, which you then discard and rewrite, revise, polish, and change some more. After all that, there may be a very slim possibility you'll sell the thing — probably for less than a secretary's starting salary. Then, when it finally gets published, the usual reaction is nothing much happens. Then it disappears.

I decided to take one more stab at it, but this time I would make it commercial, hopefully improving its chances of getting published. A writer with many unpublished manuscripts lining my closet shelves, I undertook my last attempt as a novelist with as much reservation as determination. I really meant it when I said this would be the last novel I ever wrote if it didn't sell. And I kind-of secretly wanted to open that shoe store.

It would be a special place where owner and customer would recognize each other's inexplicable desire for the perfect shoe. I could see them perched on narrow, tilted shelves: soft suede, gleaming patent leather, rounded toes, square toes, pointed toes. High heels, low heels. Buckles, straps and beads. Boots, sandals, autumn loafers. They glittered and gleamed in my imagination, which would be free to lay down the burdens of invention; I would be an impresario of fine footwear, a mother, a wife and a reader. It sounded kind of nice.

I turned my mind to the new novel, figuring I'd go down in glory with my sinking ship — no one could say I didn't try before giving up my dream — and then I would go shoe shopping.

Suspense was a fictional element I felt I had never mastered, so I decided to try it. In the past, I'd tackled plot, character, voice, linear versus abstract narrative structures, multiple point of view, single point of view, interwoven stories, humor, mystery, young adult, children's stories ... each with a novel devoted to its understanding and mastery.

(I was insane.) I enrolled in a one day how-to-write-suspense course, hoping to jump-start the learning process.

That Saturday morning, my son woke up with a fever, my husband had had insomnia and slept not a wink, and it was pouring rain. I couldn't leave my delirious husband to drag our baby daughter and her feverish brother through the deluge to the pediatrician's office, so I stayed home. The conspiracy of deterrents seemed fraught with warning: What made me think I could undertake this project, or any project, when I had small children? A few days later, I realized that I could probably learn from a book everything the class would have taught me, plus I could read a book at home. I went to the bookstore and bought *Writing the Thriller* by T. MacDonald Skillman.

It was excellent. I read it cover to cover, took notes, and read many of the novels she recommended. Then I outlined the idea that had been swimming around in the back of my mind. Thrillers are about fear and anxiety, and as a mother, I had many. I would write about what would terrify me more than anything, in a two-pronged approach: the sudden loss of a child, and the mother's inability to protect him.

It was just over a year from the first to last draft of *Five Days in Summer*, the story of a mother who vanishes at the grocery store, and whose seven-year-old son vanishes four days later. Their family is plunged into a desperate search for a serial killer whose pattern is to complete a horrific pair of crimes within five days. I scared myself writing it. Meanwhile, I kept my eye on vacant storefronts in my neighborhood, imagining how nice it would be to have a business out of the house but close to home. A business in which I could meet new people while helping them choose a perfect pair of shoes. A business I could close for an hour when there was a school play. I would be my own boss, make my own decisions; I was organized and a hard-worker; this would be fun.

My agent approved the novel (I had signed on with him during my first pregnancy, unaware of how dramatically my life would change, and he had stuck by me during years when I didn't write at all). He called me on a Thursday to go over his cover letter and list the publishers who would receive a manuscript the next day. I was prepared to wait weeks for a reaction. Six days later we were hot into an auction that would play out for five more days and leave me with a six-figure two-book contract with a major publisher.

When I recovered from the shock, I read through my new list of deadlines. I was expected to publish once a year and had a month to deliver a proposal for book number two—and I hadn't even thought about another novel. But as I *had* been thinking a lot about shoes, I solved the problem by giving myself the store after all. That is, I gave it to Alice, the protagonist of my second thriller, *Seven Minutes to Noon*. Alice, a fictional Brownstone Brooklyn mom, owns a shoe store called Blue Shoes, just a few blocks from my real-life home. The store is home base for Alice and her partner Maggie as they search for their very pregnant friend Lauren, who disappeared before picking her son up from school. As Alice digs under the surface of her quaint neighborhood, she finds a dark underside to gentrifying real estate; where there's money, there's murder, and soon Alice realizes her own life may be in danger.

To my surprise and delight, I have reinvented myself as a suspense author, just as the fictional mothers in *Seven Minutes to Noon* opened Blue Shoes as an act of personal reinvention, shedding stressful careers for flexibility, independence and, well, shoes. Needless to say, theirs is the best shoe store in town. If only it existed in real life—I would be their best customer.

Don't Go Through That Door

DAVID J. WALKER

David J. Walker is the author of eight crime novels. His most recent, called *All the Dead Fathers*, features private eye Kirsten and her lawyer-husband Dugan. It was described as "riveting" by *Publishers Weekly* and "both thought-provoking and entertaining" by the *Chicago Sun-Times,* and was a "Summer Reading" selection on Chicago Public Radio's WBEZ. His new stand-alone novel, *Saving Paulo*, is scheduled for an early 2008 release. Walker has been an Edgar nominee and is past president of the Midwest Chapter of Mystery Writers of America. He is a full-time writer and lives just north of Chicago.

M y friend Mary was trying to be polite, but she'd just finished reading *No Show of Remorse*, the fourth book in my Mal Foley series. A Chicago private eye, Mal's no Mike Hammer, mind you, but he gets around a bit. Mary's also read my Wild Onion, Ltd. series, in which the hero, Kirsten, though much different from Mal, is another PI. They both run into violence and the occasional dead body, and run over a bad guy or two when the need arises.

Anyway, Mary was trying to be polite. "What I can't figure out," she was saying, "is how you came up with these characters who're so tough and so brash, when you're so ... well ..."

She decided on "so *laid back*," as I recall, when she probably really meant "such a pushover."

"Well," I said, not giving it much thought, "it *is* all fantasy, isn't it?"

But upon reflection, the fact is that fiction is fantasy. If I sat down and wrote 85,000 words about the everyday life of Mary, or myself, or even a real private investigator — I *do* know a few — would anyone shell out for the book? We want to escape into the pages with people who are bigger, badder, prettier, sadder, wiser, better, and — most especially, for a lot of us — far more foolish than we usually let ourselves be.

It's the "don't-open-that-door" principle. It worked fifty years ago whenever Abbott and Costello got to the closed door inside that gloriously creepy house. Sensible Bud would warn Lou ... and turn the other way. Then, while one part of us screamed "No! Don't open that door!" the other part happily hyperventilated, watching foolish Lou twist the knob and stumble through. And it still works today.

Literary "doors" come in various forms, of course. Judy's about to marry plain, stable, hard-working Joe; but this new, cute, sort of offbeat guy, Rick, insists he'll call her. The phone rings. She reaches out, hesitates. "No! Don't be foolish!" we say. "That Rick ... he's nothing but trouble." But she picks ups the phone and plunges into ... what? Why, the story we've been looking forward to, naturally.

Much of the attraction of the novel is that it draws us into a world where people we care about do things we'd never dare do. In Tolkien's fantasy *The Hobbit*, Gandalf the wizard shows up at Bilbo Baggins' door, "looking for someone to share in an adventure." But we hobbits don't do adventures, objects little Bilbo, puffing on his pipe and patting his comfortable belly. Adventures indeed. "Nasty disturbing uncomfortable things! Make you late for dinner!" But guess what? Before long we're following Bilbo and Gandalf and thirteen dwarves through the door, on their way to recover the ring — meeting murderous goblins and giant spiders and great winged dragons and ... well ... much the same sort of things your average detective hero faces along the way — along with his or her own fears and reluctance.

In my own *No Show of Remorse*, Mal Foley just has to bend a little to the Illinois Supreme Court and show remorse for something he did, but he felt it was the right thing to do when he did it ... and he still feels that way. And in my Wild Onion, Ltd. book *All the Dead Fathers*,

Kirsten should know better than to try to protect people everyone despises. Common sense says they ought to back down, but both Mal and Kirsten—not being like you and me, you understand—walk through the doors put in front of them, end up in the middle of crime and corruption, and do what they can to make things right.

That's our job as mystery writers. We create people we hope readers care about, put them in front of doors—and then push them through. "Don't open that door!" the reader cries. But open it they do. And we follow them on their adventure to recover that gold ring, or get at that ugly secret, or save that doomed person—meeting dwarves and murderous goblins, Mafia hit men, rodents, and vermin of all sizes and shapes along the way.

We follow the fantasy, though we'd never go through such doors in "real" life. And we follow—in part, at least, I suspect—because in our own lives, our "real" lives, there *are* frightening doors that have to be faced from time to time. There's generally not a hit man behind the worrisome, even frightening, doors we encounter. More likely it's a new relationship, a new job, a new place, a new offer of *something*. We're not comfortable facing those doors, especially when it seems foolish to go through them. But the doors keep popping up, don't they?

So sure, Mary, I'm a "laid-back" person (read: *pushover*). I don't *do* adventures. Mal Foley does. And Kirsten does, too. They usually don't want to; they wish they were somewhere else; they wish people's problems would go away without them. And frankly, it seems, they ought to have more sense. But off they go in their separate books. And is it too grandiose of me to think that maybe their opening doors encourages a few readers here and there to be just a bit more "foolish" sometimes than they usually let themselves be?

Right now I'm working on another book, and I have a feeling that in this one, too, the hero will be facing door after door he'd really rather leave closed. Just like the rest of us.

Act Two

DIANNE EMLEY

Dianne Emley is the author of a suspense series featuring Pasadena, California, homicide detective Nan Vining. The series debut, *The First Cut*, a *Los Angeles Times* best seller, was deemed "sizzling ... hard-edged" (*Publishers Weekly*), "an edge-of-your-seat ... propulsive thriller" (*Kirkus*), and a "gripping page-turner" (*Library Journal*). Dianne is at work on the second in the series, titled *Cut to the Quick*. Visit her site at www.DianneEmley.com.

F. Scott Fitzgerald wrote that American lives have no second act. There was a time when I feared that would be the story of my writing career.

A question established writers are frequently asked by those starting out is, "Was it hard for you to get published?" They expect a tale of struggle and redemption, of rejection letters papering office walls, stacks of unpublished manuscripts in desk drawers, perseverance against all odds until, at last, *success* and a vibrant career as a published novelist.

I always answered honestly, even though my response was not what the questioner, who was likely in the rejection-slip-gathering mode, wanted to hear. "No, actually," I'd say, feeling ill at ease with the harsh truth. "It wasn't hard for me."

Being a successful novelist was my dream career since I was a child. I fell in love with writing from the moment I first picked up a crayon.

Writing was my favorite hobby through grade school, two college degrees, and, later, a business career. Then the time arrived. I felt I was finally ready to try my hand at a novel. I began rising at 4:30 A.M. to write for two hours before going to work. I spoke of this project to hardly a soul. I didn't want to be talked out of it. I feared my fragile dream would evaporate if exposed to air. After three years, I finished my first mystery novel.

Here's the first act of my career as a novelist:

I wrote my first novel.

I got an agent right away.

I got a top publisher right away.

I wrote and published four more books.

My desk drawer was not crammed with unpublished manuscripts and rejection letters. I was making a living as a novelist. I hadn't hit the bestseller lists yet, but was hopeful I would. I had a whiff of the dream, and it was good.

Then something happened. My career stalled. The reasons were due to events in both my personal world and the publishing world. The result was I got thrown off track. After having published everything I'd ever submitted, I couldn't write a story that anybody wanted. In desperation, I decided everyone else knew better than me and began passing around my ideas to friends, writers and not, seeking and taking advice, relentlessly questioning myself. My proposals were roundly rejected. I put them in my desk drawer. I wrote a novel. It was rejected. I put it in my desk drawer. I collected rejection letters. I did not put them on my walls. I shredded them.

Is this the end, I wondered. Has the magic run out? Was I done? Had I leapfrogged over my second act and gone right to the third—life as a businesswoman who had a brief, shining moment as a novelist?

I took a break to rethink my M.O. I realized all the chatter was not helping. It only clouded me. I needed clarity. I saw that I had thwarted the formula that had brought my initial success. I returned to it. I kept quiet and still. I waited for an idea, a direction to bubble up from the silence. Many ideas floated through. Nothing took hold. Months stretched into years. Finally, an idea stuck.

I started a new book. My confidence was sorely shaken, but I persevered. I had no publisher. I hadn't talked to my agent in ages. I knew if I failed this time, it would be worse than if I'd never been published.

Every day when I sat down to work, I asked, "How badly do I want this? How long will I try?" The answer always came back, "I might give up one day, *but not today.*"

That book was *The First Cut*, the first in a series featuring Detective Nan Vining. It was brilliantly published by Ballantine. There were multiple foreign and book club sales. I received my best reviews ever. It was a *Los Angeles Times* bestseller. I'm well into subsequent installments in the series, and it appears that Nan Vining will have a long and prosperous career.

And I've entered my second act.

How to Market a Five-Hundred-Pound Gorilla

JOYCE & JIM LAVENE

Joyce and Jim Lavene are currently working on four mystery series. They write the Peggy Lee Garden Mysteries and the Renaissance Festival Mysteries from Berkley Prime Crime; the Sheriff Sharyn Howard Mysteries from Avalon Books and the NASCAR Mysteries from Midnight Ink. They promote with the Carolina Conspiracy, a group of wacky North Carolina/South Carolina mystery authors who are crazier than they are. Visit their Web site at www.joyceandjimlavene.com.

T his should really be called how to market a five-hundred-pound gorilla to a woman who lives in a one-room apartment. But that title is too long to market.

See? You're already learning to be a better marketer. It doesn't take much more than a keen eye and a strange urge to write novels for a living to make even the most mild-mannered writer into Super Marketing Writer.

Marketing is everywhere, whether we like it or not. Whether it affronts our sense of dignity as artists or not. Even if it seems unfair when we'd really rather sit at home and dream up our next plots. We market to and are marketed to almost every minute of every day unless you live on a small island with no TV.

Most of the time we don't resent it too much. Oh, there's the occasional salesman in the mall who squirts eucalyptus in your eye as you walk by, but besides that, we have almost become immune to it. And there lies our problem as marketers.

Maybe it was different at some time in the far distant past. We at least like to think it was. The good old days, they call them. When editors returned calls and one book every few years paid enough to live on. The ancient texts refer to it as the time when writers could write and not worry about marketing. All we can do now is whine and complain about it in bars with fellow writers, but those days are long gone. So what can we do to survive without taking the Internet Crash Course for Salesmen?

We can have fun with it. Who says marketing your work has to be stuffy?

From the first stages of marketing, which include the hated query letter and the dreaded synopsis, we can think of it like a game. How many letters went out this week? What response did they get? Did you burn them in effigy or paper your bathroom with them? Can you go on the Internet and find a picture of the editor who keeps rejecting your work and paste it on your dart board?

It's like Risk, Monopoly, and poker all rolled into one weird game that doesn't make any sense to most people. But hey! That's life. Roll with it or let it drive you crazy.

One quick word of advice: Never play by their rules. This is *your* game. You can make your own rules. Send your work to someone whose name starts with S on Saturday. Send out 100 query letters at the same time. Don't tell anyone you're marketing to more than one house. Are they telling *you* their secret rules? We think not! Otherwise we would all know what the rejection that reads, "This is very good. Better than I ever anticipated. I love the characters and the plot is to die for! I wish every writer could write like you. Just not exactly what we were looking for," means.

Remember that buying books is a random act, not any different for *them* (editors) than say you buying a purple toothbrush instead of a green one this week. It's called being subjective. That means they don't know who you are and they don't really care unless by some off chance you have written something that is going to get *them* (editors) into an office and out of those terrible cubbies made of unsolicited manuscripts.

Once you have mastered the art of Selling To An Editor, Grasshopper, you then move on to Selling To Readers who can be even more difficult *plus* you have to sell to them face to face. The first thing you must realize: it's difficult (though not impossible) to get pictures of them for your dart board.

Sitting at a little table with the blue (green, red) tablecloth as you wait near the front door (side check out, back wall near the bathroom) it strikes you how far the reading public will go to ignore you and your little display of hot chocolate, scratch-made caramel cinnamon buns, books and expensive bookmarks. Some people actually have to go to the chiropractor after turning their heads so sharply that they develop whiplash. You might start wondering if you are cut out for this kind of thing.

It's like Risk, Monopoly and poker all rolled into one weird game that doesn't make any sense to most people.

To this, we say again; enjoy yourself! You've worked hard to get to this prestigious place where the bookstore owner gives you a free bottle of water (coffee, if you go to a bookstore with an espresso bar). Give the people who walk by without looking at you funny names like Frack and Diphead. Keep score of how many blonds vs. brunettes buy your book. Keep track of how many times the store manager comes by and smiles at you like he/she feels sorry for you. Try to get him/her to buy one of your books.

Tell sob stories to potential customers. They'll enjoy knowing how you lost your family, your home, and your dog to publish this book. They might also buy a book, but *only* if you make it good. Be knowledgeable about questions readers may ask you like, "Where is the bathroom?" or "Do you really kill people?" and "Where is the mystery section? I'm looking for a good book."

Yes, that's the life of marketing. Once you've mastered it, there are two things you must do. One: stay away from used car lots and resist the urge to stand around with your hands in your pockets offering people incredible deals on '67 Buicks. You *are* a writer, not a salesman, despite any thoughts to the contrary.

And, two: share your road warrior stories with other writers who will cringe when they hear how abused you've been as you sold ten books (your profit: fifty cents). Encourage them to go out and dare it for themselves. There's nothing like the smell of books in a bookstore on a rainy night when no one in their right mind would be out and you have to share your table with the storeowner's gerbil that keeps looking at you.

And enjoy yourself! Is this a great job or what?

Look Away
From the Review

JULIA POMEROY

Julia Pomeroy's first novel, *The Dark End of Town*, was published by Carroll & Graf in 2006. It's about Abby Silvernale, a waitress at a busy restaurant who stumbles across some ugly secrets hidden in the rural village she calls home. The sequel, with the same protagonist, is scheduled for release in September 2007. Before she began to write, Julia was a co-owner and manager of her own restaurant in upstate New York. She was born in Japan and spent her childhood in Libya and Somalia and her teens in Rome, Italy. Find her at www.juliapomeroy.com.

When my agent found a publisher for my book, I felt as if I had been air lifted to Mount Olympus, where I would finish out my days sitting amongst the gods. There aren't many things in life that can give you that feeling, but selling your first book is one of them.

As the months passed, the heady feeling settled into a more realistic one; I started writing my second book, while carefully doing all the things I was supposed to do to get ready for the publication date. I was nervous. I had a lot to learn—I was an ignoramus in a field crowded with savvy, experienced writers. But when I voiced any concerns, friends would say: "None of that matters! You've sold your book! You're gonna be a published author!"

Just before the book came out, I got my first-ever review. It was from an industry magazine which, I have since heard, is kind to writers. I read it online, before anyone else—before my editor, my publicist, my agent or my husband. And all I can say is, it wasn't kind to me. As the meaning of the words sank in, I felt the blood leave my head. I bent over and rested my forehead on my keyboard. I felt as if I had been stabbed.

The reviewer (I was certain it was a man, though it was unsigned) hated my book: he disliked the characters, he thought the plot was trivial and he sneered at the ending. He sneered at it as he gave it away, his tone implying that the whole thing was so mediocre that no one would read that far anyway, so it didn't matter if he revealed what kind of a climax it was and where it took place.

I felt naked, blindsided, shocked.

I didn't know this man. Why did he hate me? And then, while I was bent over my computer, knife sticking out of my back, a part of me walked up, stood behind me, took a handful of hair, slammed my head down on the keyboard and said: It's the emperor's new clothes, sucker. Now everyone's going to know the truth, that you're a hack, sucking up airspace reserved for real writers. Give it up, fool.

Pathetically, I read the review over and over, in case I had misunderstood, in case I had missed some little shred of approval. When I realized there was nothing to salvage, like a condemned person I forwarded it on to all the people who cared about me and had, until then, believed in my book.

Over the next few months, I got more reviews. Most were thoughtful and supportive. Some were wonderful. One or two mixed. But throughout it all, that first one lived on like an open wound, as if that knife that had been shoved between my ribs had never been pulled out, and would occasionally catch and grind against bone.

I couldn't get rid of the damn thing, either. It turned out that Amazon has a contractual agreement with the magazine and placed the soul-destroying paragraph front and center on my book's page, where it sat, unmoving, like a venomous toad. Which meant that any trusting soul with an interest in my book would immediately find out what a mediocre crap-flinger I really was. Those few times when I had to go on my Amazon page I tried not to look directly at it but forced my eyes to skip past, as if it were a dead body in my living room that I had been forbidden to remove.

As I write this, I know that it's still there. So, yes, you can go and look at it. And yes, it probably did my sales a good deal of harm. But that's it. I'm still alive, still breathing, and in spite of that reviewer, still writing. So what have I learned from all this? I'm not sure. The worst part was realizing how eager I was to believe it. Be warned: People can write reams of good things about you and your book, and you'll smile, enjoy them, and put them to one side. But let someone write something negative, and it will sit in your gut for a long, long time. As if the positive reviews were just good manners, while the negatives were somehow more real. *Truer.*

I also learned that my friends were right after all. It is wonderful to be published. No two ways about it. In fact, I was lucky I avoided a serious blow to the ego for as long as I did. And though I haven't been in this mystery world very long, I can see that it is filled with writers who are seeking approval—from their readers, other writers, their mothers, their agents, their publishers, their pets, etc. It's a thin-skinned crowd. Getting shot down hurts more than it should. That's the way it goes.

You just have to keep going. Find a way around it. For me, I've had to decide who I am going to listen to. Whose voice is going to matter to me. And how much of that voice I can listen to, without being derailed. Because I don't want to become a human yoyo, bouncing up and down, a slave to everyone's opinion of my work. I've had to put my head down more than I did before and work harder.

> Be warned: People can write reams of good things about you and your book, and you'll smile, enjoy them, and put them to one side. But let someone write something negative, and it will sit in your gut for a long, long time.

So maybe, trivial as it sounds, in the long run whatever makes you a better writer is good, and whatever makes you afraid to move forward, or afraid to try harder, is bad. If that's the case, then that first, painful review might have helped me. It was ultimately liberating. I mean, if I'm that bad, then I can write however I want, right? Who's going to give a damn?

I just went to my book page on Amazon, to gauge my response. I looked at the review and flushed with shame, all over again. But I logged off and within a few minutes I had recovered. Interesting. I'm getting tougher. But it's probably good that it still hurts. Like putting your hand on a hot stove, you don't want to stop feeling pain. That would mean you'd lost all the nerves in your fingers. You just want to learn how to keep your distance. Or wear oven mitts.

When to Read Rejection Letters? *After* You've Been Accepted Somewhere Else

CHRIS GRABENSTEIN

Chris Grabenstein's *Tilt a Whirl* was short-listed for the 2006 Gumshoe Award and won the Anthony for Best First Mystery at Bouchercon. *Mad Mouse*, the second book in the John Ceepak mystery series, was published in June 2006 and was called one of the best mysteries of the year by Kirkus. His holiday thriller *Slay Ride*, the start of a second series, came out in November 2006. *Whack a Mole*, the third book in the Ceepak series, will go on sale in June 2007. His site is www. ChrisGrabenstein.com.

Rejection letters. They're like Dear John letters from people you've never met.

Typically, these missives try to let you down gently. The writer (the rejector) makes a constructive criticism or two, tells you they wish they were writing with better news, and then thanks you (the rejectee) for thinking of them and wishes you all the luck in the world placing your work with somebody else.

Somehow, when you read that last sentence, here's how it sounds: "Good luck getting some idiot to buy this turkey. You're gonna need it."

Stephen King says he used to impale his rejection slips on a spike he had sticking out of his wall in the room where he wrote.

I did something else.

After I signed with my agent, I stopped reading them. I let Eric earn his fifteen percent doing that! He kept the negative responses hidden away in a dark, dank file somewhere in his office.

Then, when *Tilt a Whirl* (published by Carroll & Graf, the first folks who didn't say, "hasta la vista, baby") won the Anthony Award for Best First Mystery at the Bouchercon fanfest in October 2006, Eric did the coolest thing.

He dug out that depressing file and sent me all the *Tilt a Whirl* rejection letters he had received while shopping it around town.

What fun! Especially, since some of the publishers that passed had books short-listed for the same award.

But, in addition to the fun, I learned a valuable lesson: just because they're the publishers, acquiring editors with the power of life and death over your words, they may not, in the end, be right.

Take this quote from a letter now presented as writer's exhibit A: "I thought the construction was a little bit odd in that Ceepak appears to be the continuing series character yet the story is told from the first-person point of view of another character."

Yes, it's true. My character Danny Boyle does the narrating, John Ceepak solves the crimes. I think this same publisher sent a very similar rejection missive (quill pen on parchment, no doubt) to Sir Arthur Conan Doyle: "Holmes appears to be the continuing series character yet the story, heavens forefend, is told from the first-person point of view of this other character named Dr. Watson."

But, one publisher's rejection can become a book critic's cause for admiration. *Library Journal* in their starred review of *Tilt a Whirl* wrote: "The story is related by Boyle, whose youthful inexperience and desire to be a kid are the perfect foil for Ceepak's mature, by-the-book demeanor." Another mystery critic, Lesa Holstine, wrote, "In *Tilt a Whirl*, Chris Grabenstein introduces one of the best sidekick/narrators since Rex Stout's Archie Goodwin."

Here's another one: "I'm genuinely sorry to say that Chris Grabenstein's *Tilt a Whirl* doesn't seem quite right for our list at this time. I felt that the focus on moving the basic police procedural plotting along too often overwhelms the character development and keeps the reader from becoming fully engaged."

Wow. I think I may have tossed my computer out the window and called it quits if I had read that before the book ultimately found its home at Carroll & Graf, a division of Avalon Publishing, probably the smartest, best-dressed division they have, by the way, staffed, as it is, by superhumanly attractive and impossibly intelligent people.

I guess the most important thing to remember about a rejection letter is (just like those behind-the-scenes DVD extras) the views expressed are those of the actual participants. They are, in short, one person's opinion. Okay, if you receive fifteen rejection letters simultaneously saying the exact same thing, maybe there's something you need to look at in your manuscript.

But here are some other people's opinions on the same topics cited as a reasonable rationale for not taking a ride on *Tilt a Whirl*: plot and character development:

"Grabenstein brilliantly evokes the endearing seediness of a Jersey Shore town in summer but it's his development of the Ceepak-Boyle relationship that makes this an absolute triumph." *Booklist*. Starred review.

At first when I read these rejection letters after winning the Anthony Award, I couldn't help but gloat. You know, "Ha-ha-ha. You fools were sooooooo wrong. In your face. U.S.A.! U.S.A.!" Then I realized I was sounding a lot like Homer Simpson.

I also realized what could've happened.

I could've read these letters along the way.

With each letter, I could've tried to "fix" the book to make the editor happier because, let's face it, most writers are insecure lumps with inferiority complexes and major people-pleasing tendencies. We want mommy and/or daddy (pick your most appropriate Freudian fixation) to look at the ka-ka we've smeared on the wall and love it. We're like the struggling actor Dustin Hoffman played in *Tootsie*. "You want Ceepak to be the narrator? I can do that!" So now you know why I thanked my agent when I accepted the award. The book may not have been written the way it was if he hadn't shielded me from all the helpful suggestions used along the path to publication to justify a rejection.

Let's face it—some editors simply won't like your book.

They will then try to rationalize a cogent "reason why" in their attempt to let you down gently. Sure, it's better than a terse "this book sucks," but it doesn't mean you have to do what they say if you ever hope to become a published author.

A lot of the letters, I discovered, end with the same sentence: "We wish you luck in placing your work with the right house."

And you know what? They're all one hundred percent correct on that one.

Rejections are just potholes along the road to the place you need to be: The Right House.

The Path?

CATHY PICKENS

Cathy Pickens has been, under different names, a lawyer, a business professor, a university provost, a clog-dancing coach, a church organist and choir director, and a typist. She is the author of *Southern Fried* (winner of the St. Martin's Malice Domestic Award for Best Traditional Mystery), *Done Gone Wrong,* and *Hog Wild* (2007), all Avery Andrews/Southern Fried mysteries. Her site is www.Cathy Pickens.com.

I f you think publishers will pound down your door, rip your priceless prose from your reluctant fists and cram your pockets full of cash, dying to share your insights with a breathlessly waiting world …

If you think you'll make a huge splash in the publishing world, and everywhere you look, people will be reading your book …

If you think all writers are rich …

… then take a reality check.

But if you're willing to accept that writing is both art and business, both inspired and mundane, if you realize that, should you stumble, plenty of others will do anything to take your place, for even less money than you've been paid …

If you realize you'll study harder, work longer, and make less than any doctor or lawyer, and you'll either live from paycheck to paycheck or you'll struggle to maintain at least one other job …

If you're still reading … you just might have what it takes.

The Reality

Walk into a "big box" bookstore. Walk past the giant stacks of books in the front of the store (which will quickly be replaced by different books). Look around. So many books. Where will yours be? How will anyone find it? Why will they buy it, rather than one of the others?

More than 170,000 *new* titles were published in 2005 — more than double ten years ago, more than a mega-bookstore full (assuming the store carried only one copy of each title). One little book is so small, swimming in that tide.

So, why are you writing? For fame? For fortune? Because you have a burning story others *must* read? Because you want to be an author, someone others respect? Because you want to live the life of a writer? It helps to know, to be specific about *why*.

I had a fantasy about living the life of a writer, living in a cabin off in the hills somewhere, supporting myself with my writing. Fortunately for me, none of that worked out as planned. It worked out better than planned. Be realistic. Dreams are nice, but reality is … well, real. Have a dream, set goals. But be flexible.

The Apprenticeship

John D. MacDonald said fiction writers require a long apprenticeship: at least a million words. That seemed unattainable, unrealistic, un-necessary, when I started writing. Now, looking back, I see how true it is — and I'm thankful my first attempts weren't published. I wouldn't want to live down what now hides in the bottom of my filing cabinet.

Writing is important, a serious undertaking. With word processing, desktop publishing, and more leisure time than ever in history, lots of folks are writing. Some say more are writing than are reading! The question apprentice writers must answer isn't "when will I be pub-lished." The question is "when will I be *publishable*?" That's the important question — and a writer's charge.

No one has to write. Many people live long, productive lives never writing fiction. Do you love the process of writing? Not just having written, not just the idea of seeing your book on the shelf, but the research, studying others' writing, chaining yourself to your desk, rewriting endlessly, criticism from friends, editors, and idiots? (And later, from reviewers and people you'll never meet.) If you don't, there are lots easier and more predictable ways to become rich and/or famous.

There will always be another writer who is better than I am, who is more talented, who has been given a better story, or who gets a better contract or some lucky publicity. That's life. My job is to write each story as well as I possibly can.

The Path

So what most inspired me? Hearing Sue Grafton say her first, second, third, fourth, and seventh books weren't published, and that *A is for Alibi* didn't arrive until book eight. I heard her and figured that, until I had at least five unpublished books in my bottom filing cabinet drawer, I had no right to give up or complain. (The St. Martin's Malice Domestic Award for Best Traditional Mystery and my publishing contract came after two-and-a-half unpublished novels—and stacks of short stories, nonfiction books, and articles, both published and not.)

For decades, I've devoured good books, attended writers' conferences, read about writers, studied markets, submitted. Early on, I wanted to find the key, unlock the secret that would admit me to the magical world of published writers. I wanted to know the One True Secret.

Only after I published my first novel did I fully realize what Joseph Campbell (author of *The Hero with a Thousand Faces*) meant when he talked about "a thousand unseen hands" reaching to help. I found, in my search, those unseen helping hands. But I also found there's no single secret path, no one hidden door. There's a secret path for every single writer, every one who embarks on the journey, who is true to his or her calling as a writer.

The *Real* Secret

In my writing life, I've discovered a simple truth, the *real* secret: Persistence trumps talent every time.

The writing life calls for persistence at every turn. Writers must persist in writing and perfecting their craft, persist in submitting their writing, and persist in promoting their writing, in the face of rejection and overwhelming odds.

If you feel you must write, then write. Keep writing. Set goals, dream big. Realize it's all a learning process, valuable experience you'll need later. Take criticism, keep submitting, listen to feedback (and learn what to ignore), get better. Pray for discernment. Most importantly, don't look for *the* path, look for *your* path. And enjoy. It's one heck of a journey.

When Expectations Are Gone

JEFF SHELBY

Jeff Shelby's novel *Killer Swell* was a *Los Angeles Times* and *Denver Post* best-seller. The follow-up, *Wicked Break*, has been compared to the works of Robert B. Parker and Robert Crais. He lives with his family in Texas. Visit his site at www. JeffShelby.com.

I t's when the expectations are gone that things start to happen.

The summer of 2003 was chaos in my household. My wife had just given birth to our daughter. As she was our first child, we were fumbling through the act of pretending to know what we were doing as parents. We were too busy getting up in the middle of the night, entertaining well-wishers, and watching the little creature to think much about my writing career.

So when I got a call from an agent looking to represent my book amidst the chaos, it was thrilling and exciting—I'd gone through the process of being rejected countless times so this was a new break-through—but it couldn't match the luster of being a new parent. And even as I worked on the manuscript over the summer, readying it for submission to the publishing houses, the excitement in the house was more about watching this new tiny person in the house than it was about the potential possibilities of finally getting a book published.

My wife and I had made the decision that I would leave my job as a high school administrator and be a full-time stay at home dad, even before I'd signed with an agent. I wasn't leaving my job to be a writer; I was leaving it to be a father.

I left my job the first week of September, and as I started getting used to a new routine around the house, my agent submitted my manuscript to several houses in New York. I was too busy changing diapers and getting up in the middle of the night to be anxious over it.

We learned that Dutton had an interest in the book and that the editor in chief wanted to talk to me on the phone. That's when I started getting nervous. I made sure my daughter was napping when the phone call came, so we could talk in peace. The conversation went well and my hopes moved up a notch, but they weren't at the forefront of my thoughts. I was thinking more about where I'd left the diaper bag.

And then, exactly a month to the day that I'd left my job, the phone rang. It was my agent, and Dutton was offering me a two-book deal. I don't remember much about what we talked about. I'm pretty sure I asked some dumb questions because it all felt surreal.

I was holding my daughter when I answered the phone, as she was taking her morning snooze. I hung up the phone in our bedroom and sat down on the floor, too stunned to move. I started to cry—the result of excitement, wishes fulfilled, and probably lack of sleep. I hugged my daughter to my chest and screamed, "*Yes*!!!"

And, of course, she woke up, started crying, and it was back to my new reality.

But that new reality had a nice new dimension to it.

The Three Major Life Mistakes I've Made That Force Me to Write These Mysteries

VICTORIA HOUSTON

Victoria Houston is the author of the Loon Lake Mystery series, which has been featured on NPR and in *The Wall Street Journal*. She lives, writes, and fishes in northern Wisconsin. Learn more about her at www.victoriahouston.com.

T he First Mistake: I was twenty-seven when it all began—married, mother of three, and living in a suburb of Chicago where a neighbor was experiencing quite the drama in her life. So dramatic that, having had the urge to write since I was a kid, I started a novel based on her. Jennifer's life was fraught with affairs, stolen inheritances, and a rascal husband who was a prominent lawyer: *Jerry Springer, Peyton Place,* and *Oprah* in one fascinating bundle.

So I was sixty pages into documenting Jennifer's travails when she and her husband went into marriage counseling, individual therapy, etc.—and straightened their lives up! But as their world turned rosy, my book came to a skidding halt. I had made my first mistake: Never base a character on a real person.

Now, here in Wisconsin where I live, fish, and write, people swear they know who the characters are in my books—but they are wrong. My characters are distilled from memories I have from childhood. They may resemble real people in their physical characteristics—but memory works for me.

The Second Mistake: However, those sixty pages did earn me a nice rejection from an editor who said, "You show promise. Do more newspaper and magazine writing to improve." And so I did. For about six years. I was in my early thirties when I found myself working on the business side of book publishing as the Director of Publicity for a major publisher of non-fiction—though we did publish one mystery writer. I read his book. (Oh, I should mention that by now I had written and published three non-fiction books on family issues. So I had a terrific New York agent.)

Anyway, I read this guy's mystery and thought it was ... mediocre. I knew he was making in the six figures annually. I thought, "Hey, for six figures—I can be mediocre!" So over the next year, working an hour or two every evening, I wrote a mystery and sent it off to my agent. She sent it back with the comment: "It has a few problems." Okay, I rewrote the mystery. And rewrote again. The fourth time she sent it back, she said, "This is so bad don't even show it to someone who loves you unconditionally. You're a non-fiction writer, not fiction." Yikes. I had made my second mistake: I thought writing a mystery was easy.

But I'd had a good time doing a bad job. So I thought it over. Decided to give it one more try but educate myself to something I'd ignored: the conventions of the mystery genre. But where to start? I floundered.

Then, on assignment for my day job, I found myself talking to the book review editor of a national magazine who mentioned that he wrote mysteries. Whoa! I told him what a miserable job I had done, and he encouraged me to attend a mystery-writing workshop that had helped him. I was living on the east coast now—so it was easy to plan my work week attend this workshop in Greenwich Village every Monday night.

Six to eight of us attended regularly, and we only ever had one assignment: write the autobiography of a character, bring your pages, and read aloud to the class. The only person who could critique was the workshop leader. Well, I could tell when others had mastered the assignment—and I could tell, after I read a sentence or two, that I had not. It took me nine months to *get it*. She was teaching us how to "show not tell" on the page. And that is very difficult for a non-fiction writer.

The Third Mistake: But I mastered it and with great excitement started a mystery. I set it in Kansas City, where I'd lived for fifteen years; I set it against a background of art theft as I'd been the art critic for the *Kansas City Star*; and my protagonist was a lovely, intrepid, brilliant woman in her early forties—just like me!

By coincidence, Mystery Writers of America announced a mentor program just as I was fifty pages into my story. I decided to submit my pages for critique. Now, at that time, since I write without an outline, I had been surprised to discover that the stolen art had ended up at the bottom of a lake in northern Wisconsin, and a retired dentist out muskie fishing had just happened upon this strange box lurking under the water. So of the fifty pages I sent off, five pages were set in Wisconsin. Off I ran to FedEx with my fifty pages, then sat back and waited for accolades and a book contract.

What did I get? A critique that said, "I was going to recommend this writer go back to school until the story turned to Wisconsin. Then it just sparkled. It came alive."

I was stunned. I threw away forty-five pages and looked at that retired dentist with some confusion. Who knew I was born to channel Dr. Paul "Doc" Osborne—with all his neuroses, his alcohol and rehab issues, his crush on a woman who is Loon Lake's chief of police and the person who introduced him to fly fishing (one of my loves)? My third mistake was writing a character too similar to myself.

And that is how I backed into writing a series that is set in the landscape and culture that I grew up in with characters distilled from the memories of childhood. Fishing is a wonderful device for many reasons: It takes you into or on water, which can be both lovely and treacherous. It brings you into contact with a mix of people, good, bad, and evil, whom you might not meet in your everyday socio-economic strata. It is a great excuse for meditative thought: All good detectives need time and a reason to think. But best of all it works because of one simple fact: All fishermen lie. Not about the size of things but they never tell the truth about where they fish. That leaves the door wide open.

And so—no more mistakes!

The Ten Steps to Getting Published

(No Big Secrets Here)

RAY WHITE & DUANE LINDSAY

1. Join a critique group.
2. Complete your manuscript and your query letter and at least one synopsis.
3. Edit it till it screams.
4. Come up with a gripping title (and incredible concept).
5. Enter writing contests (gets you meetings with agents/editors).
6. Research literary agents and agencies (so you know what they like to represent and can personalize your query to them—and so you know what their submission guidelines are).
7. Go to conferences (fish where the fish are biting) and make yourself known to the agents and editors so you can open your query with the line, "When I met you at the blah, blah conference you said I should send this to you."
8. Develop a submissions schedule and mail queries out every week; log responses. Your critique group can help you perfect your query letter and synopsis.
9. Develop a thick skin. Remember, how you handle rejection is a matter of attitude.
10. Never Give Up.

Tenacity Over All

AIMEE AND DAVID THURLO

The Thurlos are the award winning *New York Times* best-selling authors of the acclaimed Ella Clah, Lee Nez, and Sister Agatha mystery series—that's twenty two novels and counting, too many to list here. Visit their site, www.aimeeand davidthurlo.com, for a listing.

D avid and I both had a keen interest in writing while we were in high school, and had short stories and poetry appear in school and non-commercial publications, but that creative energy became more focused once we graduated—at least for a while.

After nine years of marriage, I became bored with my part-time office job. I sat down with a legal pad and pen and decided to write a romantic intrigue novel. David was teaching at the time but couldn't resist looking over my shoulder, offering plotting suggestions, editing, and generally making a nuisance of himself whenever possible. Finally I put him to work writing action scenes, descriptions, and helping type the manuscript. But it was still essentially my project, so the novel was destined to go out in my name only.

Once the manuscript was finished, I found a local author who was willing to talk with me. The man was Norman Zollinger, who owned a small book store we patronized. Norm directed us to *Writer's Market, Literary Market Place*, and other references so we could identify publishers and editors who might be interested in seeing the completed manuscript.

I also learned as much as I could about submission protocols, formats, and writing a dynamite query letter.

Zollinger advised against making multiple submissions, but I didn't have the patience, especially when a single rejection could take several months. Anyone and everyone at publishing houses throughout the nation received a query letter from me. During the late seventies there were still many independent publishing houses, and few were left off the my list as the discouraging process of rejection after rejection continued.

But I wasn't planning on accepting defeat, and self-publishing was never considered an option, so I persisted, committed to selling the first project before beginning a second one. Eventually, not long after the sixty-eighth rejection, an offer came in from an editor in New York who'd been sent the entire manuscript. A few weeks later, I received a xeroxed, one-page contract. There were no negotiations, and, after vetting out the contract with an attorney, the terms and the pittance of an advance were finally accepted. In 1981, the first Thurlo novel was published under a pseudonym.

Soon we met more local writers, and one of them suggested I give his agent a call. A few days later we met with the literary agent, who just happened to be in Albuquerque visiting her clients and scouting out new talent. With a published novel as proof of my potential, I had a literary agent before the end of the day. The business relationship was sealed with a handshake — no contract.

We have another agent representing us now, twenty-five years and sixty published novels into our career, but we remain friends with the woman and agency where we first began.

Hard work, determination, storytelling skills, market awareness, and the never-ending desire to sell a completed manuscript are what we recommend for the aspiring writer who hopes to find a publisher. Any potential author working toward that first sale needs to have the obvious — a solid manuscript in the proper length and format for the anticipated market at the right time and place. Having very thick skin also helps when the rejections stack up, but tenacity proved most important to us when it came to making that first sale.

The best marketing advice we can give to newly published authors: make no assumptions when engaged in promoting your work. During our careers we have learned to work very closely with our publisher's staff, distributors, event coordinators, and booksellers to make certain that there *will be* copies of our featured or most recent novels present at any public relations events, which include national conventions, workshops, trade shows, panel discussions, and, of course, book signings.

We value the time we spend together creating our novels more than any other aspect of our work, but understand that our career is a business, a creative venture with many highs and lows. Our advice: Understand what you've gotten yourself into, never repeat a mistake, and find a strategy that'll help you cope with the acceptance, rejection, and never-ending pressures that run hand-in-hand with the freelance writing profession.

A Bathroom Attack

T.A. RIDGELL

T.A. (Terri) Ridgell ventured into the writing world after leaving behind a corporate position. Her novel *Operation: Stiletto* won *Romantic Times Review*'s 2005 Reviewers Choice Award, and *Fractured Souls*, the first book in her KSIS International Thriller Series, is a *Fallen Angel Reviews* Recommended Read. Visit Terri at www.taridgell.com.

After spending many years in corporate finance in the Washington, D.C., area, I decided to start writing. I finished a manuscript and then went in search of some answers. The first thing I had learned in the business world was if you want to know how to succeed, you go to those thriving in the field and ask questions.

From many successful authors, I received some excellent advice. Join local writers' organizations, find a critique group, and attend writing conferences. I took all of the advice to heart. Over the next couple of years, I went to monthly writers' meetings, finished three more manuscripts with my critique group teaching me all along the way, and attended at least five writers conferences.

For each conference, I signed up for editor and agent appointments. At home before I left, I would spend hours crafting the perfect pitch. I created clever back-of-the-book blurbs that would wow the socks off whoever was lucky enough to hear my spiel—all in hopes that an editor or agent would love my idea so much, a contract would be offered on the spot. Okay, that was an inappropriate dream, but it was mine.

The reality: the editor or agent would request a portion of my work, read it, and then send me a beautifully written rejection letter, which I am ashamed to say, I did not appreciate at all. During these years, I continued to cold-query numerous other editors and agents, racking up more and more of these unappealing letters.

Four years ago, at a writers conference full of fun activities with a ton of wonderfully talented authors, fate stepped in and changed my life. The atmosphere was festive, the mood light, and I was there to soak up the ambience.

Lori Pepio, a great friend, and I had been enjoying an evening social gathering. We needed to visit the ladies' room and made our way inside, still laughing and joking. Our lively conversation continued as we washed our hands at the sink. An author joined us for a moment, gabbing a bit before she left.

Another woman came out of a stall and we started chatting, the usual conference small talk.

"Are you a reader or a writer?"

"What do you write?"

We answered all her questions and, like most writers, enjoyed talking about our stories. Just as we started to leave, she stopped us by pulling out her business card and saying, "My name is Karen Syed, editor for Echelon Press, and I'd love for you to submit your work to me."

I'd heard those words before, but always after a prepared speech delivered during a tense one-on-one meeting. And those words didn't compare to the phone call two months later when she made an offer for the book.

You never know when opportunity will rear its head. All I can say is thank goodness. If I had known, I'd have been a lot more nervous every time I went to the restroom.

Accountants Can Do It
(So Can You)

ANTHONY BIDULKA

Anthony Bidulka is author of the Russell Quant mystery series: *Amuse Bouche*, *Flight of Aquavit*, *Tapas on the Ramplas*, and *Stain of the Berry*. Visit his site at www.anthonybidulka.com for more information.

I think it may have been the -22° Fahrenheit temperature (if you're American; but if you're Canadian or European it's -30° Celsius, or 243.1 Kelvin if you're some kind of alien). Or maybe it was that I was counting shingles. Palette after palette after palette of them, arranged by color — sandstone, granite, forest, mocha — most under a crunchy shellac coating of snow and ice. Perhaps it was the day: New Year's Eve. Everyone else in the known world was donning their sparkly best in preparation for a night of celebration, drinking champagne, and midnight kisses. I was counting shingles in the snow. I had to. I was an accountant.

Most everyone believes accountants spend their dull, drab lives punching buttons on calculators and shopping for the perfect pocket protector. Not true. Not for the kind of accountant I was becoming. For you see, I was training to be the most revered yet hated type of accountant of all: the auditor. An auditor's life is a fast-paced, at times dangerous, always-exciting series of raunchy adventures and escapades. We are sometimes liars, too.

Life got better. The shingles-in-the-snow thing — a client inventory counting procedure — was but a mere baby step on my journey to becoming the best darn accountant I could be. It was also one of the times in my life when I wondered: Is this *it*? Is this the career I will have for the rest of my (hopefully) long life? And there was an even deeper question, never verbalized outside the boundaries of my skull: What about my childhood dream of becoming a writer?

By this point I had already been a bartender, a waiter, a shoe sales-person, a uranium mine worker, and a teacher. And with each new career (or stepping stone, as I now like to think of them) I'd experienced the same niggling at the back of my mind. But the practical side of me said, "Forget it," and the "I don't want to be poor for the rest of my life" part of me agreed. I had to find a real career that paid money and offered stability.

Now, one might think bartending and selling shoes aren't real careers and don't pay very well (although not as bad as you'd imagine), but they were what I thought of as "helping" careers. Meaning, they helped me feed myself while getting an education that would suppos-edly lead to even better career opportunities. And I did a lot of this. So much, in fact, that today I could very well have a business card that reads: Anthony Bidulka, B.A., B.Ed., B.Comm., C.A.

Yup. Three degrees and one professional designation. Each repre-senting years of study, hefty student loans, too many exams, and a piece of framed paper on my home office wall.

When I look back, I find I almost need a map for my own life. The road I traveled is surprisingly long and winding, with many detours and unexpected pit stops. And you know what? I cherish every last bit of it all. Every dead-end job. Every career. Every promotion. Every convocation ceremony with a colored sash about my shoulders. Every *a-ha!* moment when I'd say to myself: It's time to quit or it's time to try something new. Now, it might sound like I was a flake, some transient who fluttered from one life experience to another not knowing what he wanted. But that's not the way it was. When I sold shoes I worked myself up to manager of a small chain of stores. My last service job was as a head bartender. In my most recent position before becoming a full-time writer, I was a senior-level audit manager with an international accounting firm for almost a decade. When I do something, I do it to become the best I can be. I do it to learn. I do it to have experiences. One of my favorite sayings is: Life is short, but it can be wide.

What many people forget is that it's up to us to make it wide.

So I made the most of what I was doing when I was doing it, but eventually I always reached a point when I knew, almost without a whiff of doubt, that it was time to move on. I suppose part of what drove me from one career to another was a sense of looking for something. So what was I looking for? I was looking for *it*. The thing that would complete me, satisfy me, excite me, challenge me, make me love getting up each morning. I wanted to be rid of that little buzz in the back of my head that was telling me something was missing, that what I was doing wasn't quite *it* yet, that I wasn't fulfilled, that I wasn't yet comfortable in my own skin. And to find that something, I finally came full circle and revisited the idea of becoming a writer and knew immediately that that was *it*.

It was a slippery slope for me. When the idea first hit my brain that I needed to at least try being a writer, it was on a beach somewhere hot, after one too many tequilas and, I think, some ice cream (not a stellar combination). At that moment of clarity, I knew that when I was eighty-five and looking back on my life, I would be sorely disappointed in myself if I didn't just try. Things moved pretty quickly after that. I was ready to take the leap. I identified the net that would catch me should I fall—in my case an amazingly supportive spouse and (now) ex-boss—and took a running jump. In my mind (still that of a logical accountant), one of the things that made it seem possible is that I, at the outset, set myself up for success.

At the very beginning, my definition of success was very simple, measurable, short-term, and stolen from a successful ad campaign: just do it.

So on my very first day, suit and tie replaced with jeans and a t-shirt, I was a successful writer. Why? Because I was doing it. My job that day was to sit behind my computer and write. It didn't matter that I hadn't yet written word one, or that I didn't have an agent and was very far from having anything worth submitting, never mind being published. I was doing it. I was a writer. Success. How great was that feeling? Pretty great.

But the story does not—cannot—end there. When I achieve success, I bask in it for a short while, brag to family and friends, maybe have some champagne. Then I move on. I identify my next goal for success and get to it. That is my writing life, really: a succession of setting goals, achieving them, celebrating them, then aiming higher. And even if I falter—and I certainly have along the way—or take longer to reach a goal than I'd hoped, I am forever empowered by the sense of accomplishment of an already established pattern of success, starting with Day One. I did it.

At the very beginning, my definition of success was very simple, measurable, short-term, and stolen from a successful ad campaign: just do it.

I've learned two important things from all this, two lessons I adhere to to this day: (1) Plan for Success, and (2) Don't Forget to Celebrate.

I celebrate the release of a new book with as much gusto as I did the first. And even more, I celebrate at every opportunity, no matter how small it might seem to an outsider: a good review, the first time I see cover art, e-mail from an especially ardent reader, whatever; I make a big deal of it. Because it is.

I have been many things in my life, and they have added up to the best thing of all: I am a writer.

The Lucky Writer's Path

M. DIANE VOGT

M. Diane Vogt published her first nonfiction in 1979 while still in law school. Since then, she's published articles, a nonfiction law practice management book, book reviews, short stories, crime puzzles, newsletters, essays, novels (including the acclaimed Judge Wilhelmina Carson legal thrillers), and more. Diane's fiction combines legal realism with characters readers care about to provide engrossing stories readers don't want to put down. Visit her at www.mdianevogt.com.

R ight up front, I want to tell you that I'm not famous. Like you didn't know that already, right? I've had a lot of luck in the writing business, though. Since I'm not famous, you're probably wondering just how much luck I've actually had. You might be surprised.

My first novel was very generously blurbed by Margaret Maron and Elizabeth Squires. Later, one of my novels was blurbed by Larry King. My first Bouchercon panel placed me right next to Walter Mosley (good thing, too, since it was the last panel on Sunday morning and no one would have come if Walter wasn't there). I was on a panel with Sue Grafton at SleuthFest, and we also had a nice long chat as I drove her to the airport. Another time, I moderated a panel with Linda Fairstein and P.J. Parrish which was humorously supported by Janet Evanovich from the audience. I've served on the board of the Florida Chapter of Mystery Writers of America and been a judge for the prestigious Edgar award. I've had dinner with David Morrell and Gayle Lynds, cocktails with Clive Cussler, wine with David Hewson, and shared a hotel room with Lee Child, Paul Levine, Michelle Martinez, and Jim Born (okay—we were using the room to prepare for a mock trial presentation at ThrillerFest, but we were all there in the room at the same time). That's just a short list of some of the luck I've had.

I published my first nonfiction article in 1979, and then I didn't publish again for twenty years. I took a few detours to get married and practice law awhile. Once I got on the right path (meaning when my biggest client suddenly filed for bankruptcy protection and all my legal work stopped immediately), it didn't take me too long to finish my first novel, find an agent, and sell the book. Four years, I think. Very lucky.

And my luck didn't end there. I'd published four novels, one nonfiction book, countless articles, and a book of crime puzzles when something truly wonderful happened. In the spring of 2006, my work appeared in *Thriller: Stories to Keep You Up All Night*, a short story anthology edited by James Patterson. My story, "Surviving Toronto," was a pilot for my new series character, Karen Brown. The story was included with others by thirty-one famous, best-selling authors. The others included David Morrell, the creator of Rambo; Gayle Lynds, not only a bestseller herself but also a woman who co-authored books with Robert Ludlum, perhaps one of the greatest spy writers ever; James Rollins, Steve Berry, M.J. Rose, David Dun, James Grippando, Heather Graham, Alex Kava, Katherine Neville, John Lescroart, the incomparable Lee Child, and more. The anthology enjoyed amazing success, and I became part of a very special group of writers who worked hard to make that success happen. I saw firsthand how hard best-selling authors work, how a classy publisher treats famous authors and major books. I participated in events where long lines of readers waited for me to sign, right alongside some of the biggest authors in the business. *Thriller* received starred reviews and significant praise from critics as well as readers. What a break all of that was for me.

See? I told you I'm lucky.

One of the things no one ever told me when I first started out in this business was that you don't need to be famous to be a successful writer.

Along the way, I learned that what every successful writer needs is to reach and build an audience. If you're reading this book, you already have everything you need to make it. (If you didn't have the right stuff, you'd be watching television or playing hockey or something else right now.) And you need luck.

One of the things no one ever told me when I first started out in this business was that you don't need to be famous to be a successful writer.

What are those necessary qualities?

Desire to write is the most important. It may seem as if everyone on the planet desires to be a writer. Not so. You think that because you hang around with people who aspire to write. You read magazines for aspiring writers, maybe join writers' groups filled with pre-published authors, attend conferences, take classes, read e-mail lists filled with aspiring writers. So you think everyone wants to be a writer and it's too competitive and too hard and you'll never make it and the odds are against you and you've never been lucky anyway and, well, hell, what's the use?

I once believed all that, too. I was wrong. I've been lucky, and you can be, too.

It may seem that everyone wants to write a book, but believe me, there are millions of people who don't even want to read a book, let alone write one. I meet these people all the time. At events in bookstores, customers tell me, "I don't read." A tragedy. But true. Other customers approach me and say, "I have a good idea for a book, but I don't have the time to write it." Or, I love this one, "I have a great idea for a book. Let me tell it to you and you can write it and I'll share the money with you." Such people are not reading this book. But you are.

True, writing is a competitive field. So is medicine or law or engineering or anything else worth doing. There's probably little value in any goal for which there is no competition. Yes, writing is competitive, but it's not impossible. Thousands of books are published every year. New authors do break in. It can be done. You can do it. How do I know? I see it all the time. I've encouraged aspiring writers to try, and I've watched them succeed.

Your desire is a wonderful gift. If you have the desire to write, that means you have some talent for it. Think about it. There are plenty of things for which you have absolutely no desire or talent. For me, it's a long list. I don't want to play football, live in a commune, travel by camel, sleep outside in the desert, or play the lute. The list goes on. But you get the point. If I have no desire to do something, I'm sure I have no talent for it, either. If you'd ever seen me try to throw a football, you'd agree. Is the gift of desire a part of the Grand Design? I like to think so. But even if you don't believe in God, you have to admit that there are a whole slew of things you have no desire to attempt nor talent to perform.

Desire to write. You have it. That's the beginning. What you must do is take that talent and develop your craft. Read a lot, write a lot, take classes, go to conferences, talk with other writers. You make a lot of false starts. After a while, you begin to finish things. Not long after that, you complete something in which you have enough confidence to send it out. And you get rejected. And then you submit something else. And something else. And something else.

Eventually, someone likes your work enough to buy it from you. And you're there. You're published. You did it. Not impossible. Not at all. A famous, experienced New York City editor once said something like, "Every piece of well-written prose eventually finds a publisher." I typed out that line and pasted it on the monitor of my computer. I believed it when I was writing my first novel, and I believe it now.

I meet aspiring writers every day who tell me they're not lucky like me. They can't get published or they can't find an agent, they say. What this usually means is that they've given up too soon. They haven't put in the time to learn the craft. They haven't completed their projects. They haven't submitted their work enough, and been rejected enough, to reach their ideal reader. The reader they've written the book or the story for. The one who really, really loves their work.

Sometimes, you worry that reader doesn't exist for you. You worry that you were given this desire, learned your craft, wrote the book, got it published, and that special reader you've written the book for isn't out there. But he is. Trust me on this. You can be lucky, too.

Maybe you're thinking, well, she's not famous. How does she know?

Because luck, you see, is what happens when your preparation, everything you've done to polish your talent and produce your best work, comes face-to-face with amazing and unforeseen opportunity.

How do you think I got asked to write an essay for this book?

If It Doesn't Sell,
Write One Better

NATHAN WALPOW

Nathan Walpow writes the Joe Portugal mystery series, including *The Cactus Club Killings*, *Death of an Orchid Lover*, *One Last Hit*, and *The Manipulated*. His short story "Push Comes to Shove" was reprinted in *Best American Mystery Stories* series. Nathan is past president of the Southern California chapter of Mystery Writers of America and a five-time *Jeopardy!* champion. His site is www.walpow.com.

The first novel I wrote was called *Cult of the Succulent Queen*. It was about a woman in modern-day Los Angeles who led a bunch of tiny aliens—their spaceships were the size of a grain of rice—into Baja, California, to find the creature who would save their race. When I finished it I studied my how-to-get-an-agent books and eagerly sent out my first round of query letters.

Responses trickled in. *Not taking any new clients* or *We only handle mystery* or simply *No thanks*. Well, I said to myself, I didn't expect it to be simple. So out went the next bunch of letters.

Two years later, I had an inch-thick pile of agent rejections. I'd gotten some interest, but no one wanted to represent me. *Cult of the Succulent Queen* was too science-fiction for the mainstream crowd and too everyday for the SF one. I put it in my electronic closet and moved on to something else, a comic novel called *Curtains*. I never finished the first draft. Looking back now, I see that it was a couple of moderately interesting characters in search of a plot.

Then a writer friend suggested I write a mystery. And I remembered something Raymond Chandler said, to the effect that *to sell a mainstream novel, it has to be great; to sell a mystery, it merely has to be good*. I took this not as a comment on quality but as one on the market. There's always room for decent mysteries. It was true in the forties when Chandler said it, and it was true in early 1997. So I wrote an amateur sleuth mystery entitled *Spines*.

When I was done, I looked back through my *CotSQ* rejections and queried someone who'd been very positive about my work. Sounds great, they said, but we're not taking any new clients. I moved to an agent who'd been encouraging, but they pointed out that they only represented crime fiction writers. If I ever wrote a mystery, they said, please look them up again. So I did. And got a summary dismissal. One of those three-word scribbles at the top of my letter. *Not for us* or some such.

Discouragement reared its ugly head. I sought other methods of getting an agent.

Somehow I'd gotten on the mailing list for a writing conference in San Diego. I read over the brochure. Included with attendance, it said, was an opportunity to submit the first seven pages of your manuscript for critique by two agents or editors. I figured if I could just get past the whole screening rigmarole, someone was bound to be so impressed that they'd give me my big break. So I wrote a check and made a hotel reservation and reviewed the list of agents and editors to see who might be a good fit.

It was a crapshoot. There wasn't enough there to make a decision. I went back to the agent book that had been gathering dust since the *CotSQ* days and checked the bios. About all I could figure out was which ones absolutely wouldn't want a mystery. So I picked a couple of names more or less at random.

The conference arrived. I discovered that one of the agents I'd chosen was a highlighted speaker. The scuttlebutt was that she was very quick to tell a writer why their manuscript was a piece of crap. Great, I thought. I had all these people to pick from, and I grabbed Cruella de Vil.

My first critique session was with the other agent. She spent ten minutes telling me all that was wrong with my sample, after which I spent an hour or two wondering why I ever took up writing. Then I slunk into my interview with Cruella.

She liked it. No, she *loved* it. Send her the whole thing, she said, and she'd get it to the person in the agency who specialized in mysteries.

One month — and a title change, to *The Cactus Club Killings* — later, I had an agent.

A month after that, I had a two-book contract with Dell.

I kept thinking back to the day I sat puzzling over the list of agents in the conference brochure. I pulled it out, looked it over, wondered why I'd chosen The Agent Formerly Known as Cruella. Wondered what would have happened if I'd picked another who felt the same as my other choice had. How many more months I might have been sending out query letters. I realized how lucky I was.

Which is the point of all this history. Sure, I had confidence in my writing (except for those couple of hours between interviews one and two). Sure, I figured I'd eventually sell a novel. But if it hadn't been for that semi-random choice of agent interview, it could have taken a whole lot longer.

On the other hand, had I chosen differently, I could have ended up with an agent who would have sold the book to another publisher. A publisher, maybe, who wouldn't have dropped me after two books as part of a purge of paperback-original authors. Or maybe I would have given up on mysteries and written the Great American Novel, and today I'd be rich and famous.

You're not fully in control of your writing career. Ultimately, there are too many random events (and too many bean counters) for you to really be in the driver's seat. All you can do is write the best book you can. Be aware of the market, let it guide you, but don't let it drive you. Just write that best book and, if it doesn't sell, write one even better.

I Want It Now, If Not Sooner

SIMON WOOD

Simon Wood is a California transplant from England. He's married to his American wife, Julie, and their lives are dominated by a long-haired dachshund and four cats. In the last seven years, he's had over 140 stories and articles published. His fiction has appeared in several anthologies, and his nonfiction has appeared in *Writer's Digest*. His previous titles include *Working Stiffs* and *Dragged Into Darkness*. His current titles are the thrillers *Accidents Waiting to Happen* and *Paying the Piper*. Visit his site at www.simonwood.net.

I suppose it's because of the times we live in — we can get anything we want and fast. Technology has placed the world in our hands. It's just as easy for me to communicate with my friends and family back in England as with my friends in this country. We can get everything in an instant — coffee, movies, music, mac 'n cheese. This godsend has a tendency to make us impatient.

I'm guilty of this. If I see more than two cars lined up in the drive-thru or people standing in front of the ATM, then screw it, I'm going elsewhere. Time and Simon wait for no man.

I've seen this trait for instant gratification amongst writers. They want to see their book in print the moment the manuscript spills off the printer. But traditional publishing isn't like that. It's a big machine that moves slowly. A lot of planning and a lot of people are involved in the book-making process. I had a book release party for *Working*

Stiffs and one of my guests asked me how quickly it took from start to finish.

"Nine months," I said, injecting a healthy dollop of incredulity.

"That slow?" my guest remarked.

They read me all wrong. Nine months is bloody fast! I worked my butt off for six months writing it, and the publisher busted his hump for three getting the cover done, copyediting, and working with the printer, etc. And this was for a small-press book not bogged down by big publishing machinery.

None of this takes into account the process of finding an agent and a publisher. Take my first book, *Accidents Waiting to Happen*. I started it in January 1999, began sending out the manuscript that September, collected a bucket-load of rejections, didn't land a contract until October 2001, and it wasn't published until July 2002. That's three-and-a-half years. If I hadn't sold a bunch of my stories in the meantime, I'm not sure I would have stuck with it. Three-and-a-half years is a long time to wait.

I won't say I felt hard done by waiting this long, but I felt I'd paid my commitment and patience dues. My story pales in comparison to some successful writers out there. I know one mystery writer who waited eight years to sell that first book. Another wrote ten novels before he sold one to a major publisher. I can't imagine writing ten books and getting nowhere. I would have given up a long time before I sat down to write the tenth book.

Vanity presses and print-on-demand (POD) services make it possible to take a freshly printed manuscript and turn it into a book in a matter of days. So I can see the appeal to the writer. Why punish yourself with the waiting game when you can have your dream today?

I won't condescend and say that just because I waited nearly four years to see my book in print, you should too. It's a lame and insulting argument.

But I will say you're doing yourself no favors going for instant gratification. Writing may be an art but it's also a craft, and crafts have to be honed. A writer, like any craftsman, needs time to develop his skills. Traditional publishing is a big machine, and not everything it produces is solid gold, but it contains a lot of talented people whether they be writers, agents, editors, etc. Whether you or I like it, it takes time to be heard. The cold, hard fact of the matter is just because a writer writes doesn't mean he or she deserves to be published. Your work may not be ready yet, your subject too controversial, or worst of all, you may not be good enough. Writing is a leap of faith. A writer's belief in his work and dedication to the craft can all be for naught. Every time I commit to writing a story or book, I have no idea whether it will be published. I have a small yet significant body of work behind me, but I hope and pray it will be good enough for publication when I send it off to the publishers.

Vanity presses can bring you publication today, but they can't give you the distribution, advances, marketing, and editing that the developing writer is going to need to become an accomplished writer. Small-press publishers have published my first three books, and getting those books seen has been tough. With POD services, those hardships are magnified. Reviewers tend not to review self-published books, and stores tend not to stock them. For a self-published book to be a success, the writer has to spend the majority of his time selling the book instead of developing his writing skills.

The hardest book to sell will be the first. It may take years, but it's worth the battle. The difference it will make to your sales and ability to build a career is immense. If you want to see your book stocked in every store and given every chance for success, then you have to be in it for the long haul. There are many ways of getting there, but going for instant gratification isn't the answer.

Every writer (new and experienced) wants his work published, but publish well, not fast. It'll make a world of difference.

More With Less—Lessons Learned By a Beginner

SUSAN SLATER

Susan Slater has lived in the Southwest for thirty-five years. She has six published mysteries—*The Pumpkin Seed Massacre*, *Yellow Lies*, *Thunderbird*, *A Way to the Manger*, *Flash Flood*, and *Five O'Clock Shadow*—all set in New Mexico. She's a member of the Tony Hillerman Conference faculty and has taught creative writing for over twenty-five years at the college level. Currently, she supports her passion for writing by working full-time for a government contractor. Her site is www.susanslater.com.

Getting sold often means going back to the basics—swallowing hard and taking another look at your manuscript. There's nothing more daunting than an editor using words like "convoluted" or "confusing" when referring to the narrative. I remember getting a "story drowns in meaningless terminology" comment and then another "slow beginning, doesn't grab me." Ow! I had work to do and needed to start at the bottom of the chain—with the building blocks: words. So, bear with me and consider the following suggestions for editing at this beginning level.

"Wordsmithing" is a word that is bandied about in writing circles, but what does it mean? Basically, it means making key choices and always asking yourself, are they the right ones? Do your words do what you want—what you expect? Is there too much passive voice? Are you painting a word picture (showing not telling)? Remember, we live in a visual society. But the question I want you to ask yourself incessantly: Have I told more, with less? Simply, have you made every word count? Whew! That's a tough one for me. I'm a little long-winded — I always feel the need to explain ... and explain and explain.

But consider what we know from the five-word opening of April Sinclair's *Coffee Will Make You Black*: "Momma, are you a virgin?" We know the approximate age of the speaker (probably preteen or just turned thirteen); we know the extent of her sexual knowledge; we know she trusts her mother with "delicate" material; and because of this we know right up front the "character roles" of these two people. And we know that the book fits into the "coming-of-age" genre.

Do we believe that editors make a decision after reading at most the first paragraph? Yes, we do. There's no such thing as hoping an editor reads past a "slow" beginning because the book "picks up" by chapter two. At no place in the novel is word choice as important as in the very beginning. Whether the reader continues is often "set" by the end of the first paragraph. The term "hook" is often used when describing how the reader is roped in, committed from the very start. You have an obligation to your readers — a lot of things rolled into one — to entice, promise something worthy of their time, set up the framework (character, setting, plot) and begin to deliver right from the very first word! My friend Craig Johnson (*A Cold Dish, Death Without Company*) said it best: "You make a $24.95 hardcover contract with your reader to make their investment pay off! You *owe* them!"

Have I made use of my own advice? Yes. I've reworked mediocre opening lines and added punch. And I've sold books! My most lucrative first paragraph rewrite was the opener for *Five O'Clock Shadow*. Initially, I opened with a lot of backstory. I explained why Pauly's name wasn't spelled Polly, why getting married was so important, why she lived with her grandmother ... you get the idea: pretty boring stuff. A lot of rewrites later I came up with:

The sharp crack of sound didn't register, hushed as it was in the whoosh of hot air being pumped into the balloon's envelope. Even when the balloon faltered some two hundred feet above the bridge and began its lopsided, rapid descent into the high voltage wires, its importance eluded her. She didn't scream. She simply dropped the camera and clung to the bridge as the gondola burst into flames.

Believe me, no one has complained about this being a slow start!

Sunrise at the Broiler

WILLIAM KENT KRUEGER

William Kent Krueger is the author of the Cork O'Connor mystery series, which is set in the great North Woods of Minnesota. His work has received numerous awards, including the Anthony Award for Best Novel, the Minnesota Book Award, the Loft-McKnight Fiction Award, and the Friends of American Writers Prize. He lives in St. Paul, Minnesota, a city he dearly loves.

It's 6:30 A.M. The sun is still well below the horizon. The streets of St. Paul, Minnesota, are quiet and, for the most part, empty. I'm sitting in my car, staring at the corner restaurant across the street, a little place called the St. Clair Broiler. There's a neon flame over the door that lights up red-orange just moments before the door is unlocked for the day's business. The flame is still dark. I see movement inside the Broiler—the cook firing up the griddle and a waitress moving toward the light switch. The flame flickers on. I grab my notebook and pen and head to my office inside: booth number four. There's a coffee pot and a clean cup already set out for me. I sit down, pour myself some java, open my notebook, and begin the work I love.

I've published eight novels in the mystery genre. All of them have been written in this way, over coffee at the St. Clair Broiler. My first novel was published in 1998, but by the time I sold it, I'd been writing at the Broiler every morning for more than ten years. The long birthing of that first book was entirely a labor of love and taught me the most important lessons about becoming a writer.

In that vague way of so many people, I always wanted to write, but I didn't know how to begin or what story to tell. When I decided absolutely that I wanted to be a writer, my wife was in law school and I was the sole support of our family, which included two small children. I knew that if I wanted to write, I had to figure a way that wouldn't interfere with my responsibilities as a breadwinner, a husband, and a father. In this, I took a lesson from Ernest Hemingway, who'd always been one of my favorite authors. One of the things I knew about Hemingway was that he loved nothing better than to rise at first light and spend two hours composing his work. For him this was the most creative time of the day. I decided that if it was good for Hemingway, it was worth a try.

I was living then a block from the St. Clair Broiler, whose doors opened at six thirty. I began to rise at five-thirty, get myself ready for work, and walk to the Broiler. I would sit down with coffee, a cheap wire-bound notebook, and a Bic pen, and write for an hour and fifteen minutes, until the bus that took me to my job pulled up in front. In those first few years, it didn't matter to me what I wrote; writing was what was important. I worked on sketches, short stories, completed a very bad novel. I filled notebook after notebook with my scribbling. I consumed vats of coffee. And I piqued the interest of the Broiler staff, who, I later learned, referred to me as "the writer guy." One day the owner of the Broiler, a terrific gentleman named Jim Theros, sat down and asked me what was up. When I told him, he laughed and said, "If you ever publish a novel, I'll throw a party here." To date, he's thrown eight.

To a young would-be writer, ten years must seem like a long apprenticeship. My perspective is different. All those years, I was not just learning how to write a book that was publishable. The daily visits to the Broiler also helped me establish the discipline that I believe is essential to becoming an artist of any kind. Eventually I understood that there was an even greater gift being given to me. I realized that writing at the Broiler fed something essential in me that in turn gave me the energy to go out into the world and accomplish whatever was required of me as a breadwinner, husband, and father. If I rose every morning knowing that the first thing I would do was the thing I loved most—writing—then I believed that nothing else the day held for me, no matter how difficult, could defeat me. Writing had become the way I centered myself, energized, and prepared to meet life.

Not only do I earn my living as a writer now, but I also teach writing. One of the most important insights I try to offer my students is this: If your goal in writing is simply to publish (with the adjunct hope of becoming rich and famous), you will probably end up disappointed. If, on the other hand, you write because it is what you love to do, then it doesn't matter if, in the end, the world ever knows your name. You will have had a rich life steeped in a satisfying enterprise. But I also tell them this: I firmly believe that if you write because it is your passion, you will eventually be rewarded with publication.

I begin every day with the magic that occurs with coffee, a notebook, and a pen. I begin every day a happy man.

Someday We'll Laugh About That

JEANNE MUNN BRACKEN

Jeanne Munn Bracken, of Littleton, Massachusetts, lives with her long-suffering husband Ray, her two daughters (including long-term cancer survivor Lisa), and four cats. She was named a *New York Times* Librarian of the Year in 2005 and much to her amazement is now listed in *Who's Who in America*.

There is nothing funny about having your child diagnosed with cancer. So it's hard to see how that event in 1977 moved me from a wannabe writer to a much-published humorist.

Books were my refuge as a child. I read all the time: under the covers in bed, on the swing when I was sent outside for fresh air, in the car, wherever. Writers were awesome. I was not. No way could I be a writer. A major in German with a minor in Speech and Drama followed by a master's degree in Library Science kept me close to books written by other people. I did read all the time: poetry, mysteries, magazines, newspapers, gonzo travel adventure, biography, everything.

Jobs in a university medical library and in a think tank research library turned out to be really good preparation for my future, even though the scientific and technical content were not "my thing," as we said then. No problem. It turned out I am a pretty good librarian, and I enjoy it.

In due course I acquired a husband, a house, and a dog, in that order. I kept reading: books, magazines, how-to manuals, gardening, dog training, interior decorating, and sewing. We branched out into parenthood. There wasn't much time with an infant in the house, but I managed to read mommy magazines, knitting periodicals, the occasional mystery, and the ubiquitous cereal boxes.

In the hot summer of 1977 our neat life fell apart when our daughter was diagnosed at the age of eleven months with a rare form of cancer. As awful as that was, it was even more shocking to discover there were no books I could read about it. My reading as coping mechanism failed me. Oh, sure, I could scan copies of *North American Clinics in Pediatric Oncology* for information on chemotherapy and laparoscopic surgery, or I could wade through the *Journal of Pediatric Hematology* in hopes of enlightenment on endodermal sinus tumors in infants. But frankly, between the weight of the professional tomes and the equally weighty *Dorland's Medical Dictionary* essential to my understanding, my muscles weren't up to it.

During the two years of her initial treatment, I was rarely both awake and functioning. But in one lucid moment I decided to write a pamphlet for parents of children with cancer. I am a librarian with experience in medical and technical libraries. How hard could it be?

Hard. Very hard. Somehow the pamphlet turned into a booklet and then into a 407-page book (*Children With Cancer: A Reference Guide for Parents*, Oxford University Press, 1986). From idea to published book took eight years. While I was working on it, I wrote a press release on a childhood cancer topic for the local weekly newspaper. The editor, clearly a woman of brilliance and fine taste, realized I could actually write and offered me freelance assignments. Shocking—the paper had advertised for writers, but I had not applied, since I had no credentials. No English literature degree. No creative writing courses. No journalism. Nada. I took the assignments.

Through the difficult days and months of dealing with childhood cancer, I realized something: there are people who cry and people who laugh. I shed very few tears during that ordeal, but it turned out I have a knack for finding humor in most situations.

So when the newspaper editor asked me for suggestions, I offered a humor column. Having a lot of space to fill every week, she went for it. My weekly column started in 1979. I wrote it for twenty-two years.

Write what you know, the experts say. So I wrote about:

- Plumbing disasters (it's hard to finish the job when the instructions are drenched).
- The challenges of raising headstrong children (nobody cared whether their socks and shoes matched—or were even the same size).
- Owning way too many cats (other people's kids bring leftover fries home from the burger joint; mine came back with a stray cat—a pregnant stray cat, of course).
- Balancing work and family (badly).
- Being married for over thirty years (to the same person).
- And of course vacations on the cheap in vehicles of questionable mechanical health (we once dropped RV parts all the way down the Jersey Turnpike).

From that beginning I wrote features, commentary, interviews, reviews, and travel articles for newspapers and magazines from coast to coast. Through it all I have continued my reference librarian day job, although I still dream of writing nonfiction for children on a full-time basis when I grow up (now defined as retirement).

Probably it's a good idea to study writing in preparation for a career in publishing. I couldn't say. Instead, my development grew from coping mechanism to silver lining.

My best advice: Work with trusted critique groups and partners. I have shared writing with several groups. One was the expansion of an adult education class. Another is through the Society of Children's Book Writers and Illustrators (SCBWI). One evolved from a weekend workshop. One is based at a Maine campground in the summer. The newest I started with support from a local literary magazine at the library where I work. Dedicated and committed writers are your best friends.

Writing doesn't have to be lonely. Find a writing partner, another working writer who will critique your manuscripts and vice versa. Not your spouse, nor one of your children, nor your agent or editor, your neighbor, your dentist, or your hairdresser.

I have been blessed with two close writing partnerships. The first woman I met through the SCBWI. We worked on many manuscripts together, supported each other, went to conferences together, and sometimes it seemed we could recite each other's words from memory. When she moved to the West Coast, I was lost.

An interim partnership didn't work out. A nurse who was going to help me update the cancer book took half of the advance and all the packages of materials I had gathered, then moved to Cairo, Egypt. I haven't heard from her in years. The new edition of *Children with Cancer* is now three years past deadline and I'm on my fifth editor.

A couple of years after my writing buddy moved to Oregon, I met my current writing partner, whose interests are similar to mine but different enough to keep it interesting. We are actually collaborating on a couple of projects, travel to conferences together, and keep in touch regularly via phone and Internet. Her advice is invaluable.

I am still a librarian, but I am also a journalist and a published writer. A selection of my columns is out (*Someday We'll Laugh About This*, Molisa Press, 2005). Silver lining, making lemonade, choose your own platitude. Just keep at it. It will happen if you don't give up. I'm still not laughing about childhood cancer, but the rest of life has turned out to be a real hoot.

My Mother, My Secret Weapon

JENNY SILER

Jenny Siler, who also writes under the pseudonym Alex Carr, is the author of several novels and numerous short stories. Her first novel, *Easy Money*, was a *New York Times* Notable Book. Her most recent book, (and her first Alex Carr novel), *An Accidental American*, is an international thriller set in Lisbon and Beirut. Jenny grew up in Missoula, Montana, and she and her family currently live in Portland, Maine. Her site is www.jennysiler.com.

Judging from the content of many of the e-mails I receive at my Web site, I can only conclude that a good half of the adult population of the English-speaking world has at least one unpublished manuscript on their hard drive or tucked into the back of a closet somewhere. Needless to say, anyone who is desperate or foolish enough to seek my advice is, to say the least, slightly behind in the game. In the four years my web site has been up and running I have received requests ranging from the presumptuous to the preposterous, but everyone seems to be looking for the same thing: the one magical piece of information published writers possess which helped them become published writers in the first place.

With the exception of a few truly frightening e-mails, I have answered every single query. After all, I was in these writers' shoes once, trying to crack the code of agents and publishers, and it's hard for me to begrudge them. Generally, I spend far more time than I should answering their misguided questions, patiently explaining that, no, I can't help them find an agent because I can't even find one for myself at the moment, or recommending various publishing guides I've found useful in the past. In the end, I always tell them there is no secret weapon, no magic insider's trick, nothing I can share that will make the process easy. Finding an agent or a publisher comes down to persistence, lots and lots of persistence, of the near-delusional kind. Keep the query letters flowing and don't give up. That's what I did.

And I am only partly lying.

The truth is that I did have a secret weapon, a very powerful one. But before I reveal what it was, there are a few things I should say about myself. I grew up in a community of writers who ran the gamut from wildly acclaimed to painfully anonymous. On any given evening in my family home, you might find a Pulitzer Prize-winning novelist sipping scotch or a penniless poet fixing a leak, or the two together engaged in a game of low-rent poker. Throw a rock here, the adage about my home town goes, and you'll hit a writer.

My mother, a poet at heart who had been forced by circumstance (namely, me) to earn a steady living, taught writing at the local university. I can't remember a single time in my childhood when she wasn't working on something. Yellow legal pads filled with her jagged handwriting lay everywhere around the house, holding, at various times, novels in progress, short stories, essays, and poems. Despite the fact that writing itself was not her main source of income, and that her real job and the care of two children and a husband limited her actual writing time to mere nanoseconds each day, it was inconceivable to think of my mother as anything other than a writer. It was how she defined herself and how we, in turn, defined her.

On the spectrum of success between poet carpenter and best-selling author, my mother fell somewhere in the middle. Occasionally, one of her poems or short stories would find a home with a respected literary publication, garnering praise or even inclusion in the occasional best-of collection. Her teaching career eventually led her to publish a composition textbook and several anthologies. But her novels, the works in which she had invested the most time, energy, and emotion, remain unpublished to this day.

Unlike my mother, who came to writing out of sheer love for the craft, I finally surrendered to the idea of being a writer out of fear. Staring down my thirties from behind a bar, with no college degree and an intense dread of returning to school, I took a gamble and wrote my first novel, hoping writing might give me at least the pretense of a career. I deliberately didn't write from the pit of my soul, didn't try for the Great American Novel, but instead chose a commercial genre in which I thought I might actually have a chance of getting published and, more importantly, making a living.

With my manuscript in hand, however, I soon found that, like those lost souls who write in to my Web site, I didn't have the vaguest clue where to begin my quest. In my desperation, I turned to the one person I knew who had experience with the process of getting published: my mother.

Unless you've been through it yourself, it's impossible to imagine the scale of self-loathing and emotional devastation that searching for an agent can bring. Most writers are fragile people to begin with, hardly suited to the dozens of rejection letters that even the most talented author inevitably receives. It doesn't matter if you are the next Sandra Brown or the next Ernest Hemingway; more people than not will pass on your work. You will be called either unmarketable or unoriginal, or both. You will be told, in the most saccharine terms, that you just don't inspire the passion necessary for agent X or Y to represent you to your full potential. And you will know in your heart that what all of this means is that you are and always will be a total failure.

I know this because I received over sixty rejection letters before finding my first agent and landing a respectable book deal which allowed me to throw in my bartender's towel for good. Yes, sixty. I often use this number when I tell those aspiring writers not to give up. What I don't tell them is that I didn't see a single one of those letters, at least not until the whole painful process was over with.

When I first went to my mother for help, she recommended that I write a query letter, saying she would send it off to a few agents whose names she knew through friends and colleagues. I did as she suggested, then handed over my letter and went back to my life, knowing the process could take some time and trying not to expect too much. What I didn't know was that while I was pushing cocktails and counting my tips, my mother was scouring every writer's guide she could find, sending my query off to anyone she thought might be even vaguely interested. It wasn't until several months into the process that she got her first real nibble, a request from the man who would eventually become my agent to see the first fifty pages of my book. Within a matter of a week he had agreed to represent me, and within a matter of a few more weeks I had a publisher. It was only then that my mother revealed the truth about just how difficult the process had been.

Despite the fact that in one sense it is, I don't mean for this to be a weepy story about a mother's love. It's remarkable what my mother did for me, and I'm well aware that I owe my career as I know it to her. But what makes this story truly remarkable is the fact that she was able to do for me what she could never do for herself.

Sometimes I wonder what would have happened if it had been me on the receiving end of all those rejections. How long would I have gone on before the demons of self-doubt defeated me? Ten letters? Maybe. Thirty? Unlikely. Certainly I would have given up long before sixty. I have distinct memories of my mother receiving similar letters, though not many. Her tolerance level for rejection, like mine, I suspect, was not high. At least not high enough.

The next time someone writes into my Web site asking for advice, I will tell them that the real secret weapon is to put all your doubts behind you. Go to your mother if you can. Leave town and hire the neighbor kid to collect your mail for you. Train your dog or cat or pet pig to sniff out rejections. Take a deep breath and tell yourself that all it takes is one "yes." Just one. Out of sixty, that is.

Semper Persistence

RAY WHITE

Never surrender, never give up, never quit. Those aren't just words to get published by; they're words to live by.

It's easy to be flip about such advice. Of course you shouldn't give up. But we all know it isn't that easy. In fact, less than one percent of writers get published in book-length fiction or nonfiction. Now I am absolutely, positively making these statistics up (though I did extrapolate them from all those agent Web sites where they claim to reject 99 percent of all submissions). But even with that being the case, it's easy to see why most writers quit trying.

Rejection hurts. So engaging in an occupation or avocation where rejection is the norm is arguably nuts. At least it would be if we writers weren't impervious to pain (not!), or maybe oblivious to reality (hmmm, gotta think about that one), or more likely we simply believe we will defy the odds, that we belong in that one percent. This is more than an unflagging belief in ourselves; it's an astounding exercise in bending objective reality to our will.

Writing is the only occupation I can think of that requires both great sensitivity and skin thicker than a T-rex.

Once again, rejection hurts. No matter how tactful the terms, each one says, "You're not good enough," at least on the emotional level. And if you think one is painful, wait till you've had dozens, or hundreds. The cumulative effect wears you down if you let it.

So here are some words to the wise. Repeat after me: "How you handle rejection is a matter of perception."

Remember the disclaimer virtually all agents included when turning you down. It was the phrase you glossed over while disappointment was setting in. It usually goes something like, "… only represents my subjective opinion and should not be taken as a conclusive judgment on the quality of your work." That's the part to take to heart. It's only one person's opinion—and most often it was an assistant and not the actual agent. In fact, by not accepting you they did you a favor, because they didn't feel strongly about your writing, and you deserve and need an agent who does.

They weren't right for you, not you weren't right for them. That's the perception to take from rejection.

You offered them a chance at your excellent work and they passed. Look how many agents turned down Jeffrey Archer or Stephen Coonts. Read how Kyle Mills' "wall of shame" bulletin board got so heavy it fell off the wall. Agents turn down superb fiction every day.

The stories you read in this book document the trials and triumphs of the authors you know and love to read. At one time they were just like you—unknown and unpublished. They did it, and so can you.

We writers get published because we are willing to keep trying until we do, because we will put up with the pain of rejection until we do. Those who don't, won't, and that is the vast majority of those who try. As Yoda said, "Do, or do not. There is no try."

We invite you to make *semper persistence* your motto, to let rejection roll off your back and even go so far as to see each rejection as another step toward success. We invite you most of all to understand and believe that if we, who had no insider connections and no realistic chance at success, can do it, you can, too.

Acknowledgments

Producing a book like this is truly a team effort and the authors would like to acknowledge all the talented and generous authors who made this book possible — most of their stories are in here. Thanks goes to our superb agent Rita Rosenkranz, who believed in us and our concept, whose suggestions helped us refine our proposal into something marketable and who then presented it to the exact right publisher. Thanks also goes to our editor at Writer's Digest, Jane Friedman, whose editorial insights improved both the structure and content of this book.

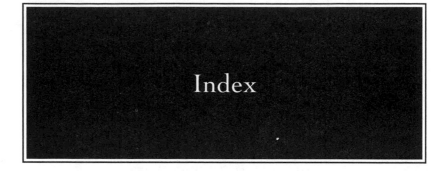

Index

About the Editors

Duane Lindsay is truly a renaissance guy. He's an electrical engineer capable of designing the control system for toxic waste incinerators (the subject of his book *Lone Rock*), and a building designer who created a business that built hundreds of houses from scratch.

Duane went to the University of Wyoming and took a good shot at an English degree. Realizing, belatedly, that this would equip him for absolutely nothing, he switched directions and used his practical side, getting an electrical engineering degree—without ever setting foot in a science class.

He's also a published songwriter, a singer and cracker-jack guitar player who has performed professionally, the last effort being the Miami Book Fair with the Rock Bottom Remainders.

His private eye manuscript, *With a Vengeance*, was a finalist in the 2006 St. Martin's Press Best New Private Eye Novel contest, and he won the Colorado Gold Writer's Contest for *The Grifter's Daughter*.

Ray White is a Louis L'Amour type storyteller and an entertaining public speaker who has taught classes and seminars on everything from writing to solar system design to tracking wounded bears through willow thickets. When he's not practicing his storytelling on friends and family, he goes to mountain man rendezvous with other 1840's era role players and entertains the attendees with his tall tales.

Before he married and settled down, he lived a dull and quiet life exploring caves, flying ultralight aircraft, and taking month long solo wilderness backpacking trips. He rode roundups as a ranch hand in the Colorado Rockies, searched for lost treasure, and prospected for gold. He was once "directionally challenged" for ten days in the jungles of Sarawak, on the island of Borneo.

Ray has written or co-authored six novels and has been a past finalist in the Colorado Gold, Pikes Peak Writer's and Southwest Writer's contests.

For more resources and updates related to this book, visit the editors' site at www.HowIGotPublished.com